The Matamoros Trade

The Matamoros Trade

CONFEDERATE COMMERCE, DIPLOMACY, AND INTRIGUE

James W. Daddysman

NEWARK: UNIVERSITY OF DELAWARE PRESS
LONDON AND TORONTO:
ASSOCIATED UNIVERSITY PRESSES

Associated University Presses
440 Forsgate Drive
Cranbury, NJ 08512

Associated University Presses
25 Sicilian Avenue
London WC1A 2QH, England

Associated University Presses
2133 Royal Windsor Drive
Unit 1
Mississauga, Ontario
Canada L5J 1K5

Library of Congress Cataloging in Publication Data

Daddysman, James W., 1936–
The Matamoros trade.

Bibliography: p.
Includes index.
1. Izúcar de Matamoros (Mexico)—Commerce—Confederate States of America—History. 2. Confederate States of America—Commerce—Mexico—Izúcar de Matamoros—History. 3. United States—History—Civil War, 1861–1865—Blockades. 4. United States—History—Civil War, 1861–1865—Economic aspects—Southern States. I. Title.
HF3240.I97D32 1983 382′.097214′075 81-72031
ISBN 0-87413-215-0

Printed in the United States of America

To Beth, with love

CONTENTS

ACKNOWLEDGMENTS

It is with deep gratitude that I acknowledge my indebtedness to those who have assisted in the preparation of this manuscript. I am especially grateful for the assistance of Dr. Wesley M. Bagby, Professor of History at West Virginia University. His gentle prods and constructive criticism seemed always to be couched in an unfailing faith in my ability to succeed. Dr. William D. Barns and Dr. Edward M. Steel, Jr., also carefully read the manuscript before it was completed and suggested numerous important corrections and improvements.

I am pleased to acknowledge the assistance of the library staffs of West Virginia University, the Eugene C. Barker Library at the University of Texas, and of the Southern Historical Collection in the Wilson Library at the University of North Carolina. Further appreciation is extended to the staffs of the Manuscript Division of the Library of Congress, and the Public Record Office and the British Museum in London for their friendly assistance.

I shall remain profoundly grateful to Alderson-Broaddus College for awarding me a two-year National Teaching Fellowship, which made this work possible. Dr. Richard E. Withers, Chairman of the Division of Social Sciences, lent editorial assistance on many points during the early drafting of the text. Professor Hilding Lind, Mrs. Karen VanHorn, and Miss Luise S. Stiefel devoted long hours to proofreading and tactfully assisting in the preparation of the manuscript. The library staff at Alderson-Broaddus College was untiring in its efforts and assistance.

I am grateful to my family, which stood by me and encouraged me at every turn. My parents' support was unfailing. To Beth, my daughter, I owe an especial gratitude. During the four years encompassing my research and writing she was far more mature in her understanding of this incomprehensible project than her young years would indicate. And finally, warm recognition is given to the memory of my wife, Peggy, whose love, devotion, and sacrifice were a continued inspiration. It is my singular regret that she did not live to see the work completed.

INTRODUCTION

As the Civil War developed and the efficiency of the Union blockade increased, Confederate and Texan authorities, as well as anxious commercial agents and leaders of foreign governments turned their attention to the sleepy little Mexican port just beyond the perimeter of American jurisdiction. Almost totally lacking in port facilities, Matamoros nevertheless became an important *entrepôt* for the Confederacy and the major lifeline for Texas and the Trans-Mississippi Department during the Civil War.

The port records for Matamoros in the Civil War period have not survived. Therefore, historians have had to search through countless pages of fragmentary manuscripts, documents, journals, and diaries scattered across several countries in order to piece together an account of the importance of that trade to the Confederacy.

Based upon portions of these records, a number of secondary books and articles have dealt, in varying degrees, with the subject. Included in these publications are Samuel B. Thompson, *Confederate Purchasing Operations Abroad* (1935), Frank L. Owsley, *King Cotton Diplomacy* (1952), Robert L. Kerby, *Kirby Smith's Confederacy* (1972), William Diamond, "Imports of the Confederate Government from Europe and Mexico," *Journal of Southern History* 6 (November 1940):470–503, and Avila Larios, "Brownsville-Matamoros: Confederate Lifeline," *Mid-America* 40 (April 1958):67–89. These studies range from portraying the Matamoros trade as an inconsequential side effect of the war to flamboyant claims and hypothetical conclusions with little basis in fact. L. Tuffly Ellis, "Maritime Commerce on the Far Western Gulf, 1861–1865," *Southwestern Historical Quarterly* 77 (October 1973):157–226, presents a refreshing reappraisal of the commercial activities through the Rio Grande port. His study, however, covers a much broader topic than the Matamoros trade and does not endeavor to reach a definite conclusion on the importance of that port to the Confederacy.

The present study is the fruition of more than fifteen years of labor. The decision to research the Matamoros trade developed in conversations with Dr. Wesley M. Bagby during the early 1960s and from a strong personal interest in Confederate diplomacy dating from the writer's childhood. The first milestone was reached in 1962 with the completion of a master's thesis on the subject at West Virginia University under the direction of Dr. Festus P. Summers. Utilizing only a limited number of sources, the thesis reflected no great departure from the generally accepted view of the Matamoros trade. With encouragement from Dr. Bagby and Dr. William D. Barns, the study was pursued further. The research has included work in materials from numerous libraries and archives in the United States and England. The most important American sources were the Confederate State Papers (formerly the John T. Pickett Papers) in the Manuscript Division of the Library of Congress, the Records of the Trans-Mississippi Cotton Bureau and the United States Consular Dispatches from Matamoros in the National Archives, and various personal papers and memoirs in the Eugene C. Barker Library of Texas History at the University of Texas. *The Official Records of the Union and Confederate Armies* and *The Official Records of the Union and Confederate Navies* also have been indispensable to the study. The major British sources included the Foreign Office Papers, the Customs Office Records, and the Admiralty Papers at the Public Record Office, and the Parliamentary Papers at the British Museum.

The Matamoros Trade

1
THE LOWER RIO GRANDE REGION

The Physical Setting

The dawn of February 1, 1862, sent silver and golden streaks across the wind-swept waters of the western Gulf of Mexico, illuminating and making clearly visible from the shore the masts and hull of a newly arrived man-of-war. The twenty-two-gun United States sloop *Portsmouth,* assigned to blockade duty at the mouth of the Rio Grande, had slipped into position during the night. With it Washington extended its shaky blockade to and beyond the furthermost reaches of the Confederate States.[1]

If it were a typical winter morning, the temperature along the Texas-Mexican coast was nearly seventy degrees and a strong northeast wind lashed heavy waves against the hull of the rolling ship. The Gulf Stream flowed along the coast from south to north, crossing the east-west trade winds, making seaborne activities off the Rio Grande uncomfortable at best. All too often heavy seas and "northers" made trading activities "impossible for ten to twelve days together."[2]

Some four miles west of the ship's position a barren shoreline stretched north and south as far as the eye could see. To the southwest, majestically breaking the coastline, was the quarter-mile wide mouth of the Rio Grande where heavy seas had built up sandbars, forcing oceangoing vessels to anchor from two to four miles off shore, there to be serviced by light-draft steamers capable of clearing the sandbars and navigating the shallow, twisting river.[3] About seven miles north of the river's mouth was the island of Brazos Santiago. Farther north the thin, arid Padre Island arched along the Texas coastline 200 miles north to Corpus Christi. It was separated from the mainland by the Laguna del Madre, which joined the sea at Port Aransas in the north and at Brazos Santiago Pass in the south. Beyond the pass, jutting out into the lagoon, was Point Isabel, once the location of the United States customhouse.

Two lighthouses, built in 1852, marked the entrance to the Texas port of Brazos Santiago. On the southern tip of Padre Island was a black wooden tower which held a beacon visible up to ten miles. Inside the lagoon, at Point Isabel, a larger, sturdier fifty-seven-foot white brick house contained a lamp that could be seen for sixteen miles to sea.[4]

From the decks of the *Portsmouth* the crew, on February 1, 1862, counted ten merchant vessels at anchor discharging their cargoes and taking on cotton. Before the end of the month the number of ships rose to fourteen, of which six or seven were British. This arithmetically illustrated the stimulating effects of the demands of war. Before the war no more than six ships visited the Rio Grande per year, of which, in 1859, none had been British.[5]

Until the arrival of the Union warship the Confederates had conducted a flourishing trade from the Texas shore through Brazos Santiago. The appearance of the *Portsmouth* forced them to transfer their operations to the Mexican side of the Rio Grande in an attempt to disguise them as neutral trade.[6] Article V of the 1848 Treaty of Guadelupe Hidalgo set "the boundary line between the two republics . . . as the center of the mouth of the Rio Grande."[7] In addition Article VII declared the river to be neutral and open to the free use of citizens of both countries.[8]

From a base that measured nearly forty miles on each side of the river at the coast the Rio Grande delta extended inland some seventy-five miles. The Mexican and Texas regions of the delta were almost identical, except that on the Mexican side the San Juan River flowed north to join the Rio Grande near Rio Grande City. On the Mexican side the delta was bordered by deserts and mountains. On the Texan side it merged into flat prairie and semiarid regions to the north. About eighty miles northwest of the mouth of the river lay El Sal del Rey, a natural salt lake about one mile in diameter, which served as a major source of salt for Spanish America and the Confederacy.[9]

Rainfall along the coast averaged nearly twenty inches annually, but decreased with the distance inland. Semitropical temperatures caused a high evaporation rate and even thirty inches was inadequate for extensive agriculture. Floods deposited a silt which made "the ground . . . as rich as the soil along the Nile and [lacking] nothing to make it as productive as the lower Mississippi except [the] seasons."[10] Until well after the Civil War there were no irrigation and flood-control projects to harness properly and utilize the waters of the river.

Much of the delta was made up of chaparrals, interspersed prairie and scrub forests. Thorn-bush thickets of mesquite, huisache, ebony, and juniper would often grow to a seventy-foot height, with prickly-pear cactus, yucca, and dense vines beneath them. Natural paths laced the chaparrals in all directions, some opening into grassy patches of several acres, with others ending abruptly in the midst of the thicket. Many local people, especially Mexicans, seemed to know every path and followed them with ease. But to the uninitiated the chaparrals were nearly impassable. They provided excellent concealment for military ambush and maneuver to within a mile of Brownsville. Gilbert D. Kingsbury, postmaster at Brownsville before the war, reported that "at a thousand points a Thermophily [sic] could be repeated by any peopl [sic] who were familiar with the country."[11] They were effectively used by marauding bandits and by filibustering expeditions sponsored by Union interests in Mexico against the Confederate trade. In Confederate-Union military clashes, the rebels consistently made superior use of the chaparrals, especially during Colonel John S. Ford's 1864 attack on the Federals in Brownsville.

Other natural barriers separated southern Texas from the rest of the state. Between Brownsville and Corpus Christi lay an arid strip, sixty-five miles wide and more than a hundred miles long, appropriately called "the Sands." Devoid of waterholes and scorched by the sun, it was a formidable barrier for travelers.[12] West of the Sands, and between the Rio Grande and Nueces rivers, stretched a flat, sandy region of prairie and chaparral, used for little except cattle raising.[13] Before the introduction of irrigation, this area was subject to dry, searing heat and vicious dust whirlwinds. In 1863 and 1864 cattle and oxen died by the thousands.[14] From Brownsville almost to the Nueces

> the country begins to look as though it had been seared with a red-hot iron. Surface water there is none, and the wells which have been dug in the deepest sink holes give a feeble supply of sickly water, highly impregnated with offensive gases and saline properties. . . . [The] dust of earth; filling the eyes, nose, mouth and hair, making one feel gritty often, and dirty always—a dust of which a man eats his peck monthly, and breathes it daily—a terrible, inhuman diabolical dust. A kingdom for a shower is a standing offer.[15]

One cavalry officer who rode through the region early in 1864 insisted, "You cannot imagine how desolate, barren and desert-like this country is; not a spear of grass, not a green shrub, with nothing but moving clouds of sand to be seen."[16] This area was extremely hostile to wagon transportation and before the Civil War the merchants of Brownsville and other towns along the Rio Grande looked to Mexico for trade rather than risk the hazards of shipping inland.

The Rio Grande is North America's sixth longest river. Indians called it *P'osoge,* or "big river," and sixteenth- and seventeenth-century Spanish expeditions called it variously El Río de las Palmas, Río de Nuestra Señora, and Río Bravo del Norte. In 1806 the American General James Wilkinson dubbed it the Grande River.[17] Often changing its course, the river sculptured its delta with dry riverbeds, ranging from eighty to a hundred yards wide and from twenty to sixty feet deep, known locally as *resacas. Bancos,* or islands, were formed as the river cut across its own loops. During the Civil War era the *bancos* were considered neutral territory and became the haven for bandits, cattle thieves, and private armies of those who preyed upon trade.[18] The river's channel averaged only four to five feet in depth. During the Mexican War, General Zachary Taylor's army had introduced steamers which were shallow-draft enough to navigate the river's four- to five-foot-deep waters and short enough to negotiate its hairpin turns. The burgeoning Civil War trade brought more of these mudskimmers to the river. While nearly all of them were American owned, many sailed under either British or Mexican registry, a privilege available from these nations' authorities in Matamoros.[19]

The river's flow was fickle and treacherous. Flash floods often inundated large areas of the delta and changed the river's channel. A soldier with the Union troops occupying Brownsville in 1864 wrote in his diary:

> The Rio Grande is again rampant. Its water is in no condition for use—I have seen the water of the Missouri, Ohio, and Mississippi when at full banks, but I have never seen such dirty muddy water as the Rio Grande is pouring forth today. . . . So sudden are the rises of this river which make constant changes in the channels that it is impossible for anyone to become a skillful pilot upon it.[20]

At other times the capricious river fell to the level of a creek.[21] When it was too shallow for the mudskimmer, goods were hauled overland by ox cart.

Lower Rio Grande Settlements and Forts

Seaborne goods consigned to Matamoros were first landed at Bagdad, Mexico, situated on the sandy flats at the mouth of the Rio Grande. Though used as early as 1780 as a port of entry for northern Mexico, Bagdad was still only "two or three board shanties" in 1861.[22] Then the Civil War boom elevated it to what Admiral Rafael Semmes of the Confederate raider *Alabama* called "a bustling town," with a polyglot population of whites, blacks, mulattoes, and Indians.[23] Visiting the booming port town in 1863, William Watson, skipper of the English blockade runner *Rob Roy,* found "everyone trying to grab what he could and many schemes there to make money out of the crisis."[24] Seemingly endless piles of cotton bales awaiting shipment to Europe lay on the waterfront along with imported goods destined for the interior. The crack of the teamsters' whip was heard in the streets almost constantly. Occasionally, an American steamboat could be seen hauled up on the flats. Mexican officials permitted individuals to cross the river freely and many Bagdad workers were Americans.[25]

Bagdad offered varied accommodations and diversions. Along with the "first class hotels, boarding houses, stores well fitted with goods . . . and restaurants without number" were saloons, gambling houses and brothels. A transient Texas parson was moved to decry Bagdad as "a veritable Babel, a Babylon, a whirlpool of business, pleasure, and sin."[26] Since the 1840s the beaches of Bagdad had attracted people from as far as Monterrey for sea bathing. For the less innocent, "fandangoes were held every night and women as beautiful as houris exhibited their charms, without the least reserve." Yet a city police force maintained "order by night and by day."[27]

Directly across the Rio Grande from Bagdad was the little town of Clarksville, Texas, with no more than 500 inhabitants. Although it too owed its existence to the wartime trade, it enjoyed neither the economic prosperity nor the exciting diversions of Bagdad.

Up the river were the twin cities of Matamoros, Mexico, and Brownsville, Texas, the major centers of the Confederate trans-Mississippi cotton trade with Europe. The distance from Bagdad to Matamoros by land was only thirty-five miles, "a ride of six hours."[28] The road to Brownsville was a more direct twenty-six miles. However, by water it was some sixty-five miles of twisting, "turbid, yellow waters of the Rio Grande."[29] Steamers could sometimes make the trip in twelve hours, but more often required twenty-four because of frequent groundings in the ever-changing channel.[30]

Founded in 1821, Matamoros was the most important Mexican city in the area. During the 1848 war with Mexico it enjoyed a brief boom as General Zachary Taylor's staging area for his drive into Mexico. This prosperity continued for a short time after the war as Taylor's veterans returned to farm the rich soil along the river. However, a series of crises, including the three-year Mexican Civil War, hurt Matamoros, and it declined from a city of 25,000 to a sleepy town of no more than 5,000. On the eve of the American Civil War it seemed to be dying, with more than half of its houses vacant and its finest brick homes renting for as little as ten dollars a month.[31]

Very little planning was evident in its construction. In the middle of the town an iron fence enclosed a plaza of some eight or nine acres, containing a few scattered benches and, in the center, a "miserable attempt" at a flower garden. Streets were ungraded, deeply rutted, and devoid of sidewalks. Rainfall turned them into quagmires sometimes eighteen inches deep. The town had neither gas nor waterworks and peons hauled silty water from the river by donkey cart for two dollars per forty-gallon barrel.[32]

Despite its filth and sporadic outbreaks of yellow fever and smallpox, Matamoros attracted an international population of thousands as it became a lucrative leak in the Federal blockade. Estimates of its Civil War population range from 9,000 to 40,000.[33] Its streets and shops were crowded with people of

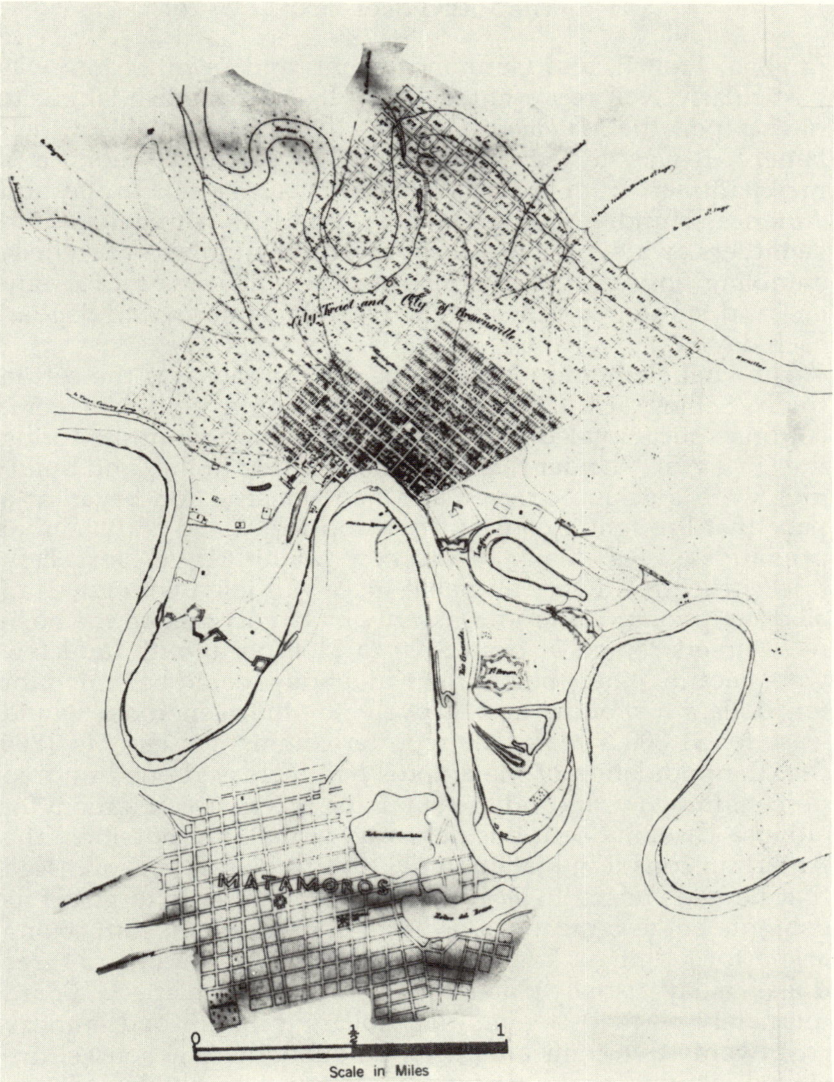

Map of Matamoros and Brownsville. *(Courtesy of the National Archives)*

English, French, and German descent, and "Yankeedom was particularly well represented."[34] By 1864 an English-language newspaper, the *Matamoros Morning Call,* was printed for their benefit. It was visited intermittently by soldiers, sailors, and merchantmen from practically every country in Europe and America. Hundreds of speculators, peddlers, smugglers, and swindlers awaited the unwary. An untold number of brothels, gambling houses, and saloons catered to natives and foreigners, and ten stagecoaches ran between Matamoros and Bagdad each day.[35]

The vital element in Matamoros's prosperity was the cotton trade. Selling at an average of fifty cents a pound in gold, cotton exports totaled an estimated $4 million monthly during the Civil War.[36] Under this stimulus deserted homes and buildings were quickly occupied and new construction began at a pace that brought a constant demand for skilled craftsmen at premium wages. Many of the new buildings were excellent brick structures. Every available space was filled with goods of all descriptions. Storerooms twenty by twenty feet on the business streets rented at from $100 to $150 per month, and few were vacant. Where before the war a house could be rented for ten dollars a month, now a twelve-by-fourteen room would lease for $1,800 a year. One reporter commented early in 1865 that the population of Matamoros had increased one hundred percent in two years and the obtaining of a house or a room for either a dwelling or a business was virtually impossible. The American consul in Matamoros, Leonard Pierce, Jr., confessed that he had chosen to sleep in his office, not only to guard its contents but as a means of escaping the exorbitant sums being asked for lodgings. Living expenses ranged from one to three dollars a day, usually paid in Spanish or Mexican specie. Board ultimately reached seventy-five dollars a month and laundry cost twenty-five cents an article. To offset these expenses, unskilled laborers could expect wages from five to ten dollars a day in specie. Owners of skiffs and lighters received twenty to forty dollars a day for their services.[37]

Across the Rio Grande River from Matamoros was Brownsville, Texas. It had been laid out in 1848 by Charles Stillman around Fort Brown of Mexican War days. Its unpaved streets were long, broad and striaght, dusty for most of the year, and muddy in the winter.[38]

Brownsville became the major Confederate port of entry for

the region, but it did not share fully in the economic boom and mushrooming population growth of Matamoros and Bagdad. Located on belligerent soil, with its chief port, Brazos Santiago, subject to blockade and under constant threat of Union invasion, the town did not have the flourishing economic activity that characterized the Mexican towns. It received financial setbacks when Union troops under General Nathaniel P. Banks occupied it from November 1863 to July 1864.

Prior to the Civil War, all the business of Brownsville was in the hands of a dozen or so American merchants who carried on a thriving trade with the mining districts of northern Mexico. A large part of this trade came in through Brazos Santiago, where the customhouse report for the year 1859 showed that there had entered from Mexico a total of 3,300,375 pounds of goods—mostly cattle, specie, gold and silver buillion, hides, wool, and grass for rope. The total amount of foreign imports other than Mexican was 2,615,040 pounds. During that year 120 sail and steam vessels were listed as having entered the port. In 1860, $12 million in specie passed through the customhouse en route to the United States.[39]

Before the Mexican War the territory between the Rio Grande and Nueces rivers was a part of the state of Tamaulipas, Mexico. Understandably, the majority of the original inhabitants were Mexicans, who composed a heavy majority of Brownsville's 1860 population of 2,672. Postmaster Kingsbury found all but 500 to be of Mexican origin. Of this number about 200 were European residents, mostly French and Spanish but some English, Italian, and German also. The other 300 were native and naturalized Americans, of which only about 75 were men. They embraced every class: merchants, shopkeepers, clerks, traders, boatmen, professional men, loafers, politicians and "blacklegs." Of the total not more than thirty had families to protect or interests to defend. He optimistically predicted, however, that "the settlement by Americans . . . is comparatively recent, indeed is yet going on."[40]

A deeply rooted antagonism, dating from the Mexican War period, existed between the Mexicans and the Americans in the town. The Mexicans resented the Americans, who, as newcomers to the region and still in a very definite minority, occupied the choice lands and economic and social positions of the community. One resident observed that "even the accusation of being an abolitionist would cause a man to be shot on the streets like a mad-dog and with far less investigation as to the merits of the case."[41] An English visitor described it as "about the rowdiest town in Texas."[42]

Fort Brown had been constructed along the banks of the Rio Grande early in 1846 by General Zachary Taylor's forces as a base for operations in northern Mexico. It came under Mexican bombardment in May of that year. Marching to its relief, General Taylor fought the first two significant battles of the war, at Palo Alto and Resaca de la Palma. Upon arriving at the fort, he ordered it named after Major Jacob Brown, who had been killed in its defense.[43] Following the Mexican conflict, it was garrisoned by a small American contingent until Texas seceded in February 1861. Then the Texas militia under the command of Colonel John S. Ford took control of the fortress and began to make repairs. When Confederate General Hamilton P. Bee became commander of the lower Rio Grande frontier, he found these repairs yet unfinished and the guns so trained that they could be "of but little use for [the] defense of Brownsville, as an enemy could without difficulty take possession of it without coming under fire from the fort."[44] Bee, however, was confident that the fort "could in a short time be made as strong as earthworks generally are."[45]

Some ninety miles up river was Fort Ringgold, also a Mexican War fortress. More commonly called Ringgold Barracks, it was linked with Fort Brown by a military road running along the north bank of the river. Around it the little town of Rio Grande City had sprung up under the promotion of Henry Clay Davis.

Further upstream, about 120 miles above Brownsville, was Roma, Texas. More than 200 miles northwest of Brownsville were located the twin cities of Laredo, Texas, and Nuevo Laredo, Mexico. Another 100 miles had to be traversed before coming to the ford between Eagle Pass, Texas, and Piedras Negras, Mexico. The distance from Brownsville to San Antonio was 200 miles, to Austin 250 miles, and to the railhead at Alleyton 300 miles. About fifty miles beyond Alleyton was Houston, the center of the small Texas railroad network. From there some 1,200 miles of railroad track spanned the distance between Texas and Richmond, Virginia.[46]

The cotton famine in Europe and the Federal blockade combined to make Matamoros and the surrounding region for a time the greatest cotton market in the world. The area's Mexican populace called this era *Los Algodones,* "the time of the cotton."[47] The commerce of this "backdoor of the Confederacy" soon came to rival that of Liverpool and New York, and gave this far corner of the world a "splendid epoch."[48]

Notes

1. Swarthout to McKean, February 3, 1862, United States Navy Department, *Official Records of the Union and Confederate Navies in the War of the Rebellion,* 30 volumes (Washington: Government Printing Office, 1894–1927), Ser. I, Vol. 17, p. 101, hereafter cited as *ORN;* Blacker to Crawford, February 9, 1862, Great Britain, Foreign Office, General Correspondence: America, United Staes, January 1861–December 1865 (Public Record Office, London), Ser. II, F. O. 97/42, hereafter cited as F. O.; L. Tuffley Ellis, "Maritime Commerce on the Far Western Gulf, 1862–1865," *Southwestern Historical Quarterly* 77 (October 1973):204; Kleiber to Reed and Company, February 6, 1862, Gilbert D. Kingsbury Papers (Eugene C. Barker Library of Texas History, University of Texas, Austin); *Tri-Weekly Telegraph* [Houston], February 2, 1862. Reports of the date of the establishment of the blockade at the Rio Grande differ. In August 1861, the reliable Confederate agent in northern Mexico, José A. Quintero, wrote R. M. T. Hunter that the blockade of the Texas coast began sometime between June 5 and 17, but he does not specifically mention the stationing of a war vessel at the mouth of the Rio Grande. Quintero to Hunter, August 16, 1861, Confederate States of America, Confederate State Papers (Manuscript Division, Library of Congress, Washington, D.C.), Vol. 58. The *New York Herald* of June 2, 1861, stated that the blockade of the Confederate coast "from the Chesapeake Bay to the Rio Grande River will be completed within the next ten days." Colonel Buchel wrote to Major Davis that the blockade began on December 5, 1861. Most records show, however, that the *Portsmouth* was not only the first ship to take up picket duty at the Rio Grande, but also was the first to take prizes there. See United States War Department, *War of the Rebellion: The Official Records of the Union and Confederate Armies,* 127 volumes (Washington: Government Printing Office, 1880–1901) Ser. I, Vol. 4, p. 155, hereafter cited as *ORA;* Lyons to Russel, March 28, 1862, Foreign Office Papers, F.O. 97/42. The *Portsmouth* was actually ordered to "cruise between Corpus Christi and the Rio Grande." Thus, her appearance at the mouth of the river on February 1, 1862, was not intended to be a permanent assignment. "Stations of Vessels Composing the Gulf Blockading Squadron," January 23, 1862; "Blockading Instructions," McKean to Swarthout, January 17, 1862; McKean to Welles, February 17, 1862, *ORN,* Ser. I, Vol. 17, pp. 71, 100, 102–03.

2. Reed to Angel, November 27, 1863, Foreign Office Papers, F.O. 5/1181; Swarthout to McKean, February 28, 1862, *ORN,* Ser. I, Vol. 17, p. 107; Watson, p. 17; James A. L. Fremantle, *The Fremantle Diary,* Walter Lord, editor (Boston: Little, Brown and Company, 1954), p. 6.

3. Pierce to Seward, May 23, 1862, *ORA,* Ser. I, Vol. 9, p. 685; Swarthout to McKean, February 28, 1862, *ORN,* Ser. I, Vol. 17, p. 108; Lyons to Russell, December 7, 1863, Foreign Office Papers, F.O. 5/1181; William Watson, *The Adventures of a Blockade Runner* (London: T. Fisher Unwin, 1892), pp. 16, 17; James A. Irby, "Line of the Rio Grande: War and Trade on the Confederate Frontier, 1861–1865" (Ph.D. dissertation, University of Georgia, 1969), pp. xvii–xix; Anne Cowling, "The Confederate Cotton Trade with Mexico" (M.S. thesis, University of Texas, 1929), p. 1. The moderate winter months

permitted the cotton trade to continue throughout the year with very little interruption, and it was not necessary for soldiers to go into winter quarters. Although the summer months were long and hot, the prevailing winds from the Gulf made life bearable during that season. Dr. Irby indicates that the tempo of activity usually increased during the winter because of the moderate temperatures and reduction in humidity. Until the early twentieth century there was no ship channel connecting Brownsville with Point Isabel as there is today. The shallow-draft steamers that navigated the Rio Grande drew about three feet of water and were called "lighters" or "mudskimmers."

4. "Lists of Light Houses, Lighted Beacons and Floating Lights of the Atlantic, Gulf and Pacific Coasts of the United States," Washington, 1862, Foreign Office Papers, F.O. 5/838.

5. Swarthout to McKean, February 3, 1862, Bailey to Welles, April 2, 1862, *ORN*, Ser. I, Vol. 17, pp. 101, 403; Pierce to Seward, March 1, 1862, *ORA*, Ser. I, Vol. 9, p. 674; Crawford to Russell, March 1, 1862, Foreign Office Papers, 1861–1865, Vol. 58 (British Museum, London), p. 510, hereafter cited as Parliamentary Papers; Robert W. Delaney, "Matamoros, Port for Texas During the Civil War," *The Southwestern Historical Quarterly* 58 (April 1955): 473, footnote 2.

6. Quintero to Browne, March 22, 1862, Confederate State Papers, Vol. 58.

7. Bell to Lewis, June 13, 1863, *ORN*, Ser. I, Vol. 20, p. 294.

8. Kathryn T. Abbey, "Incidents of the Confederate Blockade," *Journal of Southern History* 11 (May 1945):222.

9. Joseph L. Clark and Elton M. Scott, *The Texas Gulf Coast* Vol. 2 (New York: The Lewis Historical Company, 1955), pp. 31–32.

10. Ibid., p. 32; Kingsbury Papers, 2:112; *Texas State Gazette* [Austin], July 21, 1862.

11. Irby, pp. xx–xxi; Cowling, p. 6; Kingsbury Papers, 2:110–12.

12. Cowling, pp. 6–7.

13. Irby, pp. xxi, xxiii. Before the war with Mexico the Rio Grande country had been largely a land of great ranches located on huge, almost barren land grants from the King of Spain. There was only small evidence of any agricultural or commercial activity. During the 1850s changes occurred, at least along the river, where tiny wooden river-boat stations and trading posts sprang up. Merchants bought cowhides and shipped them to England, ushering in a new prosperity from the hunting and skinning of the great herds of wild longhorns and mustangs of the region. These were remnants of the vast herds formerly held by Mexican owners who were driven from the region with the outbreak of the Texas Revolution in 1836. At that time most of the people who lived in the valley, after destroying or abandoning some three million head of stock, withdrew to the south bank of the river and did not return until about 1853, when the state assured them undisputed possession of their lands.

14. Ibid., p. xx; Cowling, pp. 6–7.

15. *Tri-Weekly Telegraph* [Houston], April 29, 1863.

16. Robert L. Kerby, *Kirby Smith's Confederacy: The Trans-Mississippi South, 1863–1865* (New York: Columbia University Press, 1972), p. 179; Cowling, p. 6.

17. Irby, pp. xiv, xvi.

18. Kingsbury Papers, 2:110; Irby, p. xvi.

19. *New York Herald*, October 29, 1861; Quintero to Hunter, October 18, 1861, Confederate State Papers, Vol. 58; Fremantle, p. 6; Irby, p. xii; Kerby, p. 181.

20. Benjamin F. McIntyre, *Federals on the Frontier, The Diary of Benjamin F. McIntyre, 1863–1864*, Nannie M. Tilly, editor (Austin: University of Texas Press, 1963), pp. 334–35.

21. The water below Matamoros was not fit for drinking either. When instructed to

fill up with drinking water from the mouth of the Rio Grande, the commander of the *Portsmouth* replied: "This is not practicable, and if it were I should have a large portion of my crew on the sick list from dysentary and diarrhea. . . . [I have been informed] that it is necessary to proceed some distance up the Rio Grande before fresh water fit to drink can be obtained, and that the use of it is very injurious to those not accustomed to it." Swarthout to McKean, February 28, 1862, *ORN*, Ser. I, Vol. 17, pp. 107–08.

22. Irby, pp. xxi–xxii; *New York Herald*, January 9, 1865; Fremantle, p. 6; William Watson describes Bagdad as an "unimportant little place, very similar in appearance to other small Mexican towns." Watson, p. 22.

23. Semmes as quoted in Irby, p. 6.

24. Watson, p. 22.

25. *New York Herald*, January 9, 1865; Irby, p. 6; *ORN*, Ser. I, Vol. 19, p. 291.

26. *New York Herald*, January 9, 1865; Kerby, p. 181.

27. Irby, p. 5; *Weekly Ranchero* [Brownsville], June 15, 1867; *New York Herald*, January 9, 1865.

28. Rolando to Welles, December 1, 1863, Foreign Office Papers, F.O. 5/1182; Fremantle, p. 6.

29. Max Baron von Alvensleben, *With Maximilian in Mexico: From the Notebook of a Mexican Officer*, p. 14, as quoted in Ronnie C. Tyler, *Santiago Vidaurri* (Austin: Texas State Historical Association, 1973), p. 107; Fremantle, p. 2.

30. Fremantle, p. 7.

31. Irby, pp. xxii, 2; Matamoros was named in honor of Father Mariano Matamoros, a hero of Mexican independence. It has sometimes been misspelled as "Matamoras," "Matamaras," "Matamores." Avila Larios, "Brownsville-Matamoros: Confederate Lifeline," *Mid-America* 11 (April 1958):67.

32. *New Orleans Times*, March 3, 1865.

33. Fremantle, p. 10; *Houston Tri-Weekly Telegraph*, February 16, 1865; Paul Horgan, *Great River, the Rio Grande in North American History* (New York: Rinehart and Company, 1954), p. 837; William T. Windham, "The Problem of Supply in the Trans-Mississippi Confederacy," *Journal of Southern History* 27 (May 1951):162.

34. *Houston Tri-Weekly Telegraph*, December 30, 1864.

35. *New Orleans Times*, June 1, 1865.

36. Irby, p. 5; Horgan, p. 837; *New Orleans Daily True Delta*, March 5, 1863, December 16, 1864; *New York Herald*, January 9, 1865.

37. Wood to Seward, February 18, 23, 26, 1865, United States Department of State, Consular Dispatches, Matamoros, Record Group 59 (National Archives, Washington, D.C.), hereafter cited as Consular Dispatches, Matamoros; Fremantle, p. 10; *Daily Telegraph* [Houston], February 16, 1865; *New York Herald*, January 9, 1865.

38. Marilyn McAdams Sibley, "Charles Stillman: A Case Study of Enterpreneurship on the Rio Grande, 1861–1865," *Southwestern Historical Quarterly* 77 (October 1973):229.

39. Kingsbury Papers, "A Sketch of Brownsville," p. 106; Report of F. W. Latham, Collector of the port of Brazos de Santiago, for 1859, *The Texas Almanac* (Galveston: A. H. Belo Corporation, 1860), pp. 125, 127; Bee to the Secretary of War, October 12, 1861, *ORA*, Ser. I, Vol. 4, pp. 118–19.

40. Kingsbury Papers, 2:2–6, 108–09.

41. G. D. Kingsbury to Milton Kingsbury, May 30, 1862, Kingsbury Papers: ibid., 2:2–6; Cowling, p. 9.

42. Fremantle, pp. 10, 23.

43. Irby, pp. xii–xiv.

44. Bee to the Secretary of War, October 12, 1861, *ORA*, Ser. I, Vol. 4, p. 118. General

Bee was the brother of Confederate General Bernard E. Bee, who, lying mortally wounded at the First Battle of Bull Run, gave T. J. Jackson his nickname, "Stonewall."

45. Ibid.

46. Dana to Stone, December 25, 1863, *ORA*, Ser. I, Vol. 26, Pt. 2, pp. 876–77; Cowling, p. 41; Watson, p. 20.

47. Ellis, *SWHQ*:199, 101; Brown to Wallace, January 12, 1865, *ORA*, Ser. I, Vol. 48, Pt. 1, pp. 512–13.

48. Tyler, *Vidaurri*, p. 107. Much of the story of the Matamoros trade route has been lost with official records and private journals. No doubt other bits and pieces remain undiscovered in private collections and archives in England, France, the United States, and Mexico. Of the materials available, the most important sources are found in the Eugene C. Barker Library of Texas History at the University of Texas, Austin, the Library of Congress and the National Archives in Washington, D.C., and the Public Record Office and the British Museum in London, England.

2
THE TRADE BEGINS

Effect of the War on the Economy of the Region

At the beginning of the Civil War the Texas economy was almost entirely agricultural. By 1860 the state claimed 51,569 free farmers, 6,536 farm laborers, 1,254 overseers, and 265 planters. The industrial revolution had barely touched Texas and less than 1 percent of the state's capital was invested in industry. In contrast to New York and Pennsylvania, each of which possessed more than 22,000 manufacturing facilities, employing more than 220,000 workers, it had only 983 industrial establishments most of which employed about four people each.[1]

The Texas cattle kingdom was concentrated in the southern part of the state in the sparsely populated wedge between the Nueces and Rio Grande. By 1860 the number of cattle in the region was more than 3,700,000, five beefs for every Texan and "enough meat on the hoof to feed half of the Union."[2] Lacking railroads or other means of efficiently transporting these herds to distant American markets, some cattlemen explored the possibilities of exporting them through northern Mexico.

The decade of the 1850s also witnessed a spectacular sheep boom on the south Texas ranchlands, and it seemed that sheep would soon rival cattle in importance. Although the severe winter of 1859–1860 decimated the Texas sheep flocks, about 750,000 head remained.[3]

Of greater importance was Texas's cotton production. More than two-thirds of the state lay within the nation's 400-mile-wide major cotton-producing belt between thirty and thirty-six degrees north latitude. The state's growing population planted an ever-increasing acreage of cotton. In the decade after 1859 Texas increased its annual production from 58,072 to 431,463 bales, raising it from ninth to fifth place among cotton-growing states.[4] In the southwest cotton was king and in Texas it was the number one commodity of a strong agrarian economy.

Eighteen sixty-one was a good crop year. By midsummer Eastern newspapers were reporting that they had advice from Texas regarding the superior conditions of the crops in all sections of the state and "sugar and cotton were in excellent order."[5] According to the *Richmond Enquirer:*

> This is the greatest crop . . . known in Texas for many years. Corn is now in full roasting ear. . . . The wheat crop is all secured and is now being manufactured into flour . . . as good Texas flour as the world ever saw, enough to feed the Confederate army for three years. . . . Grass is knee high all over the prairies, and cattle and horses very fat. We make our own sugar, and our own molasses and salt. The blockade can't hurt us only in the way of coffee, but who cares for coffee.[6]

The blockade caused many Texans to turn to the Rio Grande frontier for the export of their crops. Brownsville and Matamoros were the natural outlets for cotton shipments to Europe. Merchants, speculators, and state agents converged on Matamoros. The first big load of cotton, some 3,000 bales, came from the north Texas firms of Colonel Middleton T. Johnson and the Rhyne brothers, for shipment to Europe signaled the real opening of the trade. The trickle of cotton exports that began in the summer of 1861 became a flood by fall.[7]

Although only fourteen years old when the war began, John Warren Hunter, as a teamster of a wagon hauling cotton to Brownsville, was deeply impressed with the rapidly growing trade. He later recalled "a never ending stream of cotton pouring into Brownsville." Crossing the river to Matamoros, he saw "ox trains, mule trains, and trains of Mexican carts, all laden with cotton coming from almost every town in Texas. . . . Brownsville became the greatest shipping point in the South," and Matamoros "a great commercial center [with] cotton and other commodities . . . pouring into her warehouses."[8]

By August, Brownsville merchant Charles Stillman was anticipating the shipment of the entire Texas cotton crop through Matamoros "with Mexican permits under the British flag."[9] The customhouses at Brownsville and Matamoros were overwhelmed with the processing of export and import papers. Not only was cotton "passing from Texas into Mexico by wagons . . . [but also] by light-draft vessels that [went] through the bays and bayous along the coast to the mouth of the Rio Grande."[10]

To the independent-minded Texas farmers and enterprising businessmen of the region it seemed to matter little if this trade defied the non-export and cotton destruction decrees of the Confederate government. Instead, the Confederate Congress yielded to the demands of Texas. On May 21, 1861, while voting to prohibit cotton exports, it exempted cotton shipments into Mexico, ostensibly because the trade supplied textile mills there.[11]

But from the beginning there was a scarcity of quartermaster supplies, prompting one general in the Texas Department to complain to the Confederate Secretary of War, Judah P. Benjamin, that he had found Texas "totally unprepared, confused, and defenseless . . . lacking of means, guns, arms, ammunition and a proper military organization." Its seacoast was "defenseless," and he confessed his "inability to remedy the evil."[12]

Little aid from the Confederate government was in prospect. After studying the Texas situation, Benjamin suggested "that the simplest and best plan was [for] the state of Texas to clothe her own troops, under rates and regulations to be exectued by her own officers. . . ."[13] This and other factors combined to enhance that feeling of independence which had characterized most Texans for a quarter of a century.

When shooting broke out between rival political factions in Matamoros in the fall, cotton trade along the Rio Grande was somewhat interrupted for a time, but by the end of the year order was restored and trade was burgeoning again.[14]

To handle this cotton trade, commercial firms established themselves in Matamoros and Brownsville. Among the firms doing business along the Rio Grande were Droege, Oetling and Company, Brown, Fleming and Company, Harding, Pullin and Company of London, Lloyd's of London, Treviño Brothers, and Oliver Brothers of Monterrey, Attrill and Lacosta, and Marks and Company. These companies had contacts with Europe, the United States, and the interior of Mexico. While most were operated by English or Germans, the largest and most influential one was Milmo and Company, a Mexican firm, which also had financial stakes in other companies. It was headed by Patricio Milmo, the son-in-law of Santiago Vidaurri the governor of the Mexican provinces of Nuevo León and

Tamaulipas. The governor had a personal investment in the company and wrote a letter to Confederate President Jefferson Davis claiming he could supply all the ammunition the Confederacy would be able to use. Several of the larger firms operated their own fleets of ships and controlled their own credit and capital resources. In their dealings with England, these companies usually conducted their cotton transactions through Fraser, Trenholm and Company of Liverpool, which had offices in Charleston, South Carolina, and New York City.[15]

Besides these large commercial houses, a number of private merchants were involved in the trade. Perhaps the most successful of these was José San Román. Originally from Spain, he had settled along the Rio Grande frontier sometime before midcentury, "for at least a dozen years carried on an extensive business in Brownsville,"[16] and became a multimillionaire before the outbreak of hostilities. His correspondence reveals him to be well educated, polite, formal, and discreet. In an age and area of flexible business morals, he was a quiet, honest man. Colonel John S. Ford, commander of the Texas militia on the frontier, said of him that he "never had an evil thought. He amassed a large fortune and was never accused of having wronged anyone in its acquisition."[17] These personal standards did not bar Roman from blockade running, however. Having contacts in London and New York, he negotiated cotton transactions for a number of Southern sympathizers, including Henry Clay Davis and cotton magnates Richard King, Mifflin Kenedy, and Charles Stillman. At times he engaged in gunrunning for Colonel Ford's troops at Fort Brown.[18] Further south, at Monterrey, another private merchant, German-born American citizen J. E. Schenk operated a rapidly growing business. He purchased much of the region's quicksilver, sulphur, percussion caps, and saltpeter and Confederate agents made regular visits to him.[19]

As the cotton trade grew, Matamoros and Brownsville became a center of activity for other wealthy men, including the cotton barons King, Kenedy, and Stillman. King, in the process of building one of the great ranches of the southwest some 120 miles north of Brownsville, simply called himself "a farmer." Kenedy identified himself as a "steamboat captain," and Charles Stillman, founder of Brownsville and owner of much of it and various shipping enterprises, spoke of himself as a "gentleman of leisure." Closely associated with this triumvirate were Cornelius Stillman, brother of Charles, who listed his occupation as merchant, H. E. Woodhouse, and Don Francisco Yturria, who handled much of King's, Kenedy's and Stillman's Mexican business, and Jeremiah Galvan, who most likely served as the front man for Stillman's New York operations. When the war began, these men modestly listed their estates at from $50,000 to $250,000 each.[20]

Cotton arriving on the frontier was readily transported down the Rio Grande on paddle steamers operated by King, Kenedy, and Stillman. With Stillman furnishing much of the capital, and King and Kenedy serving as steamboat captains, they had built up the river fleet in the decade before the Civil War. Constructed to be "sufficiently staunch to stand the ordinary sea and even rough weather at the mouth of the river," these boats fulfilled a twofold need.[21] They carried goods up and down the Rio Grande, and also served as lighters to haul cargoes to and from the great seagoing vessels anchored from two to four miles off the coast.

Although ostensibly destined for Matamoros, cargoes from Europe were more easily landed at Brownsville. To reach the warehouses of Matamoros, goods had to be hauled nearly a mile over a dirt road from the river. However, from the wharf it was "but a stone's cast to Stillman's levee in Brownsville on which [they] may with impunity be landed immediately . . . by the Texan purchasers." Often "this was the course of procedure . . . although owing to subtlety of the precautions taken to avoid violating the letter of international law, it [was] very difficult to establish the fact in a majority of the cases."[22]

The former president of the Brownsville branch of the Commercial and Agricultural Bank of Texas, Joseph P. Coutheuy expressed concern about the illegal trade to the American Secretary of the Navy, Gideon Welles. He said that during the four years in which he had been the bank's presiding officer he had "become well acquainted . . . with the whole commerce with Mexico, whether of exports or imports," and he could "not recall a single instance in all that time of a vessel arriving at Matamoros with a cargo of provisions, groceries, and other supplies of such magnitude and value as within the last few months [had] found its way thither almost weekly."[23] He could not remember "a solitary cargo in an English bottom" arriving prior to the Civil War. He concluded that

> [the] whole of the pseudo Mexican trade by the channel of the Rio Grande, carried on so extensively by English vessels at the present

> time has its explanation and origin in the market opened up in Texas by the necessities of that and adjacent States in arms aginst the Federal Government, consequent upon the blockade of their maritime ports. Nine-tenths of the cargoes [that went] up the Rio Grande, nominally consigned to merchants in Matamoros, were, in fact, destined to supply the rebels in Texas, and were securely stored in warehouses of Brownsville within twenty-four hours after their simulated sale on the Mexican side of the river.[24]

Texas and Confederate agents joined the many private merchants ranging across northern Mexico in search of goods, especially war materials. The three northeastern Mexican states of Tamaulipas, Nuevo León, and Coahuila offered a variety of materials, including tin, lead, copper, iron, nitrate of potash, quicksilver, sulphur, saltpeter, powder, percussion caps, cloth, blankets, shoes, and coffee. Also, Mexican lead mines along the frontier produced about 378,000 pounds each month, including 150,000 pounds from the vicinity of Monterrey. In January 1862, Confederate agents paid $15.00 per cargo of 300 pounds of lead, or 5 cents per pound in cotton. The freight costs to transport lead to Matamoros were ¾ cents per pound and ½ cents per pound more to markets in Texas. Southern agents generally negotiated for lead to be delivered in Texas at 6 ¼ cents per pound in cotton.[25]

The Confederates saw in the rapidly growing textile industry in northern Mexico a promising market for more and more cotton. On the eve of the Civil War the American businessman Edward Plumb, having carefully studied the resources of northern Mexico, wrote, "The manufacture of cotton has attained a much greater importance in Mexico than is generally understood in the United States. . . . There are now in operation in all some 40 mills running about one hundred thirty-five thousand spindles."[26] The major factories were located at Pueblo, Guadalajara, Durango, Orizara, and Quentaro. The provinces of Nuevo León and Coahuila had a total of eight mills, which, using over 1,500,000 pounds of cotton annually, were "furnishing all the necessary clothing for the slaves in Texas and could, if necessary, supply the balance of the Confederate States."[27]

For a number of reasons, however, the Mexican cotton trade failed to meet early Southern expectations. The 3,000 to 4,000 bales annually required by the mills of Nuevo León and Coahuila were but a small portion of the Texas crop. Although cotton sold reasonably at 12 to 26 cents per pound there, the "general costs of manufacturing in Mexico [was] about four times that of similar establishments in the United States,"[28] and the constant political and military turmoil in Mexico greatly increased the risks to the continuity of supply and markets. Also, the Confederates had a more pressing need for European than for Mexican materials. Consequently, the Matamoros trade was, from the beginning, oriented toward the European market.

Thus, an insignificant little Mexican town became the base of a would-be nation's supplies. Until the very end of the war Matamoros furnished Texas, Arkansas, Louisiana, and Mississippi with most of their manufactured goods and practically all of their munitions of war. Alarmed over the magnitude of the trade, the United States consul, Pierce, warned:

> Matamoros is now the great thoroughfare to the Southern States. They pass their coffee, flour, and in fact all their supplies through here. They had also a large pile of cotton on the east bank of the river, to take out when an opportunity offers.[29]

Historian J. Fred Rippy later said that "Matamoros was to the South what New York was to the North."[30]

Quickly recognizing the importance of the trade, Southern officials on the frontier from the beginning sought to impress both Texas and Confederate authorities of the importance of Matamoros and Brownsville to the Confederacy. They stressed the need not only to defend the Rio Grande frontier, but to give "proper direction" to fostering and developing its commerce.[31]

The Federal Blockade and Foreign Attitudes

As the year 1861 came to an end the blockade proclaimed earlier by President Abraham Lincoln began to have some effect on the Southern states. The trade of Galveston, Corpus Christi, and other Texas ports was interdicted. Francis Lubbock, who became governor of Texas in November, feared a Yankee invasion, and decreed that cotton could not be stored near the coast, except at the Rio Grande.[32]

Word reached Washington from Havana as well as from Matamoros that supplies of every description were going to the insurgents by way of the Rio Grande and "the mere appearance" of a gunboat at the river would effectively curtail the trade.[33]

Search-and-seizure operations were undertaken immediately against the foreign merchantmen anchored there, but the trade continued to grow. Early in 1863 Rear Admiral Theodorus Bailey, commander of the American West Gulf Fleet, complained to Washington

> that there are at present from 180 to 200 vessels of all nations, many of them Americans and having regular clearance from Northern ports, off the mouth of the Rio Grande, waiting to discharge their cargoes and receive cotton . . . and that previous to the rebellion, there were at most but half a dozen vessels trading with that port during the whole year.[34]

Union blockaders also began a concerted effort to capture the lighters servicing the merchantmen at the Rio Grande. For a time this action threatened to stop commerce through Matamoros because the pilots refused to leave port for fear of being seized. "As vessels could neither be loaded or discharged, business was entirely suspended, and Matamoros [was] virtually blockaded."[35] In Brownsville an emergency strategy meeting was called to consider the problem. Attending were José San Román, Charles Stillman, the Treviño brothers, Francisco Yturria, and Colonel John Ford. They gave consideration to an earlier offer from the British consul in Matamoros to "register any vessel under his flag sailing from that port."[36] Ford recommended that the steamboats be placed under the Mexican flag instead. This was merely a paper transaction and the same owners and crews operated the vessels. Stillman, distrusting the Mexican officials, objected and expressed a fear to King that "we shall see them with a 'Turkey buzzard' at their masthead in a day or two."[37] However, after some discussion, he agreed to the Ford proposal. The transactions were quickly completed and the commercial activities resumed.

Turbulent Mexican politics greatly affected the development of the Matamoros trade. That country's history as an independent nation, dating from 1821, was beset with internal strife, weakness, and poverty. Spanish colonialism had not prepared it for self-government. The masses remained illiterate and poor, while the army and the Church exercised preponderant military and economic powers. The shift from colony to republic provided the common man with little more than replacement of the Spanish hierarchy by home-grown Creole bosses. This changed the struggle for power between Spanish and Creole to one between Creole and *mestizo*.[38]

From the beginning of the republic these social tensions were reflected in the political divisions of the country. The Conservatives held firmly to centralism, calling for a strong national government, and the aristocratic policies of the past. The Liberals, who often split on a number of issues, advocated a federal government of autonomous states and were desirous of social and economic reforms for the benefit of the masses. Over these issues the electorate chose sides. The Creole, Castilian in temper and training, usually espoused conservatism and allied himself with the clergy, the army, the landlords, and later with the foreigner who had money to invest. He embraced centralism because an impressive and powerful national executive had similarities with a king. The *mestizo*, however, was suspicious of the affairs in the capital, identifying the pretensions of the Conservatives with the bad habits of the viceroys. His liberal views were more compatible with federalism, which divided governmental responsibility among the states.[39]

In 1855 the Liberals had united behind the Indian Benito Juárez to shift power to the *mestizo*. Civil war followed and the government treasury was soon dissipated. With the Church coffers depleted also and no hope of taxing an economically prostrated populous, Juárez ordered suspension of payments on the foreign debt in July 1861. In the following January the allied expeditionary forces of England, France, and Spain landed at Veracruz to coerce Mexico into paying the debts owed their bankers. When it became apparent that the French Emperor Louis Napoleon III had imperialistic designs on Mexico, England and Spain withdrew their forces. The French army soon captured Mexico City, chasing Juárez and his forces into the interior where they continued a guerrilla resistance. In northern Mexico several ambitious governors, while continuing to render lip-service to the Juárez government, seized the opportunity to increase their own power and prestige.[40]

The governors of the three northeastern provinces of Nuevo León, Coahuila, and Tamaulipas had virtually established their autonomy by 1862. The temptation of profits to be made from the trade and delicate Confederate diplomacy aligned these governors in sympathy with the rebels. Defying President Juárez's ban on commerce with either of the American belligerents, they connived to get supplies and essential war materials into the Confederacy.[41]

The war and turmoil in Mexico made it more difficult to determine the destination of contraband cargoes. Large-scale arms shipments to Matamoros were not necessarily bound for the South, but might be destined for the constitutional Mexican government, particularly after Juárez retreated northward and Matamoros became his only avenue of supply. So disguised, great quantities of contraband that entered Matamoros eventually found their way to the Confederate armies without molestation from Union blockaders.[42]

The Union blockade and the Confederate decision to destroy or withhold the cotton crop aroused concern in England where textile mills depended heavily upon Southern cotton. The world's largest producer of textiles, England received ninety percent of its raw cotton from the United States. The cotton famine was especially felt in Lancashire, the center of the English industry. Despite a flurry of harsh diplomatic exchanges and newspaper talk of intervention the British cabinet, influenced by public opinion, avoided a confrontation with Washington. Instead, it sought a way whereby the sorely needed cotton could be obtained under the disguise of a neutral commerce. During the war, British ships were the most numerous of the foreign callers at the Rio Grande, and it was the major recipient of the more than 300,000 bales of cotton exported through Matamoros between 1861 and 1865.[43]

In France the cotton industry was also distressed by the blockade. However, the French Emperor Louis Napoleon III found himself in a different position than the British. His troops were in Mexico in defiance of the Monroe Doctrine, and the Mexican patriots under Benito Juárez were using the northern Gulf ports to obtain supplies. Therefore, the solution to Napoleon's dilemma was not to be found in a neutral trade through Matamoros, part of which supplied the *Juaristas.* Rather, he advocated intervention, breaking the blockade and recognizing Confederate independence, which would both divide and weaken the United States, champion of the Monroe Doctrine, and would insure France a continuous supply of Southern cotton. Fearful of challenging the United States unilaterally, however, he constantly sought a policy of joint intervention with the British. This possibility prompted the *New York Herald,* in September 1861, to warn that the impending Anglo-French intervention in Mexico, ostensibly to collect debts, was actually a move to obtain cotton by placing a strong joint military force on the Rio Grande frontier. It stated "that were the Mexican frontiers in possession of English and French troops there would be no difficulty in passing cotton across them . . . [and] attempts . . . will undoubtedly be made to furnish the rebels with arms and other supplies through Mexico."[44] Apparently satisfied with her own measures to offset the cotton shortage, England was unresponsive to these overtures from Paris.

Pickett Mishandles Confederate Interests in Mexico

By early 1861, the Confederate government had concluded that the establishment of cordial relations with Mexico was, for several reasons, an expedient diplomatic move. Using their contiguous border along the Rio Grande to bypass the blockade, they hoped to receive large quantities of supplies from Mexico and Europe for the prosecution of the war. Secondly, Southerners expected some European power, probably France, to take advantage of the Civil War to intervene in Mexico. They expected Mexico "to be the lever by which Napoleon III would be toppled from his neutral perch."[45]

To develop friendly ties with the southern neighbor, Confederate President Jefferson Davis selected John T. Pickett. Forceful, bold, and shrewd, Pickett was well acquainted with Mexico, having served at Veracruz as United States consul for a number of years. At that post he had developed close association with Benito Juárez and the small group of Liberals who comprised his advisors and principal officers. Offsetting these assets were his quick and vile temper, sharp tongue, and swashbuckling characteristics that caused him to be somewhat of a troublemaker when angry. According to Frank Owsley, "Pickett was no diplomat."[46]

On May 17, 1861, the State Department appointed Pickett as special agent "of the Confederate States near the Government of Mexico."[47] While he was instructed not to insist on full diplomatic recognition at first, the Confederate government hoped that the South could ease itself into the position of friendly relations formerly held by the United States. To accomplish this, it told him to stress points that the two governments held in common:

> The people both of the Confederate States and Mexico are principally engaged in agriculture and mining pursuits, and their interests are therefore homogeneous. The institution of domestic slavery in one country, and that of peonage in the other, establish between them such a similarity in their system of labor as to prevent any tendency on either side to disregard the feelings of the other.[48]

The diplomat was instructed that conversations related to the common border were "of paramount importance." It was urgent that he get a guarantee that no United States troops would invade the Confederacy through northern Mexico. He was "to point out that the Confederacy was the only country so situated as to guarantee Mexico against foreign invasion, i.e., the United States." Finally, special attention was to be given to the prevention of border raids from each side.[49]

Pickett carried with him secret instructions to promote privateering against Union merchantships. Since Mexico had declined to sign the Declaration of Paris abolishing piracy, Confederate authorities confidently anticipated that Mexican authorities would permit privateers to operate from their ports. They expected him to use his close acquaintance with Mexican businessmen to discover their feelings on the subject, and commissioned him to grant letters of marque and reprisal.[50]

Upon his arrival in Mexico City, and before establishing official relations with the Mexican government, the Confederate agent set out to fulfill these secret instructions. On June 21, he appointed C. Markoe, a pro-Southern American merchant residing in Veracruz, as an "agent to receive applications for letters of marque and reprisal."[51] However, these plans were thwarted by the occupation of Veracruz by the allied forces of England, France, and Spain before Markoe could send a privateer to sea.

From the beginning Pickett was imprudent and tactless. When asked if he sought Mexican recognition, he replied, "To the contrary, my business is to recognize Mexico—provided I can find a government that will stand long enough."[52] Not until late July did Pickett report that he had succeeded in establishing friendly and confidential relations with Manuel Zamacona, the Mexican Minister of Foreign Relations. While endeavoring to win the confidence of the Mexican government, he continued to reveal his contempt for the country and its people in his dispatches to the State Department. Hearing a rumor that some Mexican officers might join the United States Army, he wrote:

> I have expressed the hope that they would all go and only regretted that the entire U.S. Army is not officered by Mexico. I also added that they ought to be very careful not to be taken prisinors [sic] by the South, as they would in that event, probably soon find themselves for the first time in their lives usefully employed in agricultural pursuits—i.e. hoeing corn and picking cotton.[53]

When the tactless diplomat heard that the United States had received permission to march troops across Mexican territory into Arizona, he warned that should the rumor be true there would be "at least thirty thousand Confederate diplomatic agents crossing the Mexican border in a very short time."[54] He felt that this unfriendly act relieved him of the "strictest regard" for Mexican neutrality. On September 10, he issued another set of letters of marque to Don Mateo Ramírez, a Mexican government official in Sonora and Lower California. He expressed hopes that Ramírez would seize an American gold ship from California and thereby bring about a collision between Mexico and the United States.[55] Unaware that the American minister in Mexico City, Thomas Corwin, was negotiating a loan of $11 million to the Juárez government, Pickett predicted that $1 million "judiciously applied" would purchase Mexican recognition. Since all of his messages were being seized in Matamoros and sent to President Juárez, these injudicious remarks damaged any chance he may have had for success.

Meanwhile, Thomas Corwin, the new United States minister to Mexico, arrived in Mexico City well before the Confederate agent. Using this advantage wisely, he influenced public opinion in the Mexican capital in favor of the United States before Pickett arrived. He then made the most of Pickett's indiscretions, and as the Confederate blundered from one embarrassment to another, the interests of the United States steadily gained ground with the *Juaristas.* Luckily for the Union cause, Corwin's letters were not intercepted by the Mexicans, for he had even greater designs on Mexican territory than did the Confederates.[56]

Trying desperately to outmaneuver Corwin, Pickett played his trump card. On September 28, he wrote Foreign Minister Zamacona, offering "to receive and transmit to Richmond proposals for the retrocession to Mexico of a large portion of the territory hitherto acquired from her by the late United States."[57] Still unaware that his messages were being read by Juárez, he immediately wrote to Secretary of State Robert Toombs that his message concerning the retrocession of lands was a political maneuver—nothing more or less. He could not understand why the Mexican government gave no response to his offer. However, he sensed its growing hostility.[58]

On October 29, frustrated and defeated, Pickett advised that the Confederacy should have no further dealings with the Juárez government. Insisting that its permit to allow United States troops to cross Mexican territory was a violation of neutrality, he suggested the immediate seizure of the city of Monterrey and surrounding territory in Nuevo León. Whether or not he intended that Matamoros should be included in this seizure is not clear, but there are some indications that about this time he offered the Mexican government $2 million for the use of the Rio Grande port. Further, he began to court openly the conservative Church Party of General Miguel Miramón, avowed enemies of Juárez.[59]

Determined to force his diplomatic expulsion from Mexico, he increased his insults to the Juárez government. Also, when challenged on the creditability of the Confederate government and its officials by a blustering, raw-boned Yankee, Pickett attacked him with "hands and feet." His objective was twofold: to give an enemy a "severe chatisement," and to get sent out of the country as persona non grata.[60] Apparently successful in his first objective, he failed miserably in his second. Instead of being diplomatically dismissed, he was thrown in jail as an ordinary criminal. Finally, after an imprisonment of thirty days, he bribed a judge, was released, and escorted out of the country as a disturber of the peace.[61] Richmond, no longer considering it necessary to have a minister at the seat of the Mexican government, decided not to replace him.[62]

This conclusion that a minister was no longer necessary in Mexico City matured slowly during the second half of 1861. At first President Davis and his advisers had expected France's intervention in Mexico to lead to Paris's recognition of Southern independence, but had attached very little importance to trade with and through its northern states. But while the few and dissappointing reports from Pickett were creating doubts on recognition, reports of the emerging trade across the Rio Grande were encouraging. Consequently, Confederate authorities began to revise their plans.

Quintero Serves the Confederacy in Northern Mexico

Political events in the northeastern Mexican states of Nuevo León, Coahuila, and Tamaulipas increased Confederate optimism about trading possibilities. Since 1855 the region had been under the influence of the independent-minded *caudillo,* Santiago Vidaurri. In 1859 he had combined two of the states under his control as "Nuevo León y Coahuila." Although he did not then control the mouth of the Rio Grande, he exercised a "moral influence over the state of Tamaulipas almost as great as if it were his own."[63] Then, early in 1862, he officially became governor of Tamaulipas, putting Matamoros and other important trading points along the lower Rio Grande under his control. From his capital at Monterrey, he operated a popular and progressive government that generally reflected Liberal policies.[64]

Ostensibly loyal to the Juárez administration, Vidaurri actually used the Mexican Civil War and the French intervention to strengthen his own autonomy. Feeling that his region and its people had more in common with Texas and the American southwest than with Mexico, he held thoughts of an alliance first with the United States and then, in 1861, with the Confederacy.[65] Two basic interests motivated his warm overtures toward the Confederates. First, he benefited greatly from the revenue he collected from the Rio Grande commerce. The more the cotton trade across the river increased, the more concerned he became with protecting and expanding it. Secondly, following the allied intevention by France, Britain, and Spain in Mexico, the Juárez regime, fighting for its life, was demanding greater and greater support from the various states to defend itself, and Vidaurri had no desire to sacrifice the economic and political stability of his domains for the sake of the Republic.[66]

The individual who most influenced President Davis and his

advisers to focus their attention on the Rio Grande trade was José Agustín Quintero, the leading Confederate agent in northern Mexico.[67] He was a Cuban by birth and a Southerner by choice. Born in Havana in 1829, he early demonstrated a precocious intellect which reportedly gained him entrance into Harvard College at the age of twelve, although there is no official record of his enrollment there. During his stay at Cambridge, he became friends with Henry Wadsworth Longfellow and Ralph Waldo Emerson. After his graduation he returned to Cuba, earned a law degree, and went into journalism. Moving to Texas, he edited two influential Spanish-language newspapers: *El Ranchero* in San Antonio and *Leslie's Illustrated Newspaper* published by the well-known New Yorker, Frank Leslie. He fought in the struggle for Cuban independence and lived and traveled in Mexico, where he gained a familiarity with Mexican ways and customs. He met Governor Vidaurri in Austin, in 1859, during the latter's brief, self-imposed exile and they maintained a sporadic correspondence. With the outset of hostilities, he enlisted in the Confederate army in Texas, and, after his company had been sent to Virginia, was assigned to the diplomatic corps. He proved to possess the shrewdness, insight, and tenacity necessary to achieve diplomatic success for his government.[68]

Shortly after the Confederate State Department commissioned Pickett to Mexico City, it sent Quintero to Monterrey. In May 1861, while at Austin, he was ordered to proceed to Galveston to receive instructions. On June 1, he wrote to Assistant Secretary of State William Browne acknowledging receipt of the commission and instructions dated May 22.[69] Confederate leaders expressed concern that Mexican "lawless expeditions" into Texas were about to be renewed. Quintero was instructed to present himself to Governor Vidaurri in Monterrey and to work to forestall such forays with implied threats of retaliation:

> With terms of kindness, but with firmness . . . assure the Governor that it is the wish of this Government to maintain the most friendly intercourse with the people of Mexico to prevent border raids, and lawless invasions of the soil of Mexico by our citizens, but that we require that this friendly disposition be reciprocated.[70]

His monthly salary was set at $200. He promised to "leave by water, the most expeditious route, if [no] blockading vessels [appeared] within 48 hours."[71] Optimistically citing his Cuban birth, disassociation with the civil strifes of Mexico, and his good fortune of having rendered "some personal services to . . . Vidaurri when he visited Austin during his exile," Quintero had "every reason to hope that [the governor's] reception of me will be cordial, and that I may succeed in carrying out the instructions of the State Department to its satisfaction."[72]

For some unexplained reason Quintero did not leave Galveston until June 5. Sailing on the schooner *Sam Houston,* he landed at Brazos Santiago and went to Brownsville. Entering Mexico through Matamoros, he traveled the last 300 miles to Monterrey by stagecoach, arriving on June 17. Two days later he presented his credentials and letters of introduction from Texas Governor Edward Clark and Confederate Secretary of State Robert Toombs at Vidaurri's office. In his letter, Toombs extended "friendship and good will" and anticipated "a corresponding sentiment of cordial understanding and good will in return." Suggesting that the "interests of the two Republics [were] similar and mutual . . . [he stressed that the Confederacy] disclaims all the ideas of invasion and conquest of other territories which was so conspicuous in the policy of the United States." He then called for a mutual cooperation in making the "valley of the Rio Grande" peaceful, and for Mexican support in stopping unlawful raids into Texas territory.[73]

Although Quintero's mission was supposedly secret and confidential, Union officials were, at all times, aware of his work and movements in Mexico. Soon after his first interview with Vidaurri in June, the governor's official newspaper carried documents over his name, clearly identifying him as a Confederate agent. When a few months after he arrived in Monterrey, he found it necessary to visit Matamoros and Brownsville in an attempt to settle a dispute between the contending forces of Carvajal and Vidaurri, the editor of the *Fort Brown Flag* expressed utmost confidence that "commissioer Quintero" would handle the problem ably. In May 1865, the editor of the Matamoros *Daily Ranchero* praised the diplomat for his extraordinary work. Even Union refugees, fleeing Texas, knew of him and his work. The United States consuls, M. M. Kimmey at Monterrey and Leonard Pierce, Jr., at Matamoros, were able, from newspaper coverage alone, to keep abreast of his dealings. Yet even with his cover blown from the very beginning, Quintero was the most effective agent sent to Mexico, and one of the most skillful and successful in the entire Confederate diplomatic corps.[74]

Quintero was invited to see the governor on June 21, just two days after presenting his credentials. Aiding him in getting a speedy audience were his past acquaintance and friendship with Vidaurri, and the intercession of the governor's personal physician, Dr. J. H. Means, a former resident of South Carolina. But, most importantly, Vidaurri felt threatened by President Juárez's effort to centralize authority and sought Confederate support for his autonomy. He would discuss any matter in the hope of gaining Confederate support. Once this was achieved he could negotiate with Juárez from a position of strength. It was a warm meeting of two old friends of which the young diplomat wrote, "General Vidaurri feels a great friendship for the South."[75]

After his initial interview, Quintero met officially with the governor on two more occasions. Explaining that he was on a mission that would last only a few more days, he told Vidaurri that nothing was of greater importance than cordial relations with his states. Reliable information he said, indicated that a large force was organizing in Mexico, and he hoped that the governor would assist in seeing that it never invaded Texas. The force to which he referred was under the leadership of Juan N. "Cheno" Cortina, notorious along the border for his terrorizing campaigns, especially against Texans. In 1859 he had captured and held Brownsville until he was driven out by a company of Texas Rangers. Along the Rio Grande frontier he was strongly supported by Mexican peasants with whom he had gained the status of a folk hero. He could raise a sizable force almost at will. Quintero asked for an agreement guaranteeing the security of the Rio Grande valley, and the building of defense works.

The governor's response was immediate and positive. He assured Quintero that he had been working for greater border security since 1859, when he had written to Texas Governor Hardin R. Runnels on the matter. In addition, he had unilaterally issued a decree in April 1861 calling for the arrest and punishment of anyone crossing into Texas for criminal purposes and returning to Mexico. He, too, considered Cortina an "irresponsible man" and added that he was being pursued but, regrettably, he had not yet been captured. He promised Quintero that no raids into Texas from his territory would be tolerated, for he was "determined to preserve the peace of the Rio Grande frontier with all the forces at his command."[76] A reciprocal extradition agreement, designed to reduce the number of border crossings by criminals to prevent capture, was made. Vidaurri also assured his visiting friend that he would use his influence to see that "Mr. Lincoln . . . [would] never get consent to march troops through northern Mexico to attack [the Confederacy]." This he would do, even if Juárez gave permission for such a march.[77]

Seizing the opportunity presented by the positive atmosphere, Quintero brought up the question of trade. He was instructed to inquire about the possibility of establishing commercial relations for both civilian and war supplies. Vidaurri realized that the Confederates could bring a lucrative commerce to his states, and that strengthening the informal ties he already had with Texas would put him in a more favorable position to oppose Juárez. His response was more favorable than either Quintero or the State Department had expected. While noting that he did not have the authority to conduct diplomatic relations with foreign countries, the governor stated that, because of the extraordinary circumstances, he would act on behalf of the national government in establishing commercial relations with the Confederacy.[78]

After the interviews, an elated Quintero wrote the State Department "that I have been entirely successful in my mission . . . We have gained an ally."[79] Then he set out to learn the extent of the material resources of Nuevo León y Coahuila which could be drawn on by the Confederacy. He found that lead, saltpeter, powder, copper, coarse cloth, and other products were available in large quantity and at reasonable prices. He was particularly pleased that "any quantity of lead and powder could be obtained at Monterrey . . . the former at $10.50 per cargo of 300 pounds or $12.87½ for same if delivered at Roma, Texas, and the latter at moderate prices, and available on 30 to 40 days notice."[80]

On the night before he left Monterrey for home, Quintero received another expression of Vidaurri's friendship. The governor called on the diplomat in his hotel room. In an hour-long conversation, the *caudillo* again referred to "his friendship and good will" toward the Confederacy. Before departing, he requested that the visit be regarded as a "call on his Excellency Jefferson Davis."[81]

Annexation and Transportation Proposals

By early July, Quintero was back on the Rio Grande. Here he noted that Matamoros was ideally suited for the safe importation of arms and other materials from both Mexico and Europe.

> [The] port of Matamoros will no doubt be blockaded for all intents and purposes by the Federals. But it is the best and most expedient point of entry for the Confederates in the West. If the government concludes to use Matamoros it will save much time and expense, at least one month, in transport over the use of ports further south in Mexico.[82]

In his enthusiasm Quintero misrepresented overland travel from Brownsville into the interior of Texas as "cheap and abundant . . . [with] good grass and water along the whole route of land carriage."[83] Concerned over the possibility of an accord between Juárez and the United States, he asked Richmond to "let me know of any measures, inimical to us, adopted by the General Government of Mexico that I may, if possible, defeat them on the frontier."[84] Crossing to Brownsville, he wrote to Assistant Secretary Browne that he planned to leave in a few days for Richmond, "with communications of *great importance* to our Government which I have not thought safe to send by mail."[85]

Meanwhile, in Monterrey, Governor Vidaurri moved to protect himself in case something should go amiss. He informed Juárez that a representative of the Confederate government had called upon him in a very proper manner and was concerned about mutual problems. In a more detailed note to Foreign Minister Zamacona, he wrote that Quintero had raised some very critical questions—particularly those of peace and security on the frontier—and he intended to give satisfactory answers.

Quintero arrived in Richmond on August 17. In a series of letters to the newly appointed Secretary of State R. M. T. Hunter, he divulged matters that he had chosen not to communicate by long distance because of the number of Union agents thought to be working in the post office department.[86]

Most importantly Quintero revealed a proposal from Vidaurri for the annexation of the northern states of Mexico to the Confederacy. It was well known on the border that for several years the *caudillo* had talked of secession from the cen-

The loading of wagons in Matamoros. *(Courtesy of the Texas State Historical Association)*

The interior of the city of Matamoros. *(Courtesy of the Texas State Historical Association)*

tral government and the establishment of "The Republic of Sierra Madre."[87] A union of Nuevo León y Coahuila, Tamaulipas, and perhaps even Chihuahua and Sonora with the Confederate states would be mutually beneficial, Vidaurri argued. These Mexican states not only had huge mineral deposits that could be profitably mined, but also a fledgling textile industry that could be developed under American technical skill and labor. Further, an Americanization process was already germinating in the area, and to deny its continued maturation would be unnatural.[88]

To facilitate the annexation would not be too costly, Vidaurri suggested. Of course, there would be some trouble from the Juárez government. But with a "little assistance from Texas"—perhaps 1,000 men and some "flying artillery"—success would be assured. If President Davis would appoint a trusted commissioner to negotiate with him, the governor added, discussions could begin immediately. The new commissioner could contact L. B. Cain of the New Orleans firm of K. Marks and Company, who would give him a letter of introduction to Dr. Means, who then would introduce him to Vidaurri.[89]

It was a bizarre proposal, but Quintero was convinced of the governor's sincerity. Known to be ambitious and opportunistic, Vidaurri was, in 1861, politically and militarily weak. Confederate offers of annexation and military support could give him a position of strength from which he could bargain more successfully with Juarez to continue his autonomy.

Regarding the South's great desire to purchase arms in northern Mexico, Vidaurri was less promising. He insisted that ten or eleven cannon and fewer than 10,000 rifles were all that he possessed. As long as he was struggling for survival alone against the overwhelming superiority of the Federalists, he could not allow the Confederates to obtain arms in Nuevo León y Coahuila. If the Confederacy ever became strong enough to annex northern Mexico, he said, perhaps such material could be obtained. However, he said, all the raw materials necessary to produce war material were available. One quintal (100 pounds) of copper or bronze for making cannon could be bought for $15.50. Some metals, such as lead and copper, might need refining because of the poor methods used by the Mexicans. Also, large deposits of saltpeter were available near Piedras Negras, across the river from Eagle Pass, Texas. These and other raw materials could be readily obtained by contacting Dr. Means, Vidaurri's physician, who would act as a go-between, or orders could be addressed to José Oliver, a merchant at Monterrey, or P. M. López of Treviño and Company in Brownsville and Matamoros.[90]

Transportation presented a problem, but Quintero proposed several solutions. He saw no real problem in neutral European ships landing their goods at Matamoros via Bagdad at the mouth of the river. Nor did he envision any real problem in overland transportation from Brownsville into the heart of the Confederacy. The area with the greatest transportation difficulties, he said, was northern Mexico. To meet that need, he proposed building a railroad from Matamoros on the gulf coast to Mazatlan, Sinaloa, on the Pacific. This would not only link the Confederates with an excellent deep-water port on the Pacific, but "it would bind northern Mexico in a common interest with us."[91] He suggested two possible routes: a southern coal-rich route through Durango, following the natural river pass, and another through Chihuahua. Quintero felt the Chihuahua route route would be better because passage through the mountains would be easier. Along this northern route lay numerous minerals, including iron, silver, lead, antimony, tin, gold, lime, quartz, and selenite. The area had an abundance of timber and various fruits which also could be useful to the Confederates.[92]

Quintero's final report, filed on August 22, 1861, received the same careful and long consideration as had all of his others. Pickett had not yet been heard from, and Quintero's report shifted the center of interest from Mexico City to Monterrey. Confederate leaders from President Davis through the state and war departments were greatly impressed with the possibilities he had presented to them. His stock soared in Richmond. On September 3, Browne notified Quintero that he had been appointed, "Confidential Agent of this Government in North Eastern Mexico, to reside at Monterrey."[93] According to Frank Owsley this position was most important:

> He was far more important than Pickett could have been even had the latter been a first-class diplomat. The Vidaurri government to which Quintero was accredited was in a much better position to aid or injure the Confederacy than was the Juarez government, whose

> actual power was primarily in southern and western Mexico—far from the Confederate border.[94]

Quintero was instructed to cultivate good relations with the border states, make convenient commercial arrangements, and continue to work to prevent the Yankees from moving troops and munitions across Mexican territory. However, he should politely reject Vidaurri's annexation offer. After careful study, President Davis had decided that it would be "imprudent and impolitic in the interest of both parties to take any steps at present . . . in reference to the future political relations of the Confederate States and the Northern Provinces of Mexico."[95] Davis expected several European powers to intervene in Mexico, and France to try to set up a puppet government. In such a case, the Confederate president felt that the United States would challenge them and become involved in a war which would assure Southern independence. On the other hand, should the South annex the territories, such a conflict might never occur and the Confederates would receive the wrath of the French imperialists and subject the ports of northern Mexico to Union blockade. And surely annexation would mean war with Juárez. Finally, Davis had enough independent-minded governors on his hands already. He had no desire to add another one. Nevertheless, he hoped that the interests of both peoples would continue the "intimate social and commercial relations" already begun.[96] Quintero was instructed to place an order for 500 tons of lead and 400,000 pounds of powder to be delivered at Roma, Texas. He was then to look for other articles needed by the army and for the best method of transporting them to Texas. Browne, with a special interest in small arms, had told the diplomat to request that Vidaurri reconsider his ban on the sale of guns to the South. Should the governor respond affirmative to this request, "it would be regarded as a most signal and valuable proof of his friendship."[97] If this could not be arranged, Quintero was to continue his search for arms in other Mexican states.

Having received his instructions, Quintero left Richmond to return to Monterrey "with all convenient dispatch."[98] Upon reaching New Orleans, Quintero was shocked by rumors that Governor Vidaurri had been defeated in battle by Mexican Federal troops and had fled to Texas.Supposedly Juárez had learned of the *caudillo*'s desire to secede from Mexico and join his provinces to the Confederacy. Quintero feared all was lost, for Juárez's federals would be in no mood to assist the Confederates. The Confederate agent consulted Vidaurri's confidante in New Orleans, L. B. Cain, who, although he had recently received several letters from the governor, could not with certainty dispell the rumors, Apprehensively, Quintero wrote the State Department that he would remain in New Orleans and await further instructions.[99] On September 18, much relieved, Quintero reported that "official reports" had disproved the newspaper stories of Vidaurri's exile and that he would leave the following day for Monterrey.[100]

Shifting Relations with Vidaurri

At Brownsville late in October 1861, Quintero conferred with merchants and Confederate authorities. He found Colonel John S. Ford, the Confederate commander at Fort Brown, to be "a gentleman of fine intellect and an old veteran. He is thoroughly acquainted with the Mexican character and Spanish language and ought by all means remain permanently at this post. He can be of *great service* to our government."[101] Through Ford, he met Mr. Alexander of the merchant house of R. J. Lawler and Company. Alexander revealed that his firm had "a fair prospect of procuring a lot of arms which [it was] endeavoring to smuggle out of New York and bring to Matamoros." The firm was willing to accept up to $10,000 in Confederate State Bonds on the illicit contraband. Quintero informed Secretary of State Hunter that he would "arrange the matter if possible."[102]

On his arrival in Monterrey on October 24, Quintero learned that President Juárez had proclaimed neutrality toward the American Civil War, and had given orders to close the border to the commerce of the respective belligerents. The Confederate diplomat hastened to see Governor Vidaurri regarding this crisis. Although sick in bed when Quintero arrived, Vidaurri welcomed him cordially, and assured him that the frontier would remain open to Confederate trade and that he would protect it against seizures. Quintero's report to Richmond reflected his restored confidence:

> Governor Vidaurri is much feared, not only by President Juárez but also by the people of the interior states. For years he has ruled supreme and the states of New Leon and Coahuila have under his administration been prosperous and happy. Hence his popularity on the frontier. He is our faithful friend and ally.[103]

As the trade continued, Quintero found his office besieged by merchants seeking the profits of war. After a few days of screening, he reported that Oliver Brothers of Monterrey was probably in the best position to supply the Confederacy. The company had a large capital and broad resources, and had business contacts and considerable experience in Texas and New Orleans. It offered all that the South seemed to need, blankets, shoes, cloth, lead, sulphur, saltpeter, powder, and English firearms at reasonable prices. Payment, in cash or cotton, could be made "upon delivery of the contraband articles."[104] The State Department authorized Quintero to negotiate, but Jose Oliver, excited over possibilities, decided to go to Richmond with samples of his goods. Quintero provided the Mexican merchant with a letter of introduction.[105] Once in Richmond, Oliver drove a hard bargain. His insistence that all goods be paid for in advance departed from his original proposal to Quintero, and was too much for the Confederate officials to accept. Concluding that Oliver was "fearful of responsibilities," Secretary of State Benjamin broke off the talks. However, on the possibility that the merchant might be of some help in the future, the secretary recommended that officials in Mexico keep in contact with him.[106]

Meanwhile, contrary to Vidaurri's assurances, Quintero was having difficulty locating the powder that he had been instructed to purchase. He learned that, because of inadequate machinery, powder was manufactured by a very slow process in Monterrey. Therefore it was impossible to get delivery of the 400,000 pounds desired by the War Department within the specified forty days. Oliver Brothers had informed him that some 200,000 pounds of cannon powder was available in Zacatecas, but it too could not be delivered to Texas within forty days.

At Zacatecas, Oliver Brothers hoped to purchase small arms from General Jesús González Ortega's disbanded army. Quintero asked the War Department what price it was willing to pay for the arms.[107]

Quintero also found Patricio Milmo and Company eager to trade flour for cotton. Other merchants presented attractive contract proposals, and before the middle of November, Quintero reported that he could purchase and have delivered at Roma rifle and cannon powder at $40.00 and $32.00 per 100 pounds respectively. Saltpeter and sulphur were available on the same terms at sixteen cents and nine cents per pound. He suggested that it was safer and cheaper to buy sulphur and saltpeter than powder. Mexican powder was of very poor quality, its transportation was extremely dangerous and had to be done at "our own risk." He urged that purchases be made soon because many Texas agents were buying, causing an increase in both demand and prices.[108] A short time later he found a collection of 370 "old, but serviceable" rifles, muskets, and carbines for sale at $2,000, and he expressed concern that they be purchased "immediately," before they were bought up by speculators from Brownsville and sold "to the Government at enormous prices."[109]

Meanwhile, trouble was brewing in Tamaulipas, where Vidaurri held great influence but not official authority. In the fall of 1861, Jesús de la Serna had been elected governor of Tamaulipas in a close election and his victory was sanctioned by the Federal government. However, the defeated candidate, Cipriano Guerrero refused to accept the results and prepared to seize power by force.[110]

Governor Serna turned to the well-known filibuster General José María Carvajal and his band of *rojos* for help against the threatened rebellion. Carvajal held the respect of most Americans on the border. Educated at Bethany College in Virginia (now West Virginia), he was described by the editor of the *Fort Brown Flag* as "a very intelligent gentleman," who spoke "English like a book." In an interview with the editor, Carvajal spoke of being sympathetic with the Confederacy and of having two sons protecting a Southern school from a Northern invasion.[111]

To command his force of some 800 to 1,200 *crinolinos* or *amarillos* as they were called, Guerrero chose General Guadalupe García. García was an equally able leader. When the editor of the *Fort Brown Flag* visited his camp, he came away with the impression that García was "an agreeable gentleman and a most popular officer . . . [whose men] manifest an earnest disposition to fight until the bitter end."[112]

The gathering conflict meant trouble for the Confederacy. The thriving business in Matamoros slowed to a halt. "The lately flourishing city now looks like a graveyard," it was reported. "It is dangerous to approach the town in any direction, for fear of the flying bullets."[113] As no Union blockader had yet arrived at the mouth of the river, trade could be conducted through Brownsville in Texas. But should the daily-expected Yankee gunboat appear before the struggle was settled, it could have grave consequences for the Confederate cause.

The conflict also threatened to spread to Texas. General García extracted forced loans from all those whom he suspected of favoring Serna and expelled them from Matamoros. When the ousted businessmen fled to Brownsville and began to lay plans for revenge, it seemed probable that Texans would enter the fighting. Such action by Texans could have undermined the Confederate position in northern Mexico. Thus, although sympathetic to Serna, Quintero and Colonel Ford worked diligently to maintain neutrality. When Carvajal began organizing troops on Texas soil near Brownsville, Ford dispersed them and informed both sides that he would observe strict neutrality.[114]

On November 29, Carvajal's *rojos* charged the positions of García's forces in the center of Matamoros. The Confederates blocked the ferries on the river and allowed only the wounded to be transported across to safety. Although both the assault and resistance were "fiercely" conducted, nothing was decided. To one observer there was "much powder being burned, but 'no body hurt.' "[115] Other ineffective skirmishing followed with no visible results except to curtail further the Confederate trade. By the end of December 1861, most of the trade between Matamoros and Monterrey had been halted and Governor Vidaurri, deprived of its revenues, was forced to demand a loan from the merchants of his capital. It was unpopular, especially among German-American merchants who had fled Texas to escape the Civil War.

After several months of indecisive clashes in which neither faction established control of the state, President Juárez declared martial law in Tamaulipas and appointed Vidaurri commander of all its forces with full administrative powers. It was a pragmatic decision. Despite his conflicts with the errant governor, the president recognized that Vidaurri was the most competent leader in northern Mexico. And with the allied forces of

England, France, and Spain landing at Veracruz, he needed to secure the northern coast.[116]

Upon appointment as military governor of Tamaulipas, Vidaurri raised an army to occupy the port cities of Tampico, Soto la Marina, and Matamoros. But Governor-Elect Serna, whose forces, under General Carvajal, had besieged Matamoros for several months, was not willing to surrender any authority to Vidaurri. Vidaurri requested that Serna meet him for discussions near Monterrey, but no agreement resulted.[117] He then ordered troops into Matamoros. At the same time he asked Quintero to go to Brownsville to talk with Confederate authorities, for he realized that Carvajal was a friend of many of them. By the time the Confederate diplomat reached Brownsville, Serna was already there seeking to rally support for his cause, and seemed determined not to give up.[118]

The Confederacy faced the potentially serious problem of choosing between a legally elected governor who reportedly favored the South, and a military governor, appointed by the central government, who had already demonstrated his friendship to the Richmond government. If the South should support the losing side in the conflict, the winner might retaliate against the Confederacy. Quintero favored Vidaurri, for he not only seemed to present more opportunities and support, but appeared to be the most likely victor in the impending struggle.

The major problem for Quintero was the attitude of the Confederate military at Brownsville. When he arrived from Monterrey, the garrison at Fort Brown was under the command of Colonel Philip N. Luckett while Colonel Ford was on rest leave in San Antonio. Luckett had attempted to maintain neutrality, even going so far as to disarm a band of Carvajal's *rojos* when they crossed the river into Texas.[119] But when Colonel Ford returned early in March 1862, Quintero's fears increased. Ford and Carvajal had been personal friends for a number of years a relationship upon which the Mexican filibuster sought to capitalize.[120] Word spread that Carvajal was reorganizing his forces on Texas soil with the approval and support of Colonel Ford. Vidaurri was becoming nervous and Quintero gravely concerned. When Carvajal led a band of 500 men against the Mexican town of Reynosa with weapons apparently supplied by someone in Texas, Quintero appealed directly to Governor Lubbock. He had lost faith in Ford.[121] After several other attacks by the *rojos* along the Mexican frontier and with no apparent restraint from the governor's office, the frustrated diplomat, feeling totally ineffective, requested "the Department to appoint a person to succeed me who may have more influence . . . with the military at Brownsville."[122]

As Quintero predicted, Governor Vidaurri retaliated against the South for the Carvajal raids. Early in April 1862, he completely closed the border to both individual passage and commercial traffic. When he permitted trade to resume, Matamoros had ceased to be a free port and a duty of two cents per pound was placed on cotton. The governor's interest was not to hamper the trade, but rather to coerce the Confederates into assisting him. When Quintero wrote to Vidaurri asking for an explanation of the increased duties, the governor agreed to discuss the matter. In the ensuing interview, the *caudillo* claimed that the duties were necessary to help support his army of 7,000 men. Quintero believed that no duties would have been placed on cotton if Texans had been more diligent in preventing forays into Mexico.[123]

However, both parties were eager to settle their differences and the talks quickly bore fruit. On April 5, the day after the Quintero-Vidaurri conference, the governor cut the cotton duty from two cents per pound to one cent.[124]

Meanwhile, Carvajal had established his headquarters in Texas near Brownsville. At Quintero's insistence, the Confederate government ordered Colonel Ford to arrest Carvajal if he continued to use the camp to organize forays into Mexico. Because of his close friendship with Carvajal, Ford hesitated. Quintero then suggested to Colonel Macedonio Capistrán, the new *comandante* at Matamoros, that he could initiate legal proceedings against the filibuster by charging him with violation of the international boundary. This affidavit, sworn before Commissioner John Tabor in Brownsville, forced the Confederate army to take action against Carvajal. Before the end of the month Quintero was able to report that the *rojo* party had been disbanded. Tensions between the Confederates and Vidaurri were eased.[125]

These incidents revealed to Quintero and other Confederates that Vidaurri was not as sincere about the Confederate cause as he had originally indicated, but rather his motives were to sustain and expand his personal power. Less than a year had elapsed since he had offered his entire realm of Nuevo León y Coahuila to the South. During that time he had gained economic strength from his commercial ties with the South, and had successfully defied President Juárez, retaining and expanding his autonomy. Nevertheless, he had threatened to disrupt completely his relationship with the Confederacy in order to take advantage of an opportunity to enlarge his domain. His control of Matamoros, the only neutral port open to the Confederates, gave him a strong negotiating position which enabled him to win his point against the South. While their friendship and mutually beneficial commercial relationship would continue, Quintero would no longer refer to Vidaurri as "an ally."

The conflict between Governor Vidaurri and Juan Carvajal was settled in Mexico early in 1862, but the cotton trade at Matamoros did not immediately revive. The struggle had so endangered the commodity in the vicinity that many producers had stopped shipping it to the frontier. Those which did were forced to take circuitous routes to avoid the conflict. These added transportation charges combined with the momentary shortage of cotton in Matamoros to force prices up to levels that purchasers were unwilling to pay. Reflecting on this slowdown, the editor of the *Fort Brown Flag* lamented that "there [was] neither buyer nor seller [and] no transactions [were] taking place" because the "prices offer[ed] . . . and demanded [were] so wide apart."[126] In time, however, the slow market, the low river, and "the want of steamboats under neutral flags" created a two- to three-month inventory of cotton at the Mexican port.[127]

Despite difficulties, Quintero was able to negotiate several advantageous deals for the Confederates. In February he obtained a shipment of 40,000 rifles from New York when the Mexican government, which had placed the order, was unable to pay for them. When customs officials in Matamoros notified Quintero that the shipment was on its way, he suggested that Richmond have the Confederate agent in Havana request that the French fleet not confiscate it.[128] Vidaurri's Secretary of State, Manuel G. Rejon, guaranteed the Confederates 2,500 pounds of saltpeter per month at sixteen to seventeen cents per pound. He also assured Quintero that "any quantity of ship building timber" would be supplied with payment in cash on delivery. By early March, Vidaurri was once more offering his "good will" and "all the ammunition" that the Confederates desired.[129]

As the trade resumed, trains of carts laden with powder, sulphur, saltpeter, and other contraband again moved from northern Mexico to Texas. The Confederate diplomat notified his State Department that Oliver Brothers had contracted for all of the saltpeter and powder in the state of Zacatecas, and was confident of filling all demands. *"Everything with the exception of small arms can be obtained here,"* he wrote.[130] However, many goods were being sold to individual buyers and speculators. Quintero urged Colonel H. E. McCulloch, Confederate Commander of the Western District of Texas, to purchase as much material as possible directly from Monterrey.

Large shipments of foodstuffs, including wheat, corn, flour, sugar, and coffee were imported into Texas from Mexico. Patricio Milmo and his partner, Evaristo Madero, signed an agreement in September 1862 to ship flour to Texas. A Matamoros businessman, L. Werlman, also contracted to send 332 wagon loads of that vitally needed commodity across the Rio Grande into Texas. Governor Vidaurri extended his blessings to these agreements, expressing regret that because of the unusually destructive drought then ravaging the country, he could not send more grain. Quintero told Secretary Benjamin that all the flour needed by the South was available in Mexico.[131] In December, 1862, he itemized large quantities of produce and breadstuffs on the market, including corn. While some foods later became scarce, flour remained plentiful.[132]

As his forces gained a more secure hold on Tamaulipas, Vidaurri returned to his office in Monterrey. Quintero requested and received orders from Richmond to return with him to coordinate relations with the governor. However, convinced that the expanded trade needed more attention than one man could give, he suggested that Richmond "appoint an agent to locate at Matamoros, as that place is very important to us."[133] In November, 1862, the government appointed Richard Fitzpatrick as commercial agent to Matamoros, instructing him to augment, on a local basis, the work of Quintero.[134] Fitzpatrick took up his duties with sincerity, honesty, and loyalty. Unfortunately, insufficient authority, lack of efficient communication, and ill health limited his service, and the task of maintaining friendly and cordial relations and of keeping open the channels of commerce in and through Mexico remained largely the responsibility of Quintero.

Shortly after Quintero returned to Monterrey, Governor Vidaurri gave orders for the opening of an additional hundred miles of the border from Matamoros to Mier, a town across the river from Roma, Texas. Included in this area were the strategically located border towns of Reynosa and Camargo. Reporting that the decision gave the Confederates "a longer line to introduce goods along the Rio Grande," Quintero added that Vidaurri also controlled the ports of Tampico and Soto la Marina. "The agents of the War Department will now have an opportunity of importing arms, ammunition, etc., either from the Island of Cuba or Europe," he concluded.[135]

The renewed commerce brought swarms of Southern contractors, purchasing agents, and speculators to the Rio Grande frontier. The New Orleans firm of Sandborn and Doen was one of the first to contract for Mexican goods, but others soon followed. Charles Stillman as well as Wolf and Schwartz of Brownsville made deals in Monterrey and the interior for "sundry articles of war." One Southern merchant took "into Texas a large train of war articles amounting to $30,000."[136] By the first of March, these private traders were joined at Matamoros by George A. Giddings and Major J. F. Minter, both agents of the War Department.[137]

Early in 1862 Governor Vidaurri, in an effort to gain the cooperation of the Confederacy against the marauding *rojos* of General Carvajal, began a program of customs manipulation. On occasion he allowed internal politics to dictate the tariff, but usually managed it to his own advantage.[138] Tariff manipulation soon became a favorite game among the various Mexican leaders contending for control of Matamoros, and caused Quintero and other Confederate agents continued frustration. In October 1862, the tariff was raised by General Juan B. Tranconis when he was appointed military *comandante* of Tamaulipas. But it was lowered again when Albino López became governor of the state less than a month later.[139]

The Confederate diplomat also struggled with his own government on the matter of customs. Writing to Secretary Benjamin, he encouraged the establishment of free ports along the Rio Grande:

> I wish to invite your special attention . . . to make the ports of entry on this River, free during the war with the U.S. Not only munitions of war, but large supplies of army stores would easily be encouraged to come into Texas, if they were permitted to cross the river at any point free of duty.[140]

He was convinced that such action would have a "happy effect" on the governments of the Mexican border states, bringing about a reciprocal policy. Also, military and commercial officials on the frontier complained that there were not enough Confederate officials on the Rio Grande to manage the rapidly growing trade.[141]

By the end of 1862 Quintero felt that he had made a promising beginning in northern Mexico. He had established a positive relationship with Governor Vidaurri, who seemed to be open to discussions on any problem. He had negotiated several significant trade agreements, and had facilitated contracts among government agents, private producers, and area companies. Also, he had assisted in making Matamoros a calling point for regular steamship service and an important receiving point for Confederate mails to and from Europe.[142]

Financing the Trade

When the Civil War began, Texas was a raw Southern frontier state, ill prepared for war and almost entirely without public funds. The state treasury was not only empty, but $800,000 in deficit. As true frontiersmen, Texans had not yet fully accepted the idea of supporting their state government through taxation. Most of the cost of government was being met by United States indemnity bonds which Texans had received in settlement of the boundary claim and sale of the Santa Fé region in 1850. A portion of these funds and $60,000 borrowed by E. B. Nichols, the agent of the newly appointed Committee of Public Safety supplemented by the funds surrendered by United States Major General David E. Twiggs at the beginning of hostilities, were the only means Texas had of equipping troops.[143]

Finding an adequate medium of exchange with Mexicans was a troublesome problem to Confederates in the early months of the war. At first Texas procurement officers along the Rio Grande relied on credit and Confederate notes to buy badly needed war materials. By the end of 1861 such notes were almost worthless, credit was gone, and hopes of producing a more reliable means of exchange were "so often repeated as almost to produce a smile."[144]

In the late summer and early fall, however, cotton began to arrive at Brownsville. Fully appreciative of the European demands for the white fiber, merchants gave instant credit to all who possessed it. Overnight the burgeoning cotton trade rescued the frustrated agents and officials from their financial difficulties.

Cotton soon became the basis for all commercial dealings in the Matamoros and Brownsville area. Military officials as well as private citizens used the commodity as a means of exchange. As early as October, 1861, General Paul O. Hébert, the newly appointed Texas commanding officer, reported that "arrangements have been, by my direction, made with firms . . . to procure munitions of war from Mexico, giving cotton in exchange, and with some hopes of success."[145] By November, Quintero was advising that merchants were willing to receive cotton in payment for articles and that delays and unnecessary expenses could be avoided if "money or cotton could be deposited either in New Orleans or Brownsville, Texas."[146]

In December the Confederate Ordinance Bureau sent Captain Giddings on a dual mission to the Texas border. He was instructed to purchase cotton with which to meet the government's contracts for buying arms, and to convert in Mexico one hundred United States Indemnity Bonds for the Texas State Military Board. In his cotton dealings he was moderately successful, buying over 200 bales. However, his effors to negotiate the indemnity bonds were not so fruitful.[147]

By the end of 1861, most foreign merchants were accepting cotton in payment of goods to be purchased. Arrangements made by Caleb Huse in Richmond consigned all government cotton to Fraser, Trenholm and Company of Liverpool. In return, that firm expended commercial credit and drafts that could be redeemed in cash. By 1862 the foreign consuls in northern Mexico began offering specie for cotton, and the merchants from Monterrey to Matamoros quickly followed suit.[148]

By the second half of 1862 the commerce was thriving. The "trade is immense," claimed Quintero. It "grows larger every day."[149] Union consuls in northern Mexico warned that it had reached "enormous proportions [and] large trains [carrying] goods of all kinds" were going into Texas daily.[150] Merchants talked of putting 500 wagons to work hauling the goods. Matamoros had become "the great thoroughfare to the Southern States. . . . They pass all of the supplies they receive through here."[151] By the end of the summer, Quintero reported that Texas was "well supplied with cotton," and the road to Matamoros was "one vast and almost unbroken line of wagons and carts carrying cotton to the gulf shore."[152]

United States naval officers counted hundreds of ships from various nations waiting to be loaded with cotton. "Hundreds of bales [were] brought out of the river every day in a Mexican steamer and in small Mexican lighters." Yet, "endless bales of cotton" continued to be "piled up on the Mexican side of the river" waiting to be loaded.[153] They concluded that "all the vessels fitting out in Europe and elsewhere [were] bound for Matamoros."[154] In Washington, Secretary of State Seward registered a protest to the British Minister Lord Lyons:

> It is only very recently that this especially enlarged Matamoros trade has come to our notice. Suddenly and quickly as palaces, cities, States, or Empires rise in the tales of the "Arabian Nights" under the waving of a wand, or the utterance of a spell, that trade rose from a petty barter to a commerce that engaged the mercantile activity of Liverpool and London. Simultaneously roads across the interior of Texas were covered with caravans; the cotton of disloyal citizens in the insurrectionary region became all at once the property of the treasonable conspiracy against the Union, and was hypothecated by its agents for a foreign loan to satisfy obligations contracted by them in the fitting out and equipping and clearing from British ports of steam naval expeditions to destroy the commerce of the United States.[155]

From Monterrey, a satisfied Quintero reported in December 1862 that "the frontier is quiet and commerce uninterrupted."[156] And when Governor Vidaurri's Secretary of State told him that a Union agent was in the city, he confidently replied, "He can do nothing here."[157]

Notes

1. Robert L. Kerby, *Kirby Smith's Confederacy: The Trans-Mississippi South, 1863–1865* (New York: Columbia University Press, 1972), pp. 5, 6. This sum included 192 saw

mills, 132 flour mills, 62 wagon makers, 48 saddleries, 46 farm implement and tool factories, 37 farmers, 23 commercial cotton gins, 22 breweries and distilleries, and 4 wholesale bakeries. In addition there were numerous steam cotton balers and blacksmiths almost totally engaged in repairing and renovating farm equipment. Although Texas had four small steam machinery plants, none could build a locomotive.

2. Ibid., pp. 11, 79.

3. Ibid., p. 11; Clark to Walker, September 7, 1861, *Official Records of the Union and Confederate Armies* [ORA], Ser. I, Vol. 4, p. 101.

4. Kerby, p. 6; *Cotton Supply Reporter* [Manchester], March 15, 1862.

5. *New York Herald,* June 6, 1861.

6. *Richmond Enquirer,* July 12, 1861.

7. Stillman to Morell, August 18, 19, 1861, Charles Stillman Papers (unpublished), Houghton Library, Harvard University, Cambridge, Mass.; Myers to Minter, September 14, 1861; Hébert to Benjamin, October 31, 1861; Buchel to Davis, November 30, 1861, *ORA,* Ser. I, Vol. 4, pp. 105, 130–31, 150.

8. John Warren Hunter, "The Fall of Brownsville on the Rio Grande, November, 1862" (Unpublished), Eugene C. Barker Library of Texas History, University of Texas, Austin, pp. 4–5; Ronnie C. Tyler, "Cotton on the Border, 1861–1865," *Southwestern Historical Quarterly* 73 (April 1970):456.

9. Stillman to Morell, August 18, 19, 1861, Stillman Papers.

10. McCulloch to Cooper, October 17, 1861, *ORA,* Ser. I, Vol. 4, p. 122; Dunnell to Seward, December 20, 1861, *Official Records of the Union and Confederate Navies* [ORN], Ser. I, Vol. 17, pp. 38–39.

11. *New York Herald,* August 24, 1862; Tyler, *SWHQ* 73: 457; Frank L. Owsley, *King Cotton Diplomacy* (Chicago; University of Chicago Press, 1959), p. 31; Kerby, p. 162.

12. Hébert to Benjamin, October 31, 1861, *ORA,* Ser. I, Vol. 4, pp. 130–31.

13. Benjamin to Clark, October 13, 1861, *ORA,* Ser. I, Vol. 4, p. 120.

14. Ellis, *SWHQ* 77, 204; Jonson to Russell, December 27, 1861, Foreign Office Papers, F.O. 50/355.

15. Caleb Huse, *The Supplies for the Confederate Army; How They Were Obtained in Europe and How Paid For* (Boston: T. R. Marvin and Son, 1904), p. 23; Bee to the Secretary of War, October 12, 1861, *ORA,* Ser. I, Vol. 4, pp. 118–19; Benjamin to Helm, November 30, 1863, Confederate State Papers, Vol. 8; Owsley, p. 118.

16. Couthouy to Welles, February 3, 1862, *ORN,* Ser. I, Vol. 17, p. 94.

17. José San Román, Letters, 1861–1865 (Unpublished), Eugene C. Barker Library of Texas History, University of Texas, Austin, hereafter cited as San Román Papers; Irby, p. 15.

18. Irby, p. 15; Couthouy to Welles, February 3, 1862, *ORN,* Ser. I, Vol. 17, p. 95; Purchase Order, Ford to Román, September 14, 1861, San Román Papers, 2G 61

19. Coe to Chase, January 2, 1862, *ORA,* Ser. I, Vol. 9, pp. 642–48.

20. Irby, pp. 3, 15(n). By placing a $10,000 bond, Galvan had received permission for direct commerce between New York and Matamoros.

21. Quintero to Hunter, October 18, 1861, Confederate State Papers, Vol. 8; Mann to Bee, November 30, 1863, *ORA,* Ser. I, Vol. 20, p. 684; Irby, pp. 3, 16. During the 1850s the trade along the river was valued from $10 million to $14 million annually. The owners of the new steamers had realized large profits. It was from these funds that King and Kenedy invested in and developed ranch lands north of Brownsville.

22. McCulloch to Cooper, October 17, 1861, *ORA,* Ser. I, Vol. 9, p. 123.

23. Coutheuy to Welles, May 5, 1863, *ORN,* Ser. I, Vol. 17, pp. 441–42.

24. Ibid.

25. Edward L. Plumb, Papers, Vol. 5 (unpublished), Manuscript Division, Library of Congress, Washington, D.C.; Coe to Chase, January 2, 1863, *ORA*, Ser. I, Vol. 9, pp. 642–43; Cowling, p. 5; William Diamond, "Imports of the Confederate Government from Europe and Mexico," *Journal of Southern History* 6 (November 1940):498–99; Quintero to Hunter, November 10, 1861, Confederate State Papers, Vol. 8.

26. "Notes on Cotton Manufacturer in Mexico," Plumb Papers, Letterbooks.

27. Quintero to Benjamin, September 7, 1862, Confederate State Papers, Vol. 58; *Tri-Weekly News* [Galveston], May 11, 1863; Owsley, *King Cotton Diplomacy*, p. 119.

28. "Notes on Cotton Manufacturers in Mexico," Plumb Papers, Letterbooks.

29. Pierce to Seward, March 1, 1862, *ORA*, Ser. I, Vol. 9, p. 674.

30. J. Fred Rippy, *The United States and Mexico*, p. 238; *Tri-Weekly Telegraph* [Houston], December 11, 1863; *Cotton Supply Reporter* [Manchester], December 1, 1865.

31. Quintero to Browne, March 3, 1862, Quintero to Benjamin, August 30, 1862, Confederate State Papers, Vol. 58; Bee to the Secretary of War, October 12, 1861, McCulloch to Cooper, October 17, 1861, *ORA*, Ser. I, Vol. 4, pp. 119, 123; *Texas State Weekly Gazette* [Austin], December 14, 1861.

32. Mills to Lubbock, December 4, 1861, Hutchins to Lubbock, December 7, 1861, MSS, Executive Correspondence (Texas State Archives, Austin); McCulloch to Cooper, October 17, 1861, *ORA*, Ser. I, Vol. 4, pp. 122–23.

33. Shufeldt to Seward, January 16, 1862, U.S. Consular Dispatches, Havana, as quoted in Ellis, *SWHQ* 77:204; Pierce to Seward, December 23, 1862, Consular Dispatches, Matamoros.

34. Bailey to Welles, April 4, 1863, *ORN*, Ser. I, Vol. 17, p. 403.

35. Crawford to Russell, March 1, 1862, Foreign Office Papers, F.O. 92/42; Mann to Bee, November 30, 1863, *ORA*, Ser. I, Vol. 20, p. 684. One of these lighters was the *Matamoros*, which records indicate played a major role in the Confederate commerce on the Rio Grande. It was later seized by a Union blockader.

36. Quintero to Hunter, October 18, 1861. Confederate State Papers, Vol. 8.

37. Ford to Browne, March 17, 1862, Quintero to Benjamin, August 14, 1862, Quintero to Hunter, October 18, 1861, Confederate State Papers, Vol. 58; Pierce to Seward, September 30, 1863, Consular Dispatches, Matamoros; Dunnell to Seward, December 20, 1861, *ORN*, Ser. I, Vol. 17, p. 39; Irby, p. 14; Stillman to Donahue, April 21, 1861, Stillman Papers. From the beginning of the Civil War Stillman had been apprehensive. When news reached Brownsville that hostilities had broken out at Fort Sumter, he saw little chance for protection of ships of either side. "We must all turn Turks or Japanese, and carry some of their rags at the Masthead," he confided to John Donahue, his New York agent. Initially the possibilities of Confederate privateers concerned Stillman more than the threats of a Union blockade. While admitting to Donahue that goods could be sent to Tampico and then run up to Brownsville, Stillman did not "wish to receive a dollar's worth of goods under the present appearances."

38. Hubert Herring, *A History of Latin America* (New York: Alfred A. Knopf, 1968), p. 290.

39. Ibid., pp. 291–92.

40. Ibid., pp. 292, 317–20.

41. James D. Richardson (ed.), *A Compilation of the Messages and Papers of the Confederacy*, 2 vols. (Nashville: United States Publishing Company, 1906), 2:77–80; *ORN*, Ser. II, Vol. 3, pp. 116–17, 217.

42. Bailey to Welles, March 13, 1863, *ORN*, Ser. I, Vol. 17, pp. 401–02; Delany, *SWHQ* 58, 475–77; *New York Herald*, May 26, 1861.

43. Lyons Correspondence, 1862, Foreign Office Papers, F.O. 5/829–837; Ellis, *SWHQ* 77:224; Maguire to Cracroft, November 27, 1863, Foreign Office Papers, F.O. 50/378; Austin *Weekly State Gazette,* March 22, 1865; Morse to Seward, November 28, 1862, *ORN,* Ser. I, Vol. 19, pp. 418–19; Owsley, pp. 134–43; Gideon Welles, *Diary of Gideon Welles,* 3 volumes, Howard K. Beale (editor) (New York: W. W. Norton and Company, 1960), Vol. 1, July 31, 1863, pp. 389–90, hereafter cited as Welles, *Diary.* On October 13, 1861, the *New York Herald,* in an effort to explain England's neutral stand may have initiated the "King Corn" thesis when it reported, "We are now confident that the government of the United States, in some other articles of trade, holds the balance of power in England and France over cotton. . . . In a word, the short bread crops of the present year in England and France render our surplus breadstuffs not only of more importance in this crisis to those countries than Southern cotton, but more an object to England than the success of our Southern rebellion. Anglo-French bread deficiencies this year will call for foreign supplies to the extent of at least one hundred million of bushels of grain."

44. Donaldson Jordan and Edwin J. Pratt, *Europe and the American Civil War* (New York: Octagon Books, 1969), pp. 205–13; *New York Herald,* September 25, 1861.

45. Owsley, *King Cotton Diplomacy,* pp. 87–88.

46. Owsley, *King Cotton Diplomacy,* p. 89; Toombs to Quintero, May 22, 1861, *ORN,* Ser. II, Vol. 3, pp. 29, 217. Pickett had also served in one of "Filibustering" López's expeditions to Cuba, commanding revolutionary troops against the Spanish regulars in the Battle of Cardenas.

47. Toombs to Pickett, May 17, 1861, *ORN,* Ser. II, Vol. 3, pp. 202–07.

48. Ibid.

49. Ibid.

50. William M. Robinson, *The Confederate Privateers* (New Haven: Yale University Press, 1928), p. 259.

51. Robinson, p. 260.

52. Pickett to Toombs, July 11, 1861, Confederate State Papers, Vol. 58.

53. Ibid.

54. Owsley, *King Cotton Diplomacy,* p. 93.

55. Robinson, p. 261.

56. Owsley, *King Cotton Diplomacy,* pp. 103–04.

57. Ibid., p. 95.

58. Pickett to Toombs, September 28, 1861, Confederate State Papers, Vol. 58, enclosing Pickett's note to Zamacona.

59. Pickett to Toombs, October 29, 1861, Confederate State Papers, Vol. 8; Owsley, p. 97; *New York Herald,* November 19, 1861.

60. Pickett to Toombs, November 29, 1861, Confederate State Papers, Vol. 8.

61. Pickett to Toombs, December 31, 1861, Quintero to Browne, December 12, 1861, Confederate State Papers, Vol. 58.

62. Browne to Pickett, January 28, 1862, *ORN,* Ser. II, Vol. 3, p. 322; Benjamin to Quintero, November 11, 1862, Confederate State Papers, Vol. 11.

63. Quintero to Browne, August 22, 1861, Confederate State Papers, Vol. 58.

64. Tyler, *Vidaurri,* pp. 28–29. In August 1857, a revised constitution was adopted in Nuevo León and Coahuila. Among other progressive reforms, it provided that anyone entering the state was free. Thus, it encouraged many slaves to seek refuge there, which became a source of difficulty in later negotiations with the Confederate states.

65. Ibid., pp. 28–36, 61; Tyler, *SWHQ* 63: 458(n).

66. Tyler, *Vidaurri*, pp. 14–15, 153; Mitchell Smith, "The 'Neutral' Matamoros Trade, 1861–1865," *Southwest Review* 37 (Autumn 1952): 321–22.

67. Tyler, *SWHQ* 73: 458.

68. Quintero to Browne, June 1, 1861, Confederate State Papers, Vol. 58; Owsley, p. 114; Tyler, *SWHQ* 73: 458; Tyler, *Vidaurri*, pp. 36, 45–46. Quintero's given name has often been incorrectly cited as "Juan." This error began with the indexers of the *Official Records of the War of the Rebellion*, and has been continued by some historians. Following the war he worked for the *Galveston News*, then moved to New Orleans and practiced law. There he wrote for the *Daily Picayune* and served as New Orleans consul for Belgium and Costa Rica. At the time of his death in 1885 he was editor of the *Picayune*. *Daily Picayune* [New Orleans], September 8, 1885; *Times-Picayune* [New Orleans], January 25, 1937.

69. Quintero to Browne, January 1, 1861, Confederate State Papers, Vol. 58.

70. Toombs to Quintero, May 22, 1861, Confederate State Papers, Vol. 11.

71. Quintero to Browne, June 1, 1861, Confederate State Papers, Vol. 58.

72. Ibid.

73. Quintero to Browne, July 14, 1861, Toombs to Vidaurri, May 22, 1861, Quintero to Vidaurri, June 19, 1861, Statement of Expenses, August 19, 1861, Confederate State Papers, Vol. 58; Tyler, *Vidaurri*, p. 46.

74. *Boletin Oficial* [Monterrey], July 3, 1861; *Fort Brown Flag* [Brownsville], April 17, 1862; *Daily Ranchero* [Matamoros], May 24, 1865; Pierce to Seward, various dispatches, 1861–1865, Consular Dispatches, Matamoros; Kimmey to Seward, October 29, 1862, Consular Dispatches, Monterrey, in Tyler, *Vidaurri*, p. 47; *Texas State Gazette* [Austin], June 22, 1861.

75. Quintero to Browne, July 14, 1861, Confederate State Papers, Vol. 58; Tyler, *Vidaurri*, p. 48.

76. Tyler, *Vidaurri*, p. 50; Quintero to Browne, July 14, 1861, Quintero to Hunter, August 16, 19, 1861, Quintero to Browne, August 11, 1861, Confederate State Papers, Vol. 58.

77. Quintero to Hunter, August 16, 1861, Quintero to Browne, July 14, 1861, Confederate State Papers, Vol. 58; Tyler, *Vidaurri*, pp. 49–50; Rippy, *The United States and Mexico*, pp. 236–38.

78. Quintero to Browne, July 14, 1861, Quintero to Hunter, August 16, 1861, Confederate State Papers, Vol. 58.

79. Quintero to Browne, July 14, 1861, Confederate State Papers, Vol. 58.

80. Quintero to Hunter, August 19, 1861, Quintero to Browne, August 22, 1861, Confederate State Papers, Vol. 58, with enclosures.

81. Quintero to Hunter, August 19, 1861, Confederate State Papers, Vol. 58.

82. Quintero to Browne, August 22, 1861, Confederate State Papers, Vol. 58.

83. Ibid.

84. Quintero to Benjamin, July 5, 1861, Confederate State Papers, Vol. 58.

85. Richardson, *A Compilation of the Messages and Papers of the Confederacy*, 2: 80; Quintero to Browne, July 14, 1861, Confederate State Papers, Vol. 58.

86. Quintero to Hunter, August 17, 1861, Confederate State Papers, Vol. 58.

87. Quintero to Hunter, August 19, 1861, Confederate State Papers, Vol. 58.

88. Quintero to Hunter, August 17, 19, 1861, Confederate State Papers, Vol. 58; Tyler, *Vidaurri*, p. 53.

89. Quintero to Hunter, August 19, 1861, Confederate State Papers, Vol. 58.

90. Quintero to Hunter, August 19, 1861, Quintero to Browne, August 22, 1861,

Confederate State Papers, Vol. 58; Quintero to Clark, July 11, 1861, as cited in Tyler, *Vidaurri*, p. 54.

91. Quintero to Hunter, August 20, 1861, Confederate State Papers, Vol. 58.

92. Ibid.

93. Browne to Quintero, September 3, 1861, in Richardson, 2: 77–80, and *ORN*, Ser. II, Vol. 3, pp. 253–55.

94. Owsley, *King Cotton Diplomacy*, p. 115.

95. Browne to Quintero, September 3, 1861, in Richardson, 2: 77–80.

96. Tyler, *Vidaurri*, p. 58; Owsley, *King Cotton Diplomacy*, pp. 116–17; Browne to Quintero, September 3, 1861, in Richardson, 2: 77–80.

97. Browne to Quintero, September 3, 1861, in Richardson, 2: 77–80.

98. Ibid.

99. Quintero to Browne, September 9, 1861, Confederate State Papers, Vol. 58.

100. Quintero to Browne, September 18, 1861, Confederate State Papers, Vol. 58. The rumors had anticipated a clash developing between Vidaurri and Juárez when the governor had extended refuge to a fellow Mason, former President Ignacio Comonfort. Comonfort had been exiled from Mexico following his resignation from the presidency in 1858. Juárez had ordered Vidaurri to arrest him and return him to Mexico City. When Vidaurri refused to carry out the President's order and instead replied with a long list of reasons why Comonfort should remain free, Juárez sent troops into Nuevo León to arrest the former president. Although a conflict could have occurred, it did not. Comonfort was allowed to remain in Nuevo León y Coahuila, and Vidaurri soon placed him at the head of his militia. See Tyler, *Vidaurri*, pp. 58–60.

101. Quintero to Hunter, October 18, 1861, Confederate State Papers, Vol. 8.

102. Ibid.

103. Quintero to Hunter, November 4, 11, 1861, Confederate State Papers, Vol. 8.

104. Quintero to Hunter, November 4, 1861, Confederate State Papers, Vol. 8.

105. Browne to Quintero, December 9, 1861, *ORN*, Ser. II, Vol. 3, p. 308; Quintero to Hunter, November 4, 1861, Confederate State Papers, Vol. 8; Plumb to Seward, January 31, 1862, Plumb Papers. The Oliver brothers controlled a large portion of the lead production in the Monterrey area, and held considerable influence over other mines through northern Mexico. Unionists in Mexico learned of José Oliver's trip to Richmond to sign a commercial contract that included the supplying the Confederates with their entire production of 90,000 pounds each month. They responded by moving to break Oliver's hegemony over the lead production in northern Mexico.

106. Benjamin to Lovell, March 22, 1862, *ORA*, Ser. I, Vol. 6, pp. 863–64.

107. Quintero to Hunter, November 4, 11, 1861, Confederate State Papers, Vol. 8.

108. Quintero to Hunter, November 11, 1861, Confederate State Papers, Vol. 8.

109. Quintero to Hunter, December 1, 1861, Confederate State Papers, Vol. 58.

110. Quintero to Browne, September 9, 1861, Confederate State Papers, Vol. 58.

111. *Fort Brown Flag* [Brownsville], quoted in the *Texas State Gazette* [Austin], December 21, 1861.

112. Ibid.

113. Ibid.

114. Quintero to Hunter, October 18, 1861, Confederate State Papers, Vol. 8.

115. *Fort Brown Flag* [Brownsville], quoted in the *Texas Republican* [Marshall], December 21, 1861; Quintero to Hunter, November 16, December 1, 2, 1861, Confederate State Papers, Vol. 58; *San Antonio Weekly Herald*, January 14, 1862; *Texas State Gazette* [Austin], December 14, 1861.

116. *Boletin Oficial* [Monterrey], January 14, 1862; Tyler, *Vidaurri,* p. 64; Quintero to Hunter, February 1, 1862, Confederate State Papers, Vol. 58.

117. Quintero to Hunter, February 1, 1862, Confederate State Papers, Vol. 58; *Boletin Oficial* [Monterrey], January 24, 26, 1862.

118. Quintero to Browne, March 4, 1862, Confederate State Papers, Vol. 58.

119. Ibid.

120. Ibid.; *Fort Brown Flag* [Brownsville], April 17, 1862; Luckett to Gray, May 12, 1863, *ORA,* Ser. I, Vol. 53, pp. 807–08.

121. Quintero to Browne, March 8, 22, 24, 1862, Confederate State Papers, Vol. 8; *Fort Brown Flag* [Brownsville], April 17, 1862; Quintero to Lubbock, March 24, 1862, as cited in Tyler, *Vidaurri,* pp. 70–71. Vidaurri complained to Quintero that Carvajal had openly printed and circulated proclamations in Brownsville and had purchased two cannons from Kenedy and ammunition from Treviño brothers there also.

122. Quintero to Browne, March 22, 1862, Confederate State Papers, Vol. 58.

123. Quintero to Vidaurri, April 4, 1862, Quintero to Browne, April 17, 1862, Confederate State Papers, Vol. 8.

124. Vidaurri to Quintero, April 5, 1862, Confederate State Papers, Vol. 8.

125. Quintero to Browne, April 17, 28, 1862, Quintero to Benjamin, July 5, 1862, Confederate State Papers, Vol. 8.

126. *Fort Brown Flag* [Brownsville], April 17, 1862.

127. Ibid.

128. Quintero to Browne, February 9, 1862, Quintero to Benjamin, March 1, 1863, Confederate State Papers, Vol. 8.

129. Quintero to Browne, March 4, 8, 1862, Confederate State Papers, Vol. 8.

130. Quintero to Browne, February 9, 1862, Confederate State Papers, Vol. 58.

131. Quintero to Benjamin, November 20, December 1, 1862; Milmo to Quintero, December [?], 1863, Confederate State Papers, Vol. 8.

132. Quintero to Benjamin, December 1, 11, 1862, Confederate State Papers, Vol. 8.

133. Quintero to Hunter, February 1, 1862, Quintero to Browne, March 8, 1862, Confederate State Papers, Vol. 58.

134. Benjamin to Fitzpatrick, November 15, 1862, Confederate State Paper, Vol. 11.

135. Quintero to Browne, March 22, 1862, Confederate State Papers, Vol. 58.

136. Quintero to Hunter, February 1, 1862, Confederate State Papers, Vol. 58.

137. Quintero to Browne, March 4, 1862, Confederate State Papers, Vol. 58.

138. Quintero to Browne, April 17, 1862, Quintero to Benjamin, August 14, 30, 1862, Confederate State Papers.

139. Quintero to Benjamin, September 24, October 12, November 2, 1862, Confederate State Papers, Vol. 8.

140. Quintero to Benjamin, August 30, 1862, Confederate State Papers, Vol. 8.

141. Ibid.; McCulloch to Cooper, October 17, 1861, *ORA,* Ser. I, Vol. 4, p. 123.

142. Quintero to Benjamin, July 5, 1862, Quintero to Browne, March 22, 1862, Confederate State Papers, Vol. 8; Hotze to Hunter, January 6, 1862, Henry Hotze, Papers of Henry Hotze, 1862–1865 (unpublished), Manuscript Division, Library of Congress, Washington, D.C., hereafter cited as the Hotze Papers; Pierce to Seward, December 23, 1862, Consular Dispatches, Matamoros; Pierce to Hunter, April 24, 1862, *ORN,* Ser. I, Vol. 18, p. 456.

143. C. W. Ramsdell, "The Texas State Military Board, 1862–1865," *Southwestern Historical Quarterly* 27 (April 1924): 255; Irby, pp. 64–65; Cowling, p. 59.

144. Buchel to Davis, November 30, 1861, Luckett to Yager, December 31, 1861, *ORA,* Ser. I, Vol. 4, pp. 150, 165.

145. Hébert to Benjamin, October 31, 1861, *ORA*, Ser. I, Vol. 4, p. 130.

146. Quintero to Hunter, November 10, 11, 1861, Confederate State Papers, Vol. 8.

147. Benjamin to Memminger, December 2, 1862, Giddings to Gorgas, January 5, 1862, Seddon to Davis, December 16, 1864, *ORA*, Ser. IV, Vol. 1, pp. 774, 832–33, Ser. I, Vol. 53, pp. 1033–34; Irby, p. 91.

148. Benjamin to Memminger, November 27, 1862, citing excerpts of Quintero to Benjamin, October 17, 1862, *ORN*, Ser. I, Vol. 19, p. 809; Huse, p. 16.

149. Quintero to Benjamin, September 24, October 17, 19, 1862, Confederate State Papers, Vols. 8, 58.

150. Pierce to Seward, March 1, 1862, Kimmey to Seward October 29, 1862, ORA, Ser. I, Vol. 9, p. 674, Ser. III, Vol. 2, pp. 949–51; Kimmey to Seward, November 21, 1862, Consular Dispatches, Monterrey, as quoted in Tyler, *SWHQ* 73: 466.

151. Ibid.

152. Ibid.; Quintero to Benjamin, August 14, 1862, Confederate State Papers, Vol. 8.

153. French to Farragut, September 18, 1862, *ORA*, Ser. I, Vol. 19, p. 291; Bailey to Welles, April 2, 1863, p. 283.

154. Farragut to Welles, April 11, 1862, *ORN*, Ser. I, Vol. 18, pp. 123–24.

155. Seward to Lyons, May 12, 1862, Parliamentary Papers, 1862, Vol. 72, pp. 509–10.

156. Quintero to Benjamin, August 14, 1862, Confederate State Papers, Vol. 8.

157. Quintero to Benjamin, December 11, 1862, Confederate State Papers, Vol. 8.

3
CONFEDERATE STRUGGLES TO PROTECT THE TRADE

Secession and the End of Federal Control

On February 1, 1861, a state convention at Austin adopted an ordinance of secession, chose seven delegates to represent Texas at the Confederation Convention in Montgomery, Alabama, and appointed a Committee of Public Safety to prepare the state's defenses.[1] Not willing to await the voters' ratification of the ordinance of secession, the committee on February 23 appointed four commissioners, Samuel A. Maverick, Thomas J. Devine, Philip N. Luckett, and James H. Rogers, to discuss the end of Federal authority in the state with General David E. Twiggs, the Union commander.[2]

Meanwhile, in the next four weeks Texas rebel leaders hastened to strengthen their position. An army of volunteers, under Texas Ranger Ben McCulloch, was raised to confront Union garrisons throughout the state. Rumors were rampant as to the disposition that United States General Twiggs, a Georgian with Southern sympathies, intended to make of the Federal forces. "Good authority" reported that he had already informed Texas governor Sam Houston that he would turn over all Federal property to state authorities. There were whispers that the general intended to concentrate all the troops at San Antonio and then disband them. Another rumor, supposedly from the general's son-in-law, Colonel Abraham C. Myers at New Orleans, was that Twiggs planned to parole the officers and then notify President Lincoln that "he held the Army in Texas for the Southern republic."[3]

Although these rumors were mostly ill-founded, Twiggs's

actions gave cause for alarm among Union men. In January he repeatedly wrote to his superiors concerning the restless mood in Texas and asking for instructions.[4] On January 15, he asked General-in-Chief Winfield Scott to relieve him of command. "All that I have is in the South," he wrote, "and as my health will not allow me to take an active part in the scenes that will probably be enacted, I must be a looker-on."[5] A few days later he resolved "never to fire on American citizens."[6] In addition, on January 23, he informed the Adjutant-General's office that he had been in correspondence with Governor Houston regarding his surrender of government property in Texas should the state secede.[7]

On February 18, when General Twiggs was confronted by a contingent of more than 1,000 state militia, he surrendered the entire department without firing a shot. It was agreed that the Federal command of 2,684 men would leave the state, embarking at Indianola and Brazos Santiago on the coast. The Union cavalry and infantry units would retain their arms and the artillery companies would keep two light batteries of four guns each. Except for the necessary transportation and subsistence, all other public property, valued between $1,300,000 and $3 million, was surrendered.[8]

The following day General Twiggs received word that he was to relinquish command to Colonel Carlos A. Waite. On March 1, the War Department, by direction of President James Buchanan, "dismissed [him] from the Army of the United States, for his treachery to the flag of his country, in having surrendered . . . on the demand of the authorities of Texas, the military posts and other property of the United States in [his] department and under his charge."[9]

With assurances from Washington that the steamer *Star of the West* would be waiting at Indianola, Colonel Waite ordered the scattered units to rendezvous at Green Lake, near the point of embarkation.[10] However, events overtook the withdrawal. Early in March, Texas cast her lot with the newly formed Confederate States, and on April 12 the anticipated Civil War began in Charleston harbor. Texas officials no longer felt bound by the prewar evacuation terms, and ordered Colonel Earl Van Dorn, recently appointed Confederate commander in Texas, to hold the Federal soldiers as prisoners of war and to capture the *Star of the West*.[11] The Confederates captured the ship, but Major Caleb C. Sibley succeeded in evacuating some 1,300 Federal troops at Indianola on three other vessels after agreeing to engage in no further combat against the South. Meanwhile, six companies, 300 men, enroute to the coast under Colonel Isaac V. D. Reeve were captured at San Lucas Springs, about fifteen miles west of San Antonio, on May 9. Forced to surrender all equipment including their arms, they were imprisoned at Camp Verde near San Antonio. Colonel Waite and his headquarters staff at San Antonio were also taken prisoner.[12]

Meanwhile, the Confederates made plans to seize control of the Rio Grande valley. On February 5, the Committee of Public Safety commissioned John S. Ford as Colonel of cavalry and gave him command of the Rio Grande expedition.[13]

Dr. John Salmon "Rip" Ford had followed a series of careers after migrating to Texas from South Carolina in 1836. He had practiced medicine, worked as a surveyor of Harrison County, campaigned against the Shawnees, served a term in the House of Delegates of the Texas Republic, edited and published the *Texas Democrat* in Austin, and served in the Mexican war as adjutant for Colonel Jack Hays's Texas Rangers. As adjutant, it was his duty to notify the next of kin of battle losses, and he habitually started each letter with "Rest in Peace." As casualties mounted and he was pressed for time he shortened the grim-greeting to "R.I.P." and thus earned his nickname. In 1859–60 he commanded Rangers in pursuit of the bandit Juan Cortina along the border, where he met Colonel Robert E. Lee. In 1861, he was a delegate from Cameron County at the Texas Secession Convention.

Ford was charged with a twofold mission. First, he was to "secure to the State of Texas all arms and munitions of war, together with all property of every kind now retained by and in possession of the United States of America" along the river. Secondly, he was "to use such means as will protect the Rio Grande frontier against hostile invasions."[14] His military district included all of the country between the Nueces and the Rio Grande from a point on the Rio Grande halfway between Forts Duncan and McIntosh to the Gulf.[15]

Initially he was to raise a force of not more than 600 men organized in six companies of 100 men each. If this contingent proved to be insufficient, he could "call out enough for the purpose."[16] Ford could also, if he thought it advisable, "retain any portion or all of the Federal troops in [the] district in temporary service of the State." Should the Union garrisons choose to leave, he could permit them to do so "upon such terms as will not dishonor them and as will insure the public safety and in such a way as will insure safety to their persons and private property."[17]

In the early days of secession, Texans flocked to the colors, and Ford had no trouble recruiting. Within two weeks he sailed from Galveston with 500 men. He was accompanied by Colonel Hugh McLeod, second in command, and state commissioner Ebenezer B. Nichols, who was instructed to receive the transfer of all Federal installations and property along the Rio Grande. Arriving at Brazos Santiago in the morning of November 21, Ford found it held by United States Lieutenant James Thompson and twelve artillerymen. The Union detachment had "two large pieces shotted" and ready to fire on him, he learned, should he try to enter the harbor.[18] After a two-hour conference Thompson agreed to surrender the post. In a brief ceremony the Stars and Stripes were lowered to a salute of thirty-three guns, and the Lone Star banner of Texas raised to the sound of twenty-two guns. As Thompson and his men departed for Fort Brown they were met by a reinforcing detachment bringing orders for him to destroy the property at Brazos. "Both came too late."[19]

The next day Ford went to Brownsville with Nichols and McLeod to negotiate the surrender of the Union garrison at Fort Brown. Here he ran into a subborn opponent in the person of Captain Bennett H. Hill, who commanded several companies at the fort. At first Hill refused to parley. When he did, it was a stormy session with Nichols accusing Hill of violating Texas soil and the captain threatening to arrest the commissioner as a traitor and to attack the rebels. Nothing accomplished, Hill went back to garrisoning, and Nichols started for Galveston to get more troops with which "to whale him into a knowledge that . . . Texans owned Texas."[20] McLeod returned to Brazos Santiago to work on fortifications, and Ford looked around Brownsville in search of Captain George Stoneman of the Second Cavalry, an old friend from the Cortina War, who he hoped would be more agreeable.

In a series of written exchanges, Colonel Ford made a successful, "touching appeal" to Captain Stoneman.[21] Both were anxious to avoid a clash between Federal and state troops. Ford pointed out that the danger of unintended bloodshed was great. "Texas had a considerable force in the field—volunteers are naturally restless—and every day [that] a large body of them remains within striking distance of the Federal troops the danger of collision by the mere meeting of the detachments is great."[22] This, along with the receipt of General Twiggs's order of February 18 directing the surrender of all property in the state, convinced Stoneman of the advisability of surrender. He began to work to convince Hill.[23]

Meanwhile, the rebels prepared defenses at Brazos Santiago. On March 1, McLeod informed Ford that the batteries were repaired and ready for action. Because March 2 was a holiday commemorating the proclamation of Texas secession, McLeod planned a twenty-two-gun salute in honor of the occasion. "If you hear more than 22 guns," he added, "it will be largely target practice from the Batteries firing at the sand hills with the damaged cartridges to exercise the men."[24] If Hill were foolhardy enough to attack his positions, McLeod was ready for him, he said, and felt that "he need not go into details" as to how he planned to defend Brazos Santiago from such a suicidal assault. Only a "demented" man would dare challenge his positions under the circumstances.[25] Around midday the Confederates were further strengthened when the *General Rusk* returned from Galveston with Nichols and 325 men under Lieutenant Colonel Benjamin F. Terry.[26]

Two days later Major Fitz John Porter, assistant adjutant general of the United States Army, arrived on the steamer *Daniel Webster*, carrying orders from General Winfield Scott, and $40,000 to effect, "without delay," the removal of all Union troops from the Rio Grande valley.[27] Captain Hill immediately called upon Nichols, who was ill and in bed. Explaining that he had previously been in a difficult position without orders or authorization to recognize secessionist groups, the captain said that he "was gratified that matters had taken a pacific turn . . . [and he] was under marching orders."[28]

With the threat of an armed clash now past, the transfer of authority on the Rio Grande proceeded smoothly. Using both the *General Rusk* and the *Daniel Webster*, Major Porter evacuated most of the 1,012 Union soldiers from the Rio Grande by March 19.[29] Two days later Colonel Electus Backus gave possession of Fort Brown to Nichols's secretary, H. B. Waller, and left with the last contingent of Federal troops. A police force from Brownsville occupied Fort Brown until the state troops arrived from Brazos Santiago.[30]

The arrival of rebel troops greatly disturbed the border population, especially the Mexican-Americans. Cheap labor from Mexico and the ease with which slaves could cross the river to freedom had kept the peculiar institution out of the Rio Grande frontier. The 1860 census registered only fourteen slaves and 109 free Negroes in the three southern-most Texas counties. Most labor was performed by Mexican-Americans, and they feared an extension of slavery that would threaten their livelihood. To ease their fears and reduce the growing tensions, Colonel Ford, on March 6, issued a proclamation explaining that the new government would not change the region's social and economic structure.[31]

Problems with the *Bandoleros*

In full possession of the Rio Grande frontier, Ford turned his attention to the second part of his orders, the protection of the area from hostile invasion. This primarily involved cultivating friendly relations with Mexico which was a delicate and complex matter. Mexico was torn by revolutionary turmoil, and the eastern border state of Tamaulipas was unable to control the *bandoleros* who plundered and murdered along the frontier.

Ford described the situation along the border in a series of reports to Governor Edward Clark in April 1861. Relations with Mexico were improving, he said, and he thought that the governor of Tamaulipas, General Guadalupe García, might be favorable to an extradition treaty. Already the governor had assisted in the recovery of stolen horses, and both governments had returned fugitives who had crossed the river.[32]

Juan N. Cortina, the Mexican bandit, "surrounding himself by armed men to whom he promised plunder,"[33] had terrorized the valley, burning, stealing, and massacring Americans from mid-1859 until May 1860. He excused his depredations by claiming that the territory between the Rio Grande and the Nueces rivers rightfully belonged to Mexico, and that his intentions were to liberate it from the Americans. In 1860 Ford and his Texas Rangers had joined forces with United States regulars under Colonel Robert E. Lee and had driven him into the interior of Mexico.[34] Now, reportedly, he was back on the border at his San José ranch only eighteen miles above Brownsville. One of Cortina's men told a relative on the Texas side that

Cortina would return in fifteen to eighteen days with a force of Mexicans and Indians, and advised him to find safety on the Mexican side of the river at once.[35]

Having dispatched about one-third of his command to Galveston in March, Ford and other military leaders opposed any further withdrawal of troops from the Rio Grande as some officials in Austin advocated. With Cortina threatening, he felt "confirmed" in his opinion that a further weakening of his force "would result in a war with Mexico. There would be raids from Mexico and finally hostilities between the two governments would ensue."[36]

Major E. Kirby Smith advised that a strong force of "regulars or well-disciplined troops should be employed, that amicable relations may be maintained with Mexico."[37] When Brigadier General Hamilton P. Bee toured the area in the fall of 1861, he concluded "that it is of the utmost importance to the Confederacy that Brownsville and the line of the Rio Grande should be held by them"[38]:

> Shut up and encompassed around us as we are, it is the only point through which we can communicate with the nations of Europe. By proper encouragement every necessary supply, either for our Government or people, can be brought to Matamoras [sic] from abroad, and we have no other outlet so long as the supremacy of the seas is against us. It will keep quiet and neutral a large and in some respects an efficient force of a race embittered against us by real or imaginary wrongs dating back twenty years.[39]

Further, an insurrection was brewing in Zapata County, Texas, where Mexican-American residents openly opposed joining the Confederacy. With indications that Cortina might be at the heart of the matter, Ford reported that "there [was] no telling what [might] happen." He proposed sending Captains Matthew Nolan and Santos Benavides to suppress the movement.[40]

On April 18, Ford received news of the fall of Fort Sumter and the beginning of hostilities. He also received a copy of a telegram from Confederate Postmaster General John H. Reagan, a Texan, warning that a Federal expedition was on its way to Texas, presumably headed for Brazos Santiago. Calling a council of war, Ford got his officers' support for abandoning Brazos Santiago and preparing Fort Brown to withstand a siege.[41] There were several reasons for withdrawing from

Brazos Santiago. The only water on Brazos Island was "unhealthy beachwater." The sand earthworks erected by Colonel McLeod had already been destroyed by the winds of a norther. It had no long-range guns and Ford estimated that a lone war vessel could "shell a force out of Brazos Santiago without even coming in reach of any piece we had there."[42] Also if Fort Brown were strengthened, it could serve the double purpose of a defense against possible Union invasion and of preventing attacks from Matamoros.[43]

Putting his men to work repairing the fort on April 19, Ford appealed to the mayor of Brownsville for citizen aid. Immediately a committee of aldermen called at Ford's headquarters to assure him of their complete assistance. The merchant Jerry Galvan offered anything from his inventory that might be needed. Citizens helped in the digging of trenches and other necessary work, and were organized into volunteer companies. Ford's haste was motivated as much by the expected attack from Cortina as by the threatened arrival of Yankees. To Governor Clark he wrote, "Mexicans say [Cortina] will return and they should know."[44] And if Union forces should land near Brazos Santiago, he continued, "I anticipate giving them something to do all the way up. They shall be fired upon from every place affording shelter to a sharpshooter. Their march shall be no holiday parade."[45] Further, rumors from Matamoros told of a Mexican army of 8,000 marching toward Brownsville. The supposed plan was to retake Texas on the grounds that it rightfully belonged to Mexico and no longer had the protection of the United States.[46]

While soldiers and citizens labored to put Fort Brown in first-class order, civil and military equipment was brought in from the coastal town. Using King's, Kenedy's, and Stillman's steamboats as well as mule teams, Ford moved the guns from Brazos Santiago to Fort Brown. The customhouse at the port was closed and its records and ledgers were taken to Brownsville. Choosing not to destroy the lighthouse at Point Isabel, Ford took the lenses by wagon to Brownsville and hid them in a back yard until the end of the war.[47] By the twenty-seventh the colonel was able to report the completion of the withdrawal from the coast and his satisfaction with the progress of restoring the fort.[48]

Although problems along the border in the summer of 1861 often interfered with work on the fort, Ford continued to strengthen it. On his visit in the fall General Bee found that while some details were still "unfinished [the fort] could in a short time be made as strong as earth works generally are."[49] Regarding the munitions and men at the garrison, Bee reported:

> There are twenty-five pieces of cannon of different caliber there, including a light battery, complete, with its caissons loaded, harness in good order, and ready for service in thirty minutes. The battery horses are poor and unserviceable, but in improving condition. About 300 rounds of ammunition for each piece, of the best description, and a good supply of powder and ball cartridges constitute the supply of ammunition. Lead can be bought in any quantity at 4½ cents per pound. Thre is one 10-inch mortar, and no piece larger than a 24-pounder. There are now at Fort Brown four companies of cavalry (Texan), say 400 men in all.[50]

Matamoros was greatly affected by the arrival of Texas troops at Fort Brown. Crossing the river to enjoy Matamoros's amusements, Colonel Ford's soldiers brandished revolvers and "almost took the town for the first few days after their arrival."[51] However, the local Mexican police, "strengthened considerably," began to enforce stringent laws "to arrest and disarm all disorderly persons, [and] the city became more tranquil."[52] After being required to leave their pistols at home, the Texans were less boisterous and not so "inclined to fight." One observer became convinced that "the Texans are quite as popular as the regular troops were, for though they swear at the Mexicans and make much noise they are liberal and gentlemanly, and seem disposed to be on good terms with us and with themselves."[53]

By early May rumors of Cortina's whereabouts were rampant. He was first reported within twenty miles of Fort Brown. A few days later it was said that he was moving up the river from Matamoros to invade Texas. Six recruits, on their way to join his *bandoleros*, were arrested in Matamoros. Another report stated that he had actually crossed the river and was in Texas. The stories were unfounded, and Ford continued his preparations to "give Cortina a warm welcome."[54]

In April a Mexican named Ochoa, acting under Cortina's directions, led the residents of Zapata County, Texas, in declaring themselves against the Confederacy.[55] At first the rebellion was characterized by looting and burning, but when a county judge was hanged, Colonel Ford ordered troops into the area.

A series of small skirmishes resulted that continued until Cortina invaded a month later.[56]

On May 19, the expected attack came as Cortina moved his men into Zapata County near the town of Carrizo, about 200 miles upriver from Fort Brown.[57] Having received word that Cortina's first move would be an attack on a local store, Captain Santos Benavides waited in ambush with a contingent of twenty-seven mounted riflemen. On the twentieth, three of Benavides's men, sent to reconnoiter Cortina's positions, were fired on by ten of the bandit's advance guards. Returning safely, they reported that Cortina had more than seventy men, and Benavides dispatched a rider to Fort McIntosh at Laredo for reinforcements.[58]

Around ten o'clock on the morning of May 22, Lieutenant Callahan arrived with thirty-one men to find Benavides almost entirely surrounded. Upon the appearance of these reinforcements, Cortina retreated. Although both men and horses were fatigued from their sixty-five-mile journey from Fort McIntosh, Benavides set out after the fleeing Cortina and quickly overtook him. Giving orders not to take any prisoners, the captain attacked, "and at once completely dispersed the bandits, killing seven and wounding many . . . without the loss of a single man" from his command.[59] Two of the wounded drowned while trying to cross the Rio Grande, and the eleven prisoners reportedly taken were probably executed, as was usually the fate of captured bandits on the border. Benavides discovered that at least half of the *bandoleros* were citizens of Guerrero in Tamaulipas and many of them had been involved in the insurrection under Ochoa in April.[60]

During the spring and summer 1863, other Mexican *bandoleros,* such as José María Cobos and Octaviano Zapata, attacked, looted, and burned, etching their names into the records with those of Cortina and Carvajal. They seemed to delight in harassing the Confederacy. Atrocity stories such as "murder near Brownsville . . . a wagoner who had delivered cotton . . . accompanied by a boy about fifteen years of age who was seriously wounded" regularly appeared in the Texas press.[61] Quintero constantly hurried off notes to Benjamin, describing the destructive raiding parties which attacked the citizens and property of Texas. To him, it seemed that many of these were aided by Leonard Pierce, Jr., the newly appointed United States consul at Matamoros.[62]

The governor of Tamaulipas, General Guadalupe García,

agreed to cooperate with the Confederates in Brownsville in breaking up these lawless bands. In a note to Ford he announced that he was "sending troops after Cortina [and] offering to cooperate with [Ford] in . . . the exchange of criminals escaping from justice and in suppressing all evil attempts against the peace of the country."[63] García was fearful that his failure to cooperate would result in Texas's sending a large force to the border, greatly increasing the chances of an invasion of Mexico. Confronted by this combined effort, Cortina retreated to the interior and did not return to the border for two years.[64]

Following the repulse of Cortina, the Texas frontier became reasonably quiet. The Mexican army, rumored to be on its way to invade Texas, never appeared; and the expected Federal invasion did not materialize until the fall of 1863. Goods flowed freely between Texas and Matamoros until late in the year, when the revolution in Tamaulipas again caused disruption. On May 27, Colonel Earl Van Dorn telegraphed Ford that he was "very much pleased with all you have done on your line."[65] Near the end of the year, the Austin *Texas State Gazette* called Ford's Rio Grande operations "a signal example of the right man in the right place."[66]

In the meantime a succession of military commanders wrestled with the constant problems of exchanging cotton for arms. When control passed from the Committee of Public Safety to the Confederate military on April 12, 1861, Colonel Earl Van Dorn became the commander of the Department of Texas. Within a few months Van Dorn was promoted and sent east before he could complete his organizational plans for the state. He was succeeded by Brigadier General Paul O. Hébert with Colonel Henry E. McCulloch commanding the subdistrict of the Rio Grande.[67]

Colonel Ford remained in the valley, but, as the summer wore on, some opposition to him developed. By July, opponents of Governor Clark attacked Ford as an "unsafe and disobedient officer who planned at the first opportunity to undertake the conquest of Northwestern Mexico."[68] Ford's supporters believed that much of this slander was actually an attempt to discredit and undermine the administration of Governor Clark. Because of his successful efforts in preparing the frontier defenses, and favorable reports from such influential people as José Quintero, Ford survived this effort to remove him.[69]

However, in the spring of 1862, Ford's loyalty to his old friend, José María Carvajal, caused him to be transferred to a desk job. In his unsuccessful attempt to seize Matamoros, Carvajal had used Texas as a staging area. When Ford did little to prevent these activities, Quintero, fearful of Mexican retaliation against Confederate trade, demanded Ford's removal.[70] On April 17, 1862, Colonel McCulloch ordered Ford to arrest and extradite Carvajal. Ford informed Carvajal of the order, and the filibuster fled to New York, where he remained for the rest of the Civil War. For disobeying orders, Ford was transferred from the Rio Grande to serve as superintendent of conscripts in Austin.[71]

In May 1862, Brigadier General Hamilton P. Bee took command of affairs in South Texas, with headquarters at San Antonio. Not quite forty years of age, Bee spoke Spanish fluently and was familiar with Mexican laws, character, and habits. An intelligent and courteous gentleman, he was "the most popular and efficient officer the government could have appointed."[72] Quintero felt that, had he been there from the beginning, many of the misunderstandings and disturbances which resulted from Ford's "impolitic" would have been avoided.[73] Bee assigned Colonel Philip N. Luckett and Augustus Buchel to perform the duties left by Ford on the Rio Grande.[74]

Union Sympathizers in Mexico

The first wave of recruits had enlisted for only six months service and by late summer 1861 the problem of replacing them arose.[75] This proved to be a difficult task. The initial enthusiasm faded rapidly and soldiers hesitated to join an army that was short on arms, munitions, and supplies. The state had little war material except that left behind by the retreating Federals, who had been allowed to take their small arms with them. The agents Governor Clark sent to Mexico to buy rifles had met with limited success.[76] Then, the civil war in Matamoros had interrupted the flow of supplies from Mexico on which the army greatly depended to feed and clothe its forces. Further, the Texas government, in debt from the outset of the war, fell behind in paying the troops.[77] The problem was compounded by the large German and Mexican-American populations in southern and western Texas counties. Many of these people not only refused to take the oath of allegiance to the Confederacy, but, in some areas, formed pro-Union companies or supported filibusters and *bandoleros* against the South. Union sentiment was also kept alive in Texas through a loyal Union league. The league was strong in the northern counties and also in Bexar County, especially around San Antonio, where James P. Newcomb published a pro-Union newspaper, the *Weekly Alamo Express*.[78]

Also, across the Rio Grande, Union sympathizers encouraged Confederates to desert. Near the end of 1861, the commander at Fort Brown drew a bleak picture of the problem:

> The desertions from the command have been repeatedly reported by Lieutenant-Colonel Buchel, and since my arrival several have occurred. The condition of the troops is such that I must candidly confess I am not greatly surprised at their yielding to the inducements offered by the parties on the other side of the river. The most of them are but scantily clothed, and have received no pay; they know the state of the Government's credit quite as well as I do myself, and also the difficulty heretofore experienced in raising additional troops. You cannot, therefore, considering all of these circumstances, avoid the conclusion at which I have arrived, that cause enough exists to discourage and dishearten them.[79]

The problem of recruiting and maintaining troops on the Rio Grande continued to grow. Colonel Luckett, in June 1862, appealed to the merchants on both sides of the river to assist him in devising a plan to prevent the force from being withdrawn. After discussing the difficulties, the merchants agreed that for every bale of cotton shipped across the river, the owner would exchange with the military quartermaster five dollars in specie for five dollars in Confederate currency. This procedure would give the military a profit of $5.00 Confederate or $2.50 specie for each bale exported. Although illegal, no better method of providing for the troops was suggested, and there were no complaints so long as the agreement affected only those who had entered into it. But as the volume of trade increased and domestic and foreign speculators entered the field, resistance to the requirement grew, and it was revoked after several months. By this time, however, the civil war in Matamoros had ended with the defeat of Carvajal and supplies were once more flowing into Brownsville from Mexico.[80]

Arriving in Matamoros in February 1862, the United States consul, Pierce, immediately became embroiled in this issue. In several notes to Washington, he elaborated on the never-ending line of refugees coming from Texas.[81] The American enclaves that sprang up in Monterrey, Matamoros, Piedras Negras, and other towns across the border contained over a thousand Americans. Monterrey was "full" and Matamoros looked like an "American town." Protestant services, held every Sunday in the Varieties Theater in Matamoros, were so well attended that Thomas North, one of the refugees, called it a *"religio coup d'état."*[82] Vice-consul M. M. Kimmey wrote that he was "overrun by them [and] still without instructions."[83] He had housed as many as thirty-two in his rooms, and said this was only about 3 percent of those needing assistance. In Piedras Negras some 200 of the "renegades," as the Southerners called them, had trouble finding jobs because they knew no Spanish.

Some of these emmigrants were identified as "Germans who . . . left [Texas] not with the idea of joining the U.S., but to avoid conscription,"[84] but most were loyal Union men who had forsaken their property and risked their lives in the flight to Mexico. One whose property was confiscated was Parson Lyons from San Antonio, whom Quintero called a spy who fled Texas "with Christ upon the lying lip, and Satan in the soul."[85] Some, unsuccessful in their attempt to escape, were caught by Confederate authorities and hanged as traitors, while others were "pressed into service."[86] Among those reaching Matamoros safely were more than twenty United States soldiers who had escaped from the Confederate prison at Camp Verde near San Antonio, where they had been imprisoned at the beginning of the war.[87]

The Washington government ordered Union ships at the Rio Grande to carry north all refugees who wanted to go. Hundreds took advantage of the offer and returned to enlist in the Federal army. Others formed companies and prepared to join an American invasion force if one landed along the Rio Grande. The rest waited in Mexico until the war was over when most of them returned to Texas.[88]

What infuriated patriotic Southerners most was the protection given to the refugees by the governors of the border states. Confederate pleas to the governor of Tamaulipas, Albino López, requesting that the refugees be sent to the Mexican interior or extradited in the spirit of mutual friendship, met with only polite evasions.[89] Frustrated, the Confederate State

Department gave notice that "satisfaction will hereafter be exacted by this Government," which caused United States consul Pierce to fear a rebel attack. He wrote Secretary of State Seward that an organized force of Mexicans and Texans was being formed in Brownsville to seize Matamoros and capture all the Americans and escaped rebel prisoners from Fort Brown.[90]

Although the governors of the border states repeatedly pledged neutrality, there was a real threat, during the late part of 1862 and early 1863, that the Unionists in Mexico would raid Texas.[91] Texans feared that they might combine forces with the Carvajalists or other Mexicans who held grudges against the state. A Texas newspaper reported that combined refugee and Mexican bands were as large as 1,800 men. Rumors circulated that United States vice-consul, Kimmey, at Monterrey was organizing a raid.[92] More substantial were reports that Octaviano Zapata, a former Cortinist, had formed "armed organizations" at Guerrero, Mier, and other points along the border to invade Texas and "plunder the stock ranches." Both Quintero and General Bee protested to Governor López, who informed them that steps had been taken to arrest the leaders of the movement, including Pierce if he were implicated.[93]

Late in December 1862, a party of Mexicans, flying the American flag and calling themselves the "First Regiment of Union Troops," crossed the river at Los Cuevas, attacked and robbed a Confederate wagon train "of all its contents," killed three of the teamsters, and returned to Mexico.[94] On the same day another band of about eighty Zapatists crossed into Texas near El Clareno, assassinated the chief justice of Zapata County, Isidro Vela, and then fled back to Mexico. Captain Santos Benavides, with a company of cavalrymen, followed this group across the river "and punished [them] as their crimes and atrocities merited."[95] He reported that he killed eighteen, wounded fourteen, and "dispersed and scattered" the rest.[96] He captured a cache of documents indicating that Consul Pierce had encouraged and supported the raids.[97] On the basis of the evidence presented him by the Confederates, Governor Lopez sent for Pierce and questioned him regarding the affair, but dropped the issue when the consul denied any complicity and asserted that Zapata's men had used his name to give their robberies "a political color." The Confederates were unsatisfied with the governor's handling of the matter, and Quintero wrote that "the Mexican authorities fear to come in collision with the United States and will continue to overlook the consul's improper conduct."[98]

On January 3, 1863, General Bee requested permission to move his headquarters from San Antonio to Fort Brown so as to be in a position to use his "best efforts to maintain the peace and quiet of the frontier, or, failing that, to take such measures as will compel the neighboring states of Mexico to keep her turbulent population at home."[99] He requested at least 5,000 mounted riflemen for the task.

In Monterrey, Quintero pleaded the case before Vidaurri. Explaining that he was no longer the *comandante* of Tamaulipas and did not have the authority to interfere directly in the neighboring state, Vidaurri promised to write the Juárez government offering his personal services in settling the crisis. Quintero then departed for Brownsville to confer with Bee. On his journey, he was met by a messenger from Governor López requesting an interview. The Confederate agent found the governor conciliatory and willing to permit Confederate patrols to pursue and punish the bandits wherever they could be found.[100]

The issues at the heart of the border problems were discussed in exchanges of correspondence between Bee and López during February, 1863. Both men demonstrated not only a desire to resolve their differences peacefully, but also skill, tact, and a growing respect for each other. In a spirit of cordiality they concluded, on February 25, a reciprocity agreement. Armies could engage in hot pursuit of offenders across the border, but had to give notice to the nearest military authorities. Troops would be stationed by each government at strategic towns and crossings along the Rio Grande. Passports were required of all persons crossing the border, and those moving cattle between Mexico and Texas had to have ownership permits. The Mexicans agreed to seek the recovery of goods stolen by the Zapatists, and Texas agreed to restore Mexican property seized earlier by Carvajal's band. A final, secret extradition article provided for mutual return of prisoners:

> Any person who may commit the offense of murder, arson, embezzlement, robbery, cattle or horse stealing, or larceny of chattels or personal property of the value of $20 or more in either of the two States, and who shall escape to the other, shall be delivered over to the authorities of the place where the offense was committed when the commission of the same shall be proved in such a manner that,

> according to the laws of the State where the fugitive and accused person may be found, he would be lawfully arrested and tried if he had committed the crime in that State.[101]

Quintero claimed that the governor also agreed to return fugitive slaves escaping into Tamaulipas. Apparently López already had "quietly returned" runaway slaves in the months before the treaty.[102]

The accord was soon severely tested. The refugees were led by some well-known former Texans, including Edmund J. Davis, formerly a district-court judge and later Reconstruction governor of Texas, Andrew Jackson Hamilton, a former congressman who later served as both military and provisional governor of the state, and John Haynes, a former member of the Texas legislature from Starr County. By the beginning of 1863 accusations that these men were organizers of refugee military units perpetrating crimes and atrocities against the citizens and property of Texas had made them notorious throughout the southern and western parts of the state. Newspapers fanned the growing passions against them. An Austin editorial referred to them as having fallen into "the cess-pool [sic] of Northern abolitionism."[103] The Tyler *Reporter* said they hid behind the neutrality of Mexico and "began a series of indignities which were very provoking . . . [while] their cowardly nature prompted them to peer at and insult our brave boys."[104] When Davis, as a United States colonel of the First Texas Cavalry (better known in Texas as the First Texas Traitors), returned to Matamoros from New Orleans early in March 1863, the Confederates were anxious to give him a "welcome home."[105]

On the night of March 14–15, 1863, a group of Southerners, including off-duty Confederate soldiers, crossed the Rio Grande near its mouth and seized five or six Yankee refugees. Among them were Colonel Davis and one of his lieutenants, William W. Montgomery. "This we did at 4 o'clock A.M.," one participant wrote. "Surrounding the house in which Colonel Davis was said to be, [we] . . . ordered [him] to surrender, and I regret to say, he did so."[106] After recrossing the river, the Confederates killed several of the prisoners, including Montgomery, whom they hanged from a mesquite tree near Brownsville. "I have reason to believe," Quintero wrote to Benjamin, that they "will not commit treason again in this world. They are permanently located in the soil of the Country."[107] Davis, who, according to one account, was spared because his wife, the daughter of a respected Confederate, pleaded for his life, was taken to Fort Brown as a prisoner. Reporting the incident to the adjutant general, Bee disclaimed the act, but took comfort "that the indignity cast upon us by the authorities of the United States has been avenged by the gallant sons of Texas."[108]

This violation of Mexican neutrality provoked strong reaction in Tamaulipas. On the day following the foray Matamoros was in a "blaze," as bands paraded through the streets playing patriotic music, and the people shouted *vivas* for the Lincoln government and death to the South. Knowing that he had cooperated closely with the Confederate authorities at Fort Brown, the people "hissed at" Governor López when he attended the theater. Calling the incident a flagrant violation of the recent treaty, López threatened to shut off the trade and arrest all Confederate officers found in the vicinity unless the prisoners were immediately released.[109]

Bee realized that the situation was grave. Matamoros was becoming hostile to the Confederacy, and he did not believe that any prisoner was worth the interruption of the trade. On March 16, he returned the surviving prisoners to Governor López with a formal apology to the Mexican government. Davis was welcomed as a hero, but the excitement quickly subsided and the issue passed. The trade continued uninterrupted, and the editor of the *San Antonio Herald* saw it as being "worth the lives of a thousand such traitors as Davis."[110]

A second, less threatening incident occurred a month later, when Captain Benavides followed a band of cattle thieves into Mexico with a contingent of thirty men. He trailed the rustlers directly to Guerrero and, in keeping with the agreement of February 25, informed the Mexican military authorities of his purpose and willingness to assist in arresting the culprits. But Benavides was not popular in Guerrero, the residence of many of the Cortinists he had defeated near Carrizo a year earlier, and the focal point of several other border incidents with which he had to deal. The Mexican commander told him "that the contract was not in any way binding on him," and ordered him "directly back to [his] own side of the Rio Grande."[111] Again notes were exchanged between General Bee and Governor López, and the Confederates received assurances that the stolen cattle would be returned.[112]

An opportunity for Benavides to regain favor with the people of Guerrero came early in September. Zapata's *bandoleros* attacked and routed a Mexican army detachment at Guerrero, and the *alcalde* of the town requested help from the Confederates. Benavides, recently promoted to major, immediately crossed the Rio Grande with seventy-nine cavalrymen. He trailed Zapata's party, came upon his camp the next day, and ordered an attack. After a brief exchange, the bandits broke and fled into the thick chaparral, leaving behind ten dead, including Zapata. The Confederates had no casualties. Pleased that there would "be no more trouble with this emissary of the Lincoln Government," General Bee recommended Benavides for a citation. He also congratulated himself for having negotiated the agreement which gave Confederate troops "the right . . . to cross into Mexico for just such purposes."[113]

Meanwhile, Union troop activity in Louisiana in the summer and fall of 1863 caused Major General John Bankhead Magruder, who had replaced General Hébert as commander of the Department of Texas, New Mexico, and Arizona on October 10, to rush all available forces to eastern Texas. This action stripped the Rio Grande frontier of all but a handful of men. With the scheduled departure of Captain James Duff's cavalry units on October 26, Fort Brown would be left with only nineteen men plus an unreliable militia of townsmen. Rumors now spread of an impending Yankee invasion of the Rio Grande, and reports to General Bee from his spies in New York seemed to verify the worse of them.[114]

At this juncture, and apparently influenced by the Unionists across the river, the Mexican company on picket duty below the fort mutinied under the leadership of Captain Adrian Vidal, Mifflin Kenedy's stepson, who apparently planned to seize the weakened garrison and plunder its rich commissary. The messengers were suddenly fired upon after delivering orders from Bee for Vidal's unit to return to the fort. One was killed, but the second, although severely wounded in the face, escaped to warn the general. Driving back a reconnoitering patrol sent out by Bee, and thinking that Duff's cavalry had already left for the interior, the mutinous company of some sixty men attacked the fort. But Duff had not departed, the mutineers were quickly beaten off, and Vidal and many of his men sought refuge across the river. Fearful of another attack, Bee retained Duff's command until further orders from his superiors. When he informed Manuel Ruiz, the newly appointed governor of Tamaulipas, of the incident, Ruiz, in keeping with the reciprocity agreement of February, issued orders for the arrest of the Vidal party.[115]

The Federal Invasion of 1863

Meanwhile, the long-expected Yankee invasion of the Rio Grande began. Washington early received reports of the budding Confederate commerce there. Within a month President Lincoln's top cabinet officials were exchanging notes on how to shut it off. They soon agreed that the trade was beyond the ability of the blockading ships to control. They concluded that the left bank of the Rio Grande would have to be seized, but they could not spare the required troops. By early 1863 the burgeoning trade had caught the attention of the Northern public and interest within his cabinet was renewed. On July 29, the president asked his secretary of war, Edwin Stanton, "Can we not renew the effort to organize a force to go to Western Texas? . . . I believe no local object is now more desirable." Two days later he conferred with Secretary of State William Seward and Secretary of the Navy Gideon Welles on the matter, and by August 10 Major General Nathaniel P. Banks was under orders to prepare the operation.[116] They felt that the value of the Rio Grande trade exceeded the cost of the army they planned to send to stop it. Its success would deny the South one of its greatest avenues of support, and it would free the 150 ships totalling 450 guns in the West Gulf Squadron to pursue Confederate commerce destroyers. Also it might forestall France's designs in the area.[117]

Late in October, a fleet of more than twenty transports escorted by three warships sailed from New Orleans with 6,698 men. It arrived at Brazos Santiago on November 1. Braving stormy weather and rough seas, but no Confederate resistance, the first units landed and took Brazos Island on the following afternoon. General Banks was confident, for his spies had kept him well informed, and he knew that his opponents were no match for his forces. By the evening of November 3, most of the Yankees had come ashore, chased the Confederate pickets at the mouth of the river, and were driving toward Brownsville, thirty miles away. Their only losses were five infantrymen and two sailors drowned when their landing boats were swamped while crossing the bar at the mouth of the river.[118]

At Fort Brown, General Bee, hastily piecing together the military picture from the reports of his patrols, decided to retreat. The company of Brownsville citizens "had dissolved . . . and disappeared," leaving his total strength, including Colonel Duff's tired and overworked cavalry unit, less than 200 men.[119] Already outnumbered thirty-five to one by the Federal regulars, he felt certain that hundreds of renegades also would rush upon him from Mexico. Further, General Magruder's confidential orders required that, if attacked, he was to "destroy what might fall into the hands of the enemy . . . direct all cotton in progress to Brownsville to [be shipped to Roma] . . . and . . . make the best of his way according to circumstances to join these headquarters, wherever they may be."[120] At first he thought of retreating to Roma to protect the trade at that point, but, in view of the overwhelming enemy strength in front and the threat of renegade attacks upon his rear, he decided to retire north toward King's Ranch. Impressing "all means of transportation in the vicinity," he formed a wagon train of army supplies, clothing, ammunition, and thirty-day rations for 500 men and dispatched it with a guard of ten men, from Brownsville at midday on November 3.[121] He sent the sick and wounded to Matamoros. Arrangements had been made for steamers to transport all public propety and cotton across the river, but before the vessels could arrive, word came that the Federals had reached Camp Russell just ten miles below the fort. With no time to lose, he gave orders to destroy the post and all remaining cotton. Although "several hundred bales of cotton were thrown into the river, and were in the main floated across," some 600 bales were burned.[122] The buildings were set afire and the post evacuated by midafternoon of the third. As the fire spread, it touched off the fort's store of about 8,000 pounds of powder. The explosion spread the fire to the town, burning the block of buildings in front of the ferry. Bee proceeded to King's Ranch "without interruption," turning back all cotton trains headed for Brownsville, and burning enough of the bales in each train "to enable the teams to cross the sand with balance."[123]

Although much criticism was leveled against him, Bee had followed orders explicitly.[124] Unaware of his secret orders from General Magruder, Richard Fitzpatrick, the Confederate commercial agent in Matamoros, complained to Secretary Benjamin that "the surrender of Brownsville was one of the most cowardly and scandalous affairs which has happened in any country."[125] When he claimed that "with the force at Brownsville, under brave and determined officers, the whole Yankee force could have been killed and captured,"[126] he gave evidence of why he was a commercial agent and not a commanding officer. Equally vexatious to Bee was Governor Ruiz's note to the government of Mexico accusing him of having left a detachment of soldiers to prevent the citizens of Brownsville from extinguishing the fire which had spread to the city.[127]

Some citizens, homeguards, and Mexicans organized by the exiled bandit José María Cobos fought the blaze, while others fled across the river to safety. At the ferry, armed guards were necessary to force passage for the women and children. When the powder exploded at the fort, large firebrands were showered down upon the scene. One struck the ferry boat in the middle of the river, setting it on fire. Fort Brown was destroyed and two blocks of the town were reduced to ashes.[128]

By November 6, Brownsville was occupied by some 3,000 Federals. General Banks paused at Brownsville as he contemplated his next move. After the garrison was organized, transportation established on the river, and repairs begun on the fort, Banks, "with all the troops which could be spared," struck out to claim "the passes on the coast between the Rio Grande and Galveston."[129] He left his adjutant, Major General Napoleon J. T. Dana, in command at Fort Brown. By the end of the year the only point on the Gulf Coast from Galveston to the Rio Grande open to blockade runners was the mouth of the Brazos. From Brownsville, Dana sent troops to Rio Grande City, and ordered scouting parties to roam inland as far as King's Ranch.[130]

For a brief time it seemed that the invasion would stop the Confederate trade through Mexico. On November 17, Fitzpatrick wrote Benjamin from Matamoros that "the cotton business is pretty well done within this place."[131] Major John Bruce of the Nineteenth Iowa Infantry reported that they had "stopped a large trade going on between Mexico and the so-called Confederate states."[132] In Brownsville General Dana enthusiastically reported that he had accumulated "about 800 bales" of cotton.[133]

However, contingency plans to shift the crossing of goods further upstream had been considered by the Confederates well before the Federals arrived, and within weeks trade was again flourishing along the border. At first some cotton was routed through Rio Grande City and Laredo. When Union troops threatened these towns, the trade was moved upriver to Eagle Pass some 300 miles above Brownsville. Large amounts of cotton soon converged on that point and were ferried over to Piedras Negras on the Mexican side. From there the wagons made their way along the south side of the Rio Grande to Matamoros. One Little Rock, Arkansas, merchant took one hundred wagons through Eagle Pass, and the customs inspector, Jesse Sumpter, noted that "there was scarcely a day that hundreds of bales were not unloaded . . . and crossed [over] . . . as fast as possible."[134] The cotton arrived so rapidly that a huge inventory quickly accumulated at Eagle Pass, where, early in 1864, some 5,000 bales were counted stocked up waiting transportation into Mexico. On the Texas side the trade was protected by the competent cavalry of Major Benavides, which turned back a Yankee probe into the area on February 19, 1864. On the Mexican side Governor Vidaurri gave "ample protection on all goods *intransitu*" through Nuevo León y Coahuila, a service by which he guaranteed himself an estimated $40,000 a month in revenues.[135]

Meanwhile, three quick revolutions occurred in Matamoros. Before dawn on the morning of November 6, 1863, while the Northern army was still streaming into Brownsville, General José Cobos, a conservative, forty-five-year-old supporter of the Mexican Church party, ended his ten-month exile by crossing the river with some 200 men and seizing power in Matamoros. He was joined by Juan Cortina, who, after apologizing for his errant past, recently had been appointed military commander in Tamaulipas. After arresting Governor Ruiz, Cobos in an address to his troops, raised the cry "of independence and liberty," and attacked "the accumulation of outrages" thrust upon the people of Mexico by a "tyrannical demagogue [Juárez]."[136]

Repudiating the speech and declaring Cobos a pro-French traitor, Cortina overthrew his regime before the day was over. The next morning, after a trial lasting but "a few minutes," he publicly executed Cobos and two of his lieutenants. He then released Governor Ruiz from prison and informed him that he intended to turn the government over to the "constitutionally elected governor of Tamaulipas," Jesús de la Serna.[137] He offered to provide Ruiz with an armed escort of twenty-five men for his "safe" passage into the interior, but suspicious of Cortina's intentions, Ruiz "eluded the vigilance of the sentinels and fled to Brownsville."[138]

By this time United States Consul Pierce was nervously seeking protection. He dashed off a note to General Banks stating that "we anticipate a riot (or what is called in Mexican phraseology, a revolution) tonight, and I am fearful that my house may be a point of attack."[139] The American general quickly trained his guns on the Mexican town and warned Cortina of his intentions "to protect the American flag."[140]

This action brought down upon Banks a stern lecture on American attitudes toward Mexican affairs from Secretary of State Seward. Congratulating the general on his accomplishments in Texas, Seward reminded him that the United States was "on terms of amity and friendship" with the republic, and that he was to "take no part" in the present conflict in Mexico. Rather, he was to "practice absolute non-intervention and non-interference," and consistently to "prevent aid or supplies being given from the United States to either belligerent." And while he could enter Mexico temporarily to protect his "own lines against aggression from the . . . border," he could not protect American citizens there, nor "invoke the protection of [his] forces," should the "consuls find their positions unsafe on the Mexican side of the border." If Americans wanted protection they could only get it by returning to American soil.[141]

In Matamoros, Governor Serna returned to take up the affairs of state, but Cortina, "sustained by a band of cut throats . . . obedient to his nod and beck, [remained] the power behind the throne."[142] Meanwhile, the disgruntled Ruiz collected about 800 men and, in early December, marched on the town. A fight appeared certain, and the Serna-Cortina government demanded loans from all foreigners to meet the cost of defense. Their threats to collect the loans by force if necessary alarmed both Consul Pierce and General Dana. The latter, disregarding Seward's directives, warned Serna of his intention "to protect the rights of American citizens . . . every loyal man, woman, and child of the United States [in Matamoros],"[143] and he seized the ferry boats and placed his garrison on alert. Immediately capitulating, Serna replied: "It not being the desire of the government to place any forced contributions on American citizens," he had given orders that "there shall not be molested any citizen of the United States that shall be met with at this port."[144]

Late in December several skirmishes took place between the contending Mexican parties. After negotiations, it was decided that Serna would abdicate in favor of Ruiz, and that Cortina would march off to expend his energies attacking the French at Tampico. But Cortina failed to depart and within a week one of his officers had insulted Governor Ruiz and was shot. By evening the parties were firing away at each other with artillery and muskets in the plaza at the center of town.[145] Bedlam set in. Robbers roamed the streets and roads plundering. Governor Ruiz notified General F. J. Herron, who had replaced General Dana at Brownsville, that he could no longer protect the consul. Herron then "sent the troops over" and rescued Pierce. By noon of the next day, Ruiz and several of his followers had been chased into exile in Brownsville and Cortina was the acting governor of Tamaulipas. President Juárez, retreating northward from the French, soon appointed Cortina the military *comandante,* and later governor of the state.[146]

By late February 1864, the smoldering conflict between President Juárez and Governor Vidaurri of Nuevo León y Coahuila errupted. Vidaurri, at Monterrey, was pressed by both the advancing French and the retreating Juárez for support. Hoping to retain the autonomy of his domain, he replied to a French query of February 27 that the commitment of his army to their cause was not his to make, but would have to be submitted in a referendum to the people.[147] Juárez immediately condemned him as a traitor, and moved on Monterrey. Vidaurri fled with the state archives and treasury across the Rio Grande near Laredo, and spent several days with his good friend Colonel Benavides. Then he continued to Houston, where he was welcomed by General Magruder and put up in one of the city's finest hotels.[148]

After Vidaurri's flight, Juárez entered Monterrey with nearly 6,000 troops. In spite of the uncertainty, the Confederate agent, Quintero, who had worked closely with Vidaurri, stood his ground in Monterrey and sought an interview with the president. Juárez greeted him cordially, invited him to dinner, introduced him to his cabinet, and assured him that he expected to keep the channels of trade open to the Confederacy.[149]

However, Quintero soon had reason for concern. The former Mexican secretary of state, Manuel Rejon, fled to Brownsville hoping to get passage to Havana. At Brownsville, however, General Herron had him arrested and returned to the *Juaristas* who shot him as a traitor. The Yankees had already succeeded in extraditing from Mexico one of the killers of William Montgomery, and now requested that the Mexicans turn Quintero over to them in the spirit of a mutual extradition of "political offenders." However, Juárez, realizing the importance of the revenue that he received from the Confederate trade, reassured Quintero in their discussions on April 6. The president spoke of Mexico's long practice of granting political asylum, and said that both Unionists and Confederates were safe there. During the four and one-half months that the Juárez government remained in Monterrey the two men cooperated for the mutual benefits of the trade.[150]

The Confederates Regain Control

The fall of Brownsville to the Federals brought the return of Colonel John Ford to the Rio Grande frontier. On December 22, 1863, General Magruder excused him from conscript duty and ordered him to raise a command at San Antonio to regain control of the region. Cautioning him to be "very particular and . . . not let a soul know of [his] intended movements," Magruder suggested that he give the impression that he was "coming to Indianola, via Goliad, to meet the enemy . . . [but then] strike off to the west."[151] Ford was authorized to sell 200 bales of cotton at Piedras Negras for the purchase of needed supplies and to impress all transportation "absolutely necessary to fit out [the] expedition."[152] The colonel requested permission to use "the camels now here as pack animals," for they "would answer admirably for the expedition."[153]

By late January 1864, Ford was able to report that he expected to have a command of about 1,600 men when complete. Comprised of scattered elements of state cavalry and mounted riflemen, it was designed to be the highly mobile force suited for effectively operating in the prairie and chaparral expanses of southwestern Texas. Once the expedition was underway, it would be joined by the commands of Colonel Benavides at Laredo and Captain George H. Giddings at Eagle Pass.[154]

On March 17, Ford swung his columns into line and marched out of San Antonio. Within a week he had passed through Helena and pushed on to Banquete. From there he hastened to Laredo to join Benavides, who had reported that he was threatened by Yankees. Ford retained the element of surprise, as Union intelligence estimated his forces at no more than 650 men, and dismissed reports of his movements as "mere rumor."[155]

In spite of Washington's directives to transfer units from the Rio Grande "for other operations in the spring," the Federals remained strong along the river. Some 3,000 Union soldiers occupied positions from Brazos Santiago to Los Rucias Ranch, twenty-four miles above Brownsville. They had worked hard on the fortifications around Brownsville, and early in January estimated that "with a garrison of 500 men, the defenses [were] capable of withstanding the attack of 5,000 good troops."[156] However, Major General Edward O. C. Ord, Commander of the Thirteenth Army Corps, who inspected the area in mid-February, was "convinced they [were] not reliable either in arms or construction." He also found "the so-called cavalry there" incapable of rendering effective "service on account of want of forage . . . and the horses rapidly dying."[157]

Arriving in Laredo, Ford collected his forces and planned to attack. He hoped "to cut up, disperse, or drive in, all the mounted troops of the enemy and induce them to believe I feel myself too weak for anything greater."[158] At the same time he would probe for a vulnerable point in the Union defenses which, once found, he would exploit to destroy them. Calling in Benavides and Giddings, he left only small forces at Eagle Pass and Laredo, and pushed cautiously downriver. In front of him reconnaissance patrols sought the enemy. It was a good time to move for the "rains [had] been abundant and the grass [was] becoming plentiful."[159]

On June 25, he surprised two companies of Union First Texas Cavalry at Los Rucias and completely routed them. He killed or wounded thirty of the "renegades" and captured thirty-six. "A good many escaped across the laguna, many of them wounded," he reported. "Some of them crossed the Rio Grande and secreted themselves in the cane. . . . Those wounded in the laguna were drowned."[160] Among the spoils were two wagons, twenty-eight horses, and a number of "badly needed" saddles and weapons.[161]

The skirmish cleared the country between Las Rucias and Brownsville of Federal cavalry and Ford moved to take advantage of it. He drove to a point just five miles from Brownsville and felt out the main Federal defenses. Finding them to be stronger than anticipated, he broke off contact, doubled back to Edinburg, thirty miles upriver, and set out pickets. To the Union commander at Brownsville, it seemed that Ford's intentions were "to keep us in as close quarters as possible, which he can do to a certain extent owing to our want of cavalry or horses to mount infantry."[162]

Ford waited another three weeks while he purchased additional ordnance and quartermaster supplies from firms in Matamoros. On July 19, he broke camp and moved down the road toward Brownsville. Small sharp engagements were fought with Union outposts at Ebonal Ranch on the twenty-second and at Dead Man's Hollow on the twenty-fifth. In both exchanges the Yankees were scattered and their relief columns dispersed. By July 20, Herron had concluded that Brownsville was indefensible. Declaring it to be an open city, he evacuated his positions around it and pulled back to Brazos Santiago. The following day, Ford's troops paraded into Brownsville, and were welcomed by the Mayor E. W. Cave and a delegation of ladies who presented the colonel with a new battle flag. With the Texas side of the Matamoros trade route securely in Confederate hands, it was expected that a huge trade would soon again crowd the river.[163]

Notes

1. Twiggs to Nichols, February 4, 1861, Waite to Nichols, February 12, 1861, *Official Records of the Union and Confederate Armies,* [ORA], Ser. I, Vol. 1, pp. 586, 522–23.

2. Robertson to Lubbock and Green, February 4, 1861, *ORA,* Ser. I, Vol. 1, p. 512.

3. Hill to Cooper, February 19, 1861, *ORA,* Ser. I, Vol. 1, pp. 591–93.

4. Twiggs to Thomas, January 2, 7, 1861, *ORA,* Ser. I, Vol. 1, p. 580.

5. Twiggs to Scott, January 15, 1861, *ORA,* Ser. I, Vol. 1, p. 581.

6. Twiggs to Adjutant-General, January 18, 1861, *ORA,* Ser. I, Vol. 1, p. 581.

7. Twiggs to Houston, January 22, 1861, Twiggs to Cooper, January 23, 1861, *ORA,* Ser. I, Vol. 1, pp. 582–83.

8. Devine, Maverick and Luckett to Robertson, February 18, 1861, McCulloch to Reagan, February 25, 1861, Devine, Luckett and Maverick, Circular, February 18, 1861, Twiggs to Thomas, February 19, 1861, Waite, Report of number of troops to be removed from Texas, February 16, 1861, Robertson to Roberts, March 22, 1861, *ORA,* Ser. I, Vol. 1, pp. 503–04, 516, 524, Vol. 53, p. 657, Ser. II, Vol. 1, pp. 8, 33, 35; U.S. Troops evacuated from Texas, February 24, 1861, Thomas J. Devine, Letters, 1861–1867 (unpublished), Eugene C. Barker Library of Texas History, University of Texas, Austin, Texas, hereafter cited as Devine, Letters, 1861–1867. Devine's figures show a total of 2,752 Union troops to be evacuated from Texas.

9. Thomas to Waite, February 4, 1861, Twiggs to Waite February 19, 1861, Holt,

General Orders No. 5, March 1, 1861. *ORA,* Ser. I, Vol. 1, pp. 586, 591; 597, *Richmond Enquirer,* March 3, 1861.

10. Townshend to Chandler, March 12, 1861, Waite to Adjutant General, April 17, 1861, *ORA,* Ser. I, Vol. 1, p. 487, Ser. II, Vol. 1, p. 39.

11. McCulloch to Walker, April 17, 1861, Cooper to Van Dorn, April 11, 1861, *ORA,* Ser. I, Vol. 1, p. 627, Ser. II, Vol. 1, p. 56. On March 19, General Scott telegraphed Colonel Waite to set up a strong defensive perimeter of some 500 to 1,200 troops to protect Indianola "against hostile Texans until further orders." This move was to be subject to the approval of Governor Houston and other Union leaders in Texas. The plan was dropped, however, when Houston, fearful that it would incur the wrath of all Texans against him, rejected it and requested that the evacuation of U.S. troops continue as rapidly as possible. Scott to Waite, March 19, 1861, Lander to Waite, Houston to Waite, March 29, 1861, *ORA,* Ser. I, Vol. 1, pp. 551–52, 598–99.

12. *New York Herald,* May 11, 28, June 18, 1861; Sibley to Adjutant-General, April 25, 1861, Reeve to Thomas, May 12, 1861, Reeve to Thomas, May 12, 1861, Waite to Townshend, May 25, 1861, Sibley to Thomas, June 3, 1861, Van Dorn to Cooper, June 3, 1861, *ORA,* Ser. I, Vol. 1, pp. 567–68, Ser. II, Vol. 1, pp. 39, 40, 43, 49, 60. Some of the Yankee prisoners offered to fight for the South provided the Confederates assume the responsibility of their back pay. This was refused, however, on the grounds "that no appropriation had been made for such purpose." In the spring of 1863, the prisoners were exchanged for an equivalent number and rank of North Carolina troops held in Fort Warren at Boston, Massachusetts. McAllister to Hébert, November 11, 1861, Maclin to Hébert, November 16, 1861, Dimick to Thomas, January 25, 1862, Irwin, General Orders No. 34, April 25, 1863, *ORA,* Ser. I, Vol. 4, p. 136, Ser. II, Vol. 1, pp. 77, 114.

13. Committee of Public Safety to Ford, February 5, 1861, *ORA,* Ser., I, Vol. 53, pp. 650–51.

14. Irby, p. 27 (n.3), Marcus J. Wright, *Texas in the War, 1861–1865,* Harold B. Simpson, editor (Hillsboro, Texas: Hill Junior College Press, 1965), p. 111.

15. Ibid.; Ford to Robertson, February 22, 1861, *ORA,* Ser. I, Vol. 53, p. 651.

16. Committee of Public Safety to Ford, February 5, 1861, *ORA,* Ser. I, Vol. 53, pp. 650–51.

17. Ibid.

18. Ford to Robertson, February 22, 1861, *ORA,* Ser. I, Vol. 53, p. 651.

19. Ibid.; Thompson to Bailey, February 22, 1861, *ORA,* Ser. I, Vol. 1, pp. 537–38.

20. Nichols to Texas Delegation, February 27, 1861, Ford to Robertson, February 25, 1861, Nichols to Robertson, March 23, 1861, *ORA,* Ser. I, Vol. 53, pp. 619–20, 655.

21. Smith to Nichols, April 8, 1861, *ORA,* Ser. I, Vol. 1, pp. 600–601.

22. Ford to Stoneman, March 6, 1861, *ORA,* Ser. I, Vol. 53, p. 653.

23. Nichols to Texas Delegation, February 27, 1861, Ford to Robertson, February 25, 1861, *ORA,* Ser. I, Vol. 53, pp. 619–20, 655.

24. McLeod to Ford, March 1, 1861, John S. Ford Collection of Military Correspondence (unpublished), Daughters of the Confederacy Museum, Austin, Texas, as cited in Irby, p. 29.

25. Ibid.

26. Nichols to Robertson, February 28, March 23, 1861, *ORA,* Ser. I, Vol. 53, pp. 655–61.

27. Thomas to Waite, February 7, 1861, Ford to Robertson, March 6, 1861, *ORA,* Ser. I, Vol. 1, p. 587, Ser. I, Vol. 53, p. 652.

28. Nichols to Robertson, March 23, 1861, *ORA,* Ser. I, Vol. 53, p. 664.

29. *Ranchero* [Corpus Christi], March 16, 1862, Nichols to Robertson, March 23, 1861,

Statement of the number of troops to be removed from the Department of Texas, February 26, 1861, Porter, Report, March 30, 1861, *ORA,* Ser. I, Vol. 53, p. 664, Ser. II, Vol. 1, pp. 21–22.

30. Backus to Cooper, March 30, 1861, *ORA,* Ser. I, Vol. 1, pp. 560–61.

31. Irby., p. 30; Ford to the People of the Valley of the Rio Grande, March 6, 1861, *ORA,* Ser. I, Vol. 53, p. 654; The *New York Herald,* August 20, 1861, predicted that the slaves' "natural asylum will be Mexico, on account of its convenience and the consideration and sympathy . . . enjoyed by the negro race. Besides the climate and soil are both favorable. [There] the negro can hope to have a future; while at the North he is certain to remain the servile, as both the climate and institutions of the Northern people place a barrier to his rising much above the social station he enjoys in the slave states. . . . If the Civil War continues Mexico will assuredly be overrun by the slaves from the Southern States."

32. Ford to Clark, April 16, 1861, Austin to Ford, April 17, 1861, Ford Military Correspondence as cited in Irby, p. 31.

33. Kingsbury Papers, 2: 113, 115.

34. John S. Ford, Memoirs (unpublished), Eugene C. Barker Library of Texas History, University of Texas, Austin, Vol. 4, pp. 783–835; Lyman L. Woodman, *Cortina: Rogue of the Rio Grande* (San Antonio: Naylor Company, 1950), p. 70.

35. Ford to Clark, April 16, 1861, Ford Military Correspondence, as cited in Irby., p. 31.

36. Ibid.

37. Kirby Smith to Secretary of War, April 20, 1861, *ORA,* Ser. I, Vol. 1, pp. 627–28.

38. Bee to the Secretary of War, October 12, 1861, *ORA,* Ser. I, Vol. 4, pp. 118–19.

39. Ibid.

40. Ford to Clark, April 16, 21, 1861, Ford Military Correspondence, as cited in Irby., p. 32.

41. Ford to Clark, April 21, 1861, ibid.

42. Ibid.

43. Ibid.

44. Ibid., p. 33.

45. Ibid.

46. *Richmond Enquirer,* April 4, 1861.

47. Ford, Memoirs, 5: 1004.

48. Ford to Clark, April 27, 1861, Ford Military Correspondence, as cited in Irby., pp. 33–34.

49. Bee to the Secretary of War, October 12, 1861, *ORA,* Ser. I, Vol. 4, pp. 118–19.

50. Ibid.,

51. *New York Herald,* May 31, 1861.

52. Ibid.,

53. Ibid.

54. *New York Herald,* May 16, 21, 31, 1861.

55. Ibid.; Ford, Memoirs, 5: 1102.

56. Ford, Memoirs, 5: 1002–03.

57. Benavides to Ford, May 23, 1861, Ford Military Correspondence, cited in Irby, p. 34.

58. Benavides to Ford, May 23, 1861, Ford Military Correspondence, cited in Irby, p. 35.

59. Ibid.

60. Ibid.

61. *San Antonio Herald,* May 24, 1862.

62. Quintero to Benjamin, January 30, February 26, March 21, 1863, Confederate State Papers, Vol. 8.

63.*New York Herald,* May 31, 1861.

64. Ibid.; Ford to Benavides, May 26, 1861, cited in Irby., p. 36 (n); *Texas State Gazette* [Austin], June 8, 1861.

65. Van Dorn to Ford, May 27, 1861, *ORA,* Ser. I, Vol. 1, pp. 577–78.

66. *Texas State Gazette* [Austin], December 14, 1861.

67. Van Dorn to Cooper, June 3, 1861, Van Dorn to Ford, May 27, 2862, *ORA,* Ser. I, Vol. 1, pp. 573–74, 577–78.

68. Reynolds to Ford, July 30, 1861, Ford Military Correspondence, as quoted in Irby, pp. 36–37.

69. Ibid., Quintero to Hunter, October 18, 1861, Confederate State Papers, Vol. 58.

70. Quintero to Browne, March 8, 24, 1862, Confederate State Papers, Vol. 58; Quintero to Lubbock, March 24, 1862, as cited in Tyler, *Vidaurri,* pp. 70–71. A note of April 30, 1862, from Secretary Benjamin gives insight into the influence that Quintero had in Richmond. "In order to avoid as far as possible the recurrence of such acts as seem to be complained of on both sides of the river, the President has directed that an officer of higher grade than Colonel Ford shall be assigned to the command of the frontier, and the fact stated by you that General Vidaurri has reason to believe that Colonel Ford is connected by close personal relations of friendship with Carvajal has not been without influence in the adoption of this course." Benjamin to Quintero, April 30, 1862, Confederate State Papers, Vol. 11.

71. Irby, p. 38.

72. Quintero to Benjamin, February 26, 1863, Confederate State Papers, Vol. 8; Special Orders No. 101, May 2, 1862, *ORA,* Ser. I, Vol. 9, p. 709; Maverick Family Papers, Correspondence 1850–1872 (unpublished), Eugene C. Barker Library of Texas History, University of Texas, Austin.

73. Quintero to Benjamin, February 26, 1863, Confederate State Papers, Vol. 8.

74. Irby, p. 38.

75. Debray to Walker, August 28, 1861, *ORA,* Ser. I, Vol. 4, p. 99.

76. McCulloch to Clark, March 31, May 14, 1861, Nichols to Clark, May 27, July 27, August 31, September 18, 1861, cited in Cowling, p. 59; Irby., pp. 65, 66.

77. Luckett to Yager, December 31, 1861, *ORA,* Ser. I, Vol. 4, p. 166.

78. Ford to Stith, November 11, 1861, Brewin to Ford, November 7, 1861, McCulloch to Davis, March 21, 1862, Bell to Flewellen, November 28, 1862, Turner to Flewellen, December 6, 1862, Magruder, Special Orders No. 135, January 5, 1863, Bee to Dickinson, February 25, 1863, *ORA,* Ser. I, Vol. 4, pp. 132, 137, Vol. 9, pp. 705–06, Vol. 15, pp. 887, 890, 931, 991–92; *New York Herald,* October 18, 1861, January 7, 1864; Claude Elliott, "Union Sentiment in Texas 1861–1865," *Southwestern Historical Quarterly* 1 (1947): 463–64. See Elliott, *SWHQ 50: 450–51, 454.*

79. Luckett to Yager, December 31, 1861, *ORA,* Ser. I, Vol. 4, p. 165.

80. *Tri-Weekly Telegraph* [Houston], September 28, 1863.

81. Pierce to Seward, March 1, 16, 1862, Consular Dispatches, Matamoros.

82. Pierce to Seward, March 16, 24, 1862, April 30, 1862, March 4, 1863, Consular Dispatches, Matamoros, Kimmey to Seward, November 21, 1862, April 7, 1862, 1863, Consular Dispatches, Monterrey; Tyler, *Vidaurri,* pp. 83, 86.

83. Kimmey to Seward, September 21, 1863, Consular Dispatches, Monterrey, as quoted in Tyler, *Vidaurri,* p. 83.

84. Quintero to Benjamin, October 19, 1862, Confederate State Papers, Vol. 8.

85. Quintero to Benjamin, March 22, 1862, Confederate State Papers, Vol.8.

86. Pierce to Seward, May 5, 1862, Blood to Seward, May 23, 1862, *ORA*, Ser. I, Vol. 9, pp. 684–85, 686.

87. Pierce to Hunter, April 21, 1862, *Official Records of the Union and Confederate Navies*, [*ORN*], Ser. I, Vol. 18, p. 454.

88. Seward to Stanton, July 11, 1862, Luckett to Dickinson, January 26, 1863, Ser. I, Vol. 9, p. 684, Vol. 15, p. 961; Pierce to Hunter, April 21, 1862, Hunter to Pierce, April 23, 26, 1862, Hunter, Report, May 5, 1862, Hunter to Farragut, July 5, 1862, Hunter to State Department, June 16, 1862, Farragut to Bell, September 12, 1862, Emmons, Report, October 7, 1862, *ORN*, Ser. I, Vol. 18, pp. 454, 455–56, 457–58, 501, 668, Vol. 19, pp. 75–76, 127, 265–266; Davis to Luckett, June 6, 1862, Confederate State Papers, Vol. 58; Pierce to Seward, April 8, 1862, Consular Dispatches, Matamoros.

89. Buchel to Gray, December 28, 1862, Buchel to López, December 27, 1862, Luckett to Dickinson, January 26, 1863, *ORA*, Ser. I, Vol. 15, pp. 923, 924, 960–61.

90. Pierce to Seward, March 24, 1862, Blood to Seward, May 23, 1862, ORA, Ser. I, Vol. 9, pp. 656, 685–86; Pierce to Seward, March 4, 1863, Consular Dispatches, Matamoros; Hunter to Pierce, April 23, 1862, *ORN*, Ser. I, Vol. 18, pp. 456–57; Benjamin to Quintero, November 26, 1862, Confederate State Papers, Vol. 11; *Washington Evening Post*, March 23, 1865.

91. Quintero to Benjamin, January 25, 1864, Confederate State Papers, Vol. 58.

92. Quintero to Benjamin, August 30, 1862, October 19, 1862. Confederate State Papers, Vol. 8; *Tri-Weekly Telegraph* [Houston], November 10, 1862.

93. Quintero to Benjamin, November 2, 1862, December 1, 11, 1862, Confederate State Papers, Vol. 8; Vidaurri to the Minister of Foreign Relations, May 18, 1862, United States Congress, *House Executive Documents*, 37th Congress, 3rd Session, Document No. 54 (Washington: Government Printing Office, 1863), pp. 19–20; *Boletin Oficial* [Monterrey], November 30, 1862.

94. The exact date of the attack is difficult to determine. Quintero refers to December 18, and General Bee indicates December 26, 1862, as being the date for the atrocity. Quintero also reported that most of Zapata's men were not Mexicans, but Texans residing in Mexico to escape the draft. Quintero to Benjamin, January 30, 1863, February 26, 1863, Confederate State Papers, Vol. 8; Bee to López, February 3, 1863, *ORA*, Ser. I, Vol. 15, pp. 966–67.

95. Quintero to Benjamin, January 30, 1863, Confederate State Papers, Vol. 8; Bee to López, February 3, 1863, *ORA*, Ser. I, Vol. 15, pp. 966–67.

96. Quintero to Benjamin, January 30, 1863, Confederate State Papers, Vol. 8.

97. Ibid.; Quintero to Benjamin, February 26, 1863, Confederate State Papers, Vol. 8.

98. Quintero to Benjamin, February 26, 1863, Confederate State Papers, Vol. 8.

99. Bee to Dickinson, January 3, 1863, *ORA*, Ser, I, Vol. 15, p. 923.

100. Bee to Dickinson, February 3, 1863, *ORA*, Ser. I, Vol. 15, pp. 965–66; Quintero to Benjamin, January 30, 1863, Confederate State Papers, Vol. 8.

101. Bee to López, February 3, 18, 1863, López to Bee, February 11, 22, 23, 1863, Confederate State Papers, Vol. 8; Bee to López, February 26, 1863, March 1, 1863, López to Bee, February 28, 1863, *ORA*, Ser. I, Vol. 15, pp. 991–1008.

102. Quintero to Benjamin, November 2, 1862, February 26, 1863, Confederate State Papers, Vol. 8.

103. Quintero to Benjamin, February 26, 1863, Confederate State Papers, Vol. 8; in 1862 Hamilton was appointed military governor of Texas by President Lincoln and after the war President Johnson designated him the provisional governor on June 17, 1865. Quintero to Benjamin, November 30, 1862, January 20, 1863, February 26, 1863, March

21, 1863, Confederate State Papers, Vol. 3; *Texas State Gazette* [Austin], November 5, 1862; Elliott, *SWHQ*, 50: 451.

104. *Reporter* [Tyler], April 16, 1863.

105. *Texas Almanac Extra* [Austin], March 26, 1863.

106. Bee to Dickinson, March 15, 1863, *ORA*, Ser. I, Vol. 15, pp. 1016–17; *Reporter* [Tyler], April 16, 1863; Pierce to Seward, March 26, 1863, Consular Dispatches, Matamoros.

107. Tyler, *Vidaurri*, pp. 86–87; Quintero to Benjamin, March 21, 1863, Confederate State Papers, Vol. 8.

108. Fremantle, *Diary*, pp. 7–9; *Tyler Reporter*, April 16, 1863; Bee to Dickinson, March 15, 1863, Confederate State Papers, Vol. 8; *Texas State Gazette* [Austin], April 1, 1863.

109. Quintero to Benjamin, March 21, 1863, April 20, 1863, Confederate State Papers, Vol. 8.

110. Bee to López, March 16, 1863, *ORA*, Ser. I, Vol. 26, Pt. ii, p. 70, also in Confederate State Papers, Vol. 8; Quintero to Benjamin, March 21, April 20, 1863, Confederate State Papers, Vol. 8. *San Antonio Herald*, April 11, 1863.

111. Benavides to Gray, April 4, 1863, *ORA*, Ser. I, Vol. 15, pp. 1040–41.

112. López to Bee, April 17, 1863, Bee to López, April 22, 1863, *ORA*, Ser. I, Vol. 15, pp. 1044–45, 1051–53.

113. Benavides to Yager, September 3, Bee to Turner, September 11, 1863, *ORA*, Ser. I, Vol. 26, Pt. 1, pp. 284–85.

114. Special Orders No. 237, October 10, 1862, Turner to Scurry, May 7, 1863, Kimmey to Seward, June 4, 1863, Bee to Dye, October 24, 1863, *ORA*, Ser. I, Vol. 15, pp. 826, 1079–80. Vol. 26, Pt. 1, p. 657, Pt. 2, p. 350; Quintero to Benjamin, December 19, 1862, April 20, 1863, Fitzpatrick to Benjamin, February 1, 1863, Confederate State Papers, Vol. 8; Magruder to Turner, December 3, 1862, Magruder to Cooper, June 8, 1863, Bee to Turner, August 13, 14, 24, 1863, October 11, 1863, *ORA*, Ser. I, Vol. 15, p. 886, Vol. 26, Pt. 2, pp. 63, 164–65, 166–67, 180–81, 302; *Texas State Gazette* [Austin], September 2, 1863, from the *Fort Brown Flag* [Brownsville], August 14, 1863.

115. Bee to Turner, October 28, 1863, Bee to Ruiz, October 28, 30, 1863, Bee Report, October 31, 1863, *ORA*, Ser. I, Vol. 26, Pt. 1, pp. 448–51; Quintero to Benjamin, September 16, 1863, Confederate State Papers, Vol. 8; *Texas State Gazette* [Austin], September 2, 1863, from the *Fort Brown Flag* [Brownsville], August 14, 1863.

116. Chase to Seward, January 24, 1862, Pierce to Seward, March 1, 1862, Seward to Stanton, March 13, 1863, April 25, 1863, Blood to Seward, May 23, 1862, *ORA*, Ser. I, Vol. 9, pp. 642, 648, 667, 674, 686; Walker to Farragut, c. September 20, 1862, *ORN*, Ser. I, Vol. 19, p. 214; *New York Times*, February 7, 19, 1863; Welles, *Diary*, 1: 283, 387–88; Welles to Seward, April 16, 1863, Welles to Stanton, April 23, 1863, Welles to Seward, June 9, 1863, Ser. I, Vol. 18, pp. 415–16, Vol. 20, pp. 155, 291; Lincoln to Stanton, July 29, 1863, *ORA*, Ser. I, Vol. 26, Pt. 1, p. 659; Kerby, pp. 186–87.

117. Banks to Stanton, Report, April 6, 1865, Banks to Halleck, August 8, 1863, *ORA*, Ser. I, Vol. 26, Pt. 1, pp. 21, 697; Woolsey to Gillis, August 1863, *ORN*, Ser. I, Vol. 20, p. 467; *New York Daily News*, September 7, 1863, found in Edmund Kirby Smith Papers (unpublished), Southern Historical Collection, Wilson Library, University of North Carolina, Chapel Hill, 3: 3; Welles, *Diary*, 1: 442–43.

118. Banks to Stanton, October 26, 1863, April 6, 1865, Banks to Halleck, November 4, 1863, Table of Strength and Composition of the Rio Grande Expedition, October 31, 1863, *ORA*, Ser. I, Vol. 26, Pt. 1, pp. 20, 397, 398, 776; Strong to Bell, November 4, 1863, Banks to Bell, November 3, 1863, Gillis to Bell, November 8, 1863, Tarver to Dickinson,

November 8, 1863, Bee to Turner, November 2, 1863, *ORN*, Ser. I, Vol. 20, pp. 646, 647–48, 649; *Richmond-Enquirer*, November 21, 1863; Kingsbury to Strong, August 20, 1862, Kingsbury to McMahon, November 10, 1863, Kingsbury Papers, Letters and Papers, 1: 86, 136. Not only had Gilbert Kingsbury constantly apprised Banks of the conditions on the Rio Grande and the strength of the Confederates there, but he had also reported regularly for the *New York Herald* under the pseudonym of W. W. Fenn.

119. Bee to Turner, November 8, 1863, Duff to Tarver, November 11, 1863, Taylor to Duff, November 3, 1863, Davis to Caldwell, November 11, 1863, enclosed with Bradfute to Turner, November 24, 1863, *ORA*, Ser. I, Vol. 26, Pt. 1, pp. 435, 442, 443–45; Bee to Turner, November 2, 1863, *ORN*, Ser. I, Vol. 26, p. 649; Note on the size of Bee's command, Maverick Papers; Quintero to Benjamin, November 26, 1863, Confederate State Papers, Vol. 58.

120. Turner, Confidential Circular, October 26, 1863, Turner to Bee, October 27, 1863, *ORA*, Ser. I, Vol. 26, Pt. 2, pp. 357–58, 361; Note on Turner's orders to Bee, Maverick Papers.

121. Bee to Turner, November 5, 1863, Duff to Tarver, November 11, 1863, Quintero to Benjamin, November 26, 1863, *ORA*, Ser. I, Vol. 26, Pt. 1, pp. 433, 441, 443, Vol. 34, Pt. 2, pp. 888–89.

122. Bee to Turner, November 8, 1863, Duff to Tarver November 11, 1863, *ORA*, Ser. I, Vol. 26, Pt. 1, pp. 434, 442; Quintero To Benjamin, November 9, 26, 1863. Confederate State Papers, Vol. 58; *Richmond Enquirer*, November 29, 1863.

123. Bee to Turner, November 8, 1863, Duff to Tarver, November 11, 1863, *ORA*, Ser. I, Vol. 26, Pt. 1, pp. 434, 442.

124. Bee's actions and route of retreat were approved by his superiors. Boggs to Magruder, November 23, 1863, *ORA*, Ser. I, Vol. 26, Pt. 2, pp. 441–42.

125. Fitzpatrick to Benjamin, November 17, 1863, Confederate State Papers, Vol. 8.

126. Ibid.

127. Bee to Vidaurri, November 22, 1863, *ORA*, Ser. I, Vol. 26, Pt. 1, pp. 438–39.

128. Banks to Halleck, November 6, 1863, *ORA*, Ser. I, Vol. 26, Pt. 1, p. 399; Irby, pp. 61–62; Kerby, p. 192.

129. Dana to Banks, November 16, 1863, Banks to Stanton, April 6, 1865, *ORA*, Ser. I, Vol. 26, Pt. 1, pp. 20, 413.

130. Strong to Bell, December 28, 1863, *ORN*, Ser. I, Vol. 20, p. 742; Kerby, pp. 192–93.

131. Fitzpatrick to Benjamin, November 17, 1863, Confederate State Papers, Vol. 8; Boggs to Magruder, November 27, 1863, *ORA*, Ser. I, Vol. 26, Pt. 2, pp. 449–50.

132. Bruce to Baker, December 1, 1863, *ORA*, Ser. I, Vol. 26, Pt. 1, p. 425.

133. Dana to Stone, December 2, 1863, *ORA*, Ser. I, Vol. 26, Pt. 1, p. 830.

134. Quintero to Benjamin, July 5, 1862, Confederate State Papers, Vol. 8; Bee, Report, October 31, 1863, *ORA*, Ser. I, Vol. 26, Pt. 1, p. 451; Tyler, *SWHQ* 73: 463; *Richmond Enquirer*, November 29, 1863.

135. McManus to Dana, February 13, 1864, ORA, Ser. I, Vol. 34, Pt. 2, p. 318; Quintero to Benjamin, November 26, 1863, Confederate State Papers, Vol. 8; Tyler, *SWHQ* 73: 463; Windham, *Journal of Southern History* 27: 164.

136. Quintero to Benjamin, November 26, 1863, Confederate State Papers, Vol. 8; Banks to Halleck, November 6, 1863, Cobos to His Companions in Arms, November 6, 1863, *ORA*, Ser. I, Vol. 26, Pt. 1, pp. 399–401.

137. Quintero to Benjamin, November 26, 1863, Confederate State Papers, Vol. 8; Banks to Halleck, November 6, 1863, *ORA*, Ser. I, Vol. 26, Pt. 1, pp. 399–401.

138. Quintero to Benjamin, November 26, 1863, Confederate State Papers, Vol. 8.

139. Pierce to Banks, November 7, 1863, *ORA,* Ser. I, Vol. 26, Pt. 1, pp. 404–05.

140. Banks to Halleck, Banks to Pierce, November 7, 1863, *ORA,* Ser. I, Vol. 26, Pt. 1, pp. 403–04.

141. Seward to Banks, November 23, 1863, *ORA,* Ser. I, Vol. 61, Pt. 4, pp. 410–11.

142. *Tri-Weekly Telegraph* [Houston], January 5, 1864; Banks to Halleck, November 9, 1863, *ORA,* Ser. I, Vol. 26, Pt. 1, p. 405.

143. Dana to Stone, December 11, 15, 1863, Dana to Serna, December 26, 1863, Pierce to Dana, December 26, 1863, *ORA,* Ser. I, Vol. 26, Pt. 1, pp. 844, 856–57, 883, 884–85; *Tri-Weekly Telegraph* [Houston], January 20, 1864.

144. Serna to Dana, December 26, 1863, *ORA,* Ser. I, Vol. 26, Pt. 1, p. 885.

145. Quintero to Benjamin, December 30, 1863, January 25, 1864, Confederate State Papers, Vol. 8; *Tri-Weekly Telegraph* [Houston], January 20, 1864; Herron to Stone, January 16, 1864, *ORA,* Ser. I, Vol. 34, Pt. 2, p. 92.

146. Banks, Special Orders No. 322, December 24, 1863, Herron to Stone, January 1, 1864, *ORA,* Ser. I, Vol. 26, Pt. 1, p. 879, Vol. 34, Pt. 2, p. 93; Kerby, p. 192; Quintero to Benjamin, January 25, 1864, Confederate State Papers, Vol. 8.

147. Quintero to Benjamin, February 28, 1864, Confederate State Papers, Vol. 8; Vidaurri to Bazaine, March 1, 1864, in *Boletin Oficial* [Monterrey], March 3, 1864.

148. Quintero to Benjamin, March 8, 1864, Confederate State Papers, Vol. 8; Benavides to Slaughter, April 10, 1864, *ORA,* Ser. I, Vol. 53, pp. 980–81; Kimmey to Seward.

149. Quintero to Benjamin, April 3, 1864, Confederate State Papers, Vol. 8.

150. Quintero to Benjamin, April 7, 1864, Confederate State Papers, Vol. 8; *Daily Telegraph* [Houston], May 25, 1864; *San Antonio News,* June 18, 1864.

151. Turner to Ford, December 22, 1863, *ORA,* Ser. I, Vol. 26, Pt. 2, p. 525.

152. Turner to Ford, December 22, 29, 1863, *ORA,* Ser. I, Vol. 26, Pt. 2, p. 560.

153. Ford to Turner, December 29, 1863, *ORA,* Ser. I, Vol. 26, Pt. 2, p. 560.

154. Turner to Ford, December 22, 1863, Ford to Turner, January 6, 1864, *ORA,* Ser. I, Vol. 26, Pt. 2, p. 525, Vol. 53, pp. 922–23; Ford to Benavides, Ford Military Correspondences, cited in Irby, p. 146.

155. Kimmey to Herron, February 3, 1864, Herron to McClernand, April 16, 1864, *ORA,* Ser. I, Vol. 34, Pt. 2, p. 222; Pt. 3, p. 176; Irby, p. 152.

156. Halleck to Stanton, January 1, 1864, Dana to Stone, January 7, 1864, Herron to Ord, February 11, 1864, *ORA,* Ser. I, Vol. 34, Pt. 2, pp. 29–30, 39, 295; Kerby, pp. 367–68; *Tri-Weekly Telegraph* [Houston].

157. Ord to Herron, February 12, 1864, Ord to Stone, February 16, 1864, *ORA,* Ser. I, Vol. 34, Pt. 2, pp. 309, 344.

158. Ford to Slaughter, May 16, 1864, Ford Military Correspondence, as quoted in Irby, p. 155.

159. Ford to Slaughter, June 15, 1864, *ORA,* Ser. I. Vol. 53, p. 1001.

160. Ford to Slaughter, June 23, 1864, *ORA,* Ser. I, Vol. 34, Pt. 1, pp. 1054–56.

161. Ibid.

162. Herron to Owight, June 26, 1864, *ORA,* Ser. I, Vol. 34, Pt. 1, pp. 1053–54; *Weekly State Gazette* [Austin], June 29, 1865.

163. Kerby, pp. 368–69.

4
THE OVERLAND TRADE

Texas Cotton Transportation

Through the cooperative efforts of Quintero and other Confederate authorities, Matamoros became what United States Consul Pierce called the "great thoroughfare" of the South. It was "to the rebellion west of the Mississippi . . . [what] New York [was] to the United States."[1] Nevertheless, the Confederates always had to wrestle with troublesome commercial entanglements created by self-interest groups on both sides of the border. From the beginning, periodic political disturbances in Tamaulipas interrupted the trade. And even when they could deal with the Mexicans, they had no central trade coordinating body. As a result, too many agents were in the market trying to make deals for themselves or for clients, usually working at cross purposes and to the disadvantage of the Confederacy.

Furthermore, the confederates experienced great difficulties in getting cotton to Matamoros. On both sides of the border transportation was "very slow owing to their having neither railroads nor water communication."[2] Some 300 to 400 miles of semiarid and desert country lay between the San Antonio and Alleyton collecting points and the Mexican border. In good weather the cumbersome cotton wagons could traverse these distances in four to six weeks. But those coming from the more distant interior terminals often took several months to plod their way to the border towns.[3]

A number of wagon trails were used to haul the cotton from the plantations of Texas, Louisiana, Arkansas, and even states east of the Mississippi River. The most popular route, suggested by Texas purchasing agent Pryor Lea, stretched from the railroad terminus at Alleyton to Brownsville by way of

Richard King's ranch. Usually teamsters broke the journey into three parts. The first segment extended from Alleyton to Goliad, the second from there to the King ranch, and the final one to Brownsville. Once the planters got their cotton to Alleyton or Goliad, Mexican teamsters often hauled it over the last stretches. Another trail led from central and western Texas through Austin, San Antonio, and then to the King ranch and Brownsville, or to Roma, Laredo, or Eagle Pass. A third route passed through Gonzales and on to Laredo or Eagle Pass. Wagon trails paralleled the Rio Grande on both sides from Eagle Pass and Piedras Negras down to Brownsville and Matamoros. The river, navigable as far up as Roma, was often used to carry goods between that Texas town and Matamoros.[4]

Alleyton, San Antonio, and the King ranch became important cotton depots. San Antonio became the focal point for cotton from central and western Texas. It was reported that "carts and wagons loaded with cotton [were] passing daily through [the] city for Mexico," and Eliza Ripley counted "hundreds of . . . [others] 'parked' with military precision outside [the city] waiting their turn to enter the grand plaza, deliver packages of goods, and load with cotton," for their return to Mexico.[5] One San Antonio merchant advertised "Mexican Goods" for sale, including bagging, bailing rope and twine, blankets, leather, lead, various foodstuffs, and "segars." Another sold Mexican flour from the Taylor and Black mills of Monclova, Coahuila.[6] Alleyton, located about sixty-five miles west of Houston, was the western terminus of the Texas railroad system. As large amounts of cotton from east Texas and beyond rolled into the "little wooden village . . . [it was soon] crammed full of travelers and cotton speculators."[7] From Alleyton wagons hauled the cotton to the King ranch, where "all roads from every cotton section of the state in the direction of Brownsville converged."[8]

At the depots small wagon trains were organized, water and provisions taken on, repairs made, and additional draft animals acquired, if available, for the push to the border. Each train consisted of ten or fifteen wagons, a few saddle horses, and twenty or thirty spare draft animals. The train generally had one wagon master, two section captains, twelve teamsters, a couple of armed outriders, and a "corporal" to ride herd on the extra animals. The business grew quickly as "nearly everybody [became] wild with the cotton mania [and] about

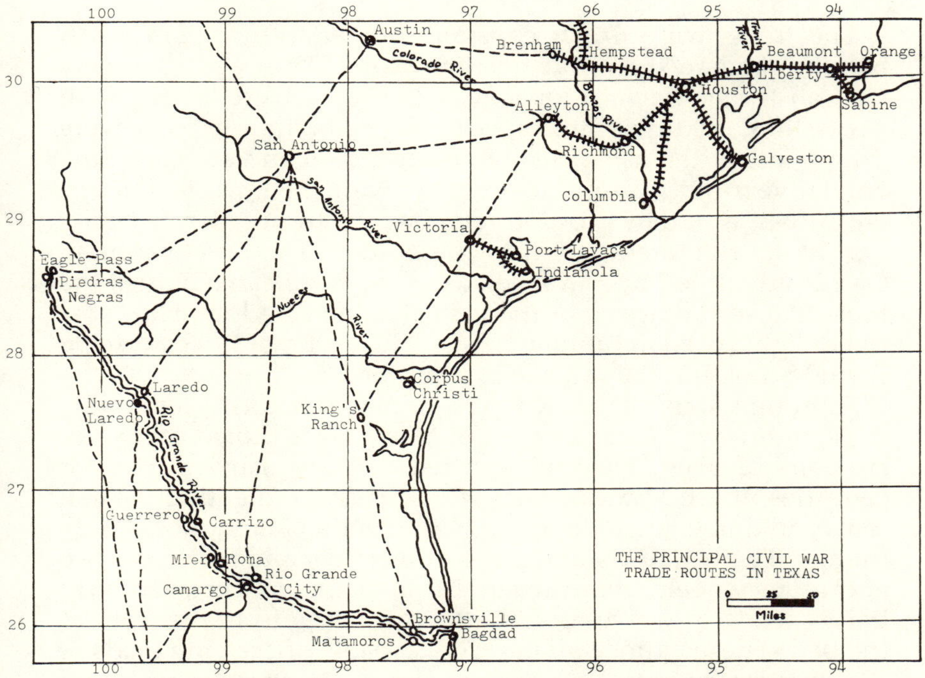

Map of principal trade routes, railroads, and military installations.

5,000 wagons [were] employed in hauling cotton from Louisiana, Texas and the Indian territory to Matamoros."[9]

South of the King ranch was "the Sands," the most difficult part of the journey. With few watering places, it was a dreary waste of mesquite, prickly pear, salt licks and sand, infested with rattlesnakes, tarantulas, scorpions, ticks, and fleas. To cross this treacherous strip of more than 120 miles, the teamsters took extra oxen along to assist in pulling through the more difficult places and to replace animals that became too weak to continue. Sometimes the hardships of the trail so weakened the animals that loads had to be lightened by dumping some cotton bales along the way. Often there were long droughts when neither food nor water was available. In time the trails were marked by "hundreds of domestic animals, dead, their flesh seemingly dried up on their bones."[10] In spite of these difficult conditions, the Sands "became a broad thoroughfare along which continuously moved two vast, unending trains of wagons; the one outward bound with cotton, the other homeward bound with merchandise and army supplies."[11]

The trains were under constant danger from Indian raids, bandits, jayhawkers, and bushwhackers. This was especially true on the homeward journey, when they were loaded with necessities, luxuries, and specie. At night the wagons were drawn into a defensive circle to protect men and animals. Seventeen-year-old "Corporal" August Santleben wrote that he encountered outlaws, Union refugees, and Confederate "sulkers" as he freighted cotton to the border. The outlaw Abram García, identified by Santleben as *"Caballero Blanco,"* struck the most fear in the hearts of the teamsters and traders. His "special delight [was] in humiliating . . . [his victims] . . . by forcing them to dance at the muzzle of a six shooter."[12]

Although some light two- and four-wheel carts were used, most cotton was hauled in large, heavy carts pulled by five or six pairs of oxen. Having been used in Spanish America for centuries, these Mexican carts were constructed entirely of cottonwood timbers held together with wooden pegs and rawhide thongs. The bed measured six by fifteen feet and rested on two enormous wheels, about seven feet in diameter. The oxen were harnessed to a twelve-foot tongue projecting from the front of the bed. These clumsy affairs were capable of carrying loads of 10,000 pounds, or twenty cotton bales. Because the wheels and axles were made of wood, they soon produced a peculiar wobbling motion accompanied by a constant creaking noise. To reduce the friction and the noise, prickly-pear leaves were often pushed into the hub as a lubricant. Sturdy poles at each corner of the bed supported a thatched straw covering which protected men and cargo from the weather. Many drivers later abandoned the slow-moving Mexican carts for newer and more efficient wagons, but they continued to serve as an important means of freighting until the end of the war.[13]

As the war progressed, the Mexican cart was generally replaced by the larger, mule-drawn freight wagon. The bed was twenty-four by four and a half feet, and five and a half feet high. With a running gear of solid iron, these vehicles could haul immense loads and stand hard service. Fully loaded, they carried sixteen cotton bales. A tarpaulin, often bearing the owner's name and the train number, was stretched over a frame to cover the cargo. Whenever available, ten or twelve mules were used in the team rather than the larger but less durable oxen. Small and tough, the mules could travel faster and could be shod so as to protect their feet on rough roads.[14]

Wagons, teams, and particularly teamsters were hard to get.

Many teamsters were conscripted by the army, and merchants usually outbid the financially restricted and less energetic state agents for the services of those who remained. Consequently, the government had to use some enlisted men as teamsters. In 1863, General Edmund Kirby Smith, commander of the Trans-Mississippi Department, sought to replace these conscript teamsters with Negroes. But the planters were reluctant to release them because of "the delicate tenure by which [they] would hold this species of property on or near the Rio Grande."[15] The shortage of teamsters, teams, and wagons became so critical that advertisements for them appeared daily in the Texas newspapers.[16]

Because of their scarcity and the dangers of the trail, private teamsters received substantial wages. Those working for private merchants were the better paid, reportedly getting $9.00 per day and ox feed. According to the editor of the *San Antonio Herald,* their high wages contributed to the inflationary prices of civilian commodities.

> One thing that contributes largely to the high prices of corn, meal, flour, salt and other necessaries of life in this city, is the difficulty, almost impossibility of procuring hauling. A great majority of teamsters are conscripts and unless they haul for the Government, they are compelled to go into the army. The army thus monopolizes the transportation and consequently the provisions, and the citizens are compelled to pay for their food such prices as dealers see fit to extort from them.[17]

Government haulers, being either conscripted or impressed, received only $5.00 a week and ox feed.[18]

The directives of general headquarters, designed to overcome these transportation difficulties, were not always followed in the loose military administration in the Southwest. Petty frontier army officers almost constantly interfered with outgoing and incoming trains by conscripting teamsters and seizing wagons, teams, cotton, and especially importations of military supplies.[19]

These problems often combined to push the cost of transportation up to half the value of the cargo. In southwestern Texas the freight rates ran as high as twenty cents per ton per mile even before the war. By early 1862 complaints were made that handling costs were from 300 to 400 percent higher than in peace time.[20]

For cotton, the rate early in 1862 was five and six cents a

pound from Alleyton to the Rio Grande. The drought that summer and the fear of impressment of teams or teamsters sent the prices up to eight and ten cents. In September, the freight from San Antonio to Brownsville was set at one and one-half cents in specie plus three cents in Confederate notes per pound per one hundred miles for all commodities. A year later, complaints were made against a bill raising the rates to twelve cents in specie per pound for transporting cotton from Alleyton to the river. Opponents of the bill asserted that the rate previously had been nine cents.[21]

In addition to the overland trade, commerce was conducted in Texas's coastal waterways that lay behind the offshore islands and sandbars. Safely out of reach of the large Union blockaders, shallow-draft schooners sailed these lagoons and bays running cotton and contraband between the Gulf ports of Texas and the neutral waters of Mexico. Drawing about three feet of water and manned by crews of three to six men, these small, swift ships usually carried forty to eighty bales of cotton. Frequently, smaller sloops carrying from fifteen to forty bales and two- to three-man crews were used. A few larger ships, such as the schooner *Water Witch* and the bark *Teresita*, could carry up to 300 bales. In 1863, the freight charge on cotton transported along the inland waterway was fourteen cents a pound delivered to a neutral port. In addition the owner of the vessel was given a bonus of $7.00 per bale for all cotton carried through the blockade.[22]

The owners of these schooners realized tremendous profits on both outbound and return voyages. Capable of carrying 171 bales, the *Rob Roy* netted about $13,000 for each load of cotton delivered to Matamoros. Purchasing a cargo at the Rio Grande for $2,000 the *John Douglas* brought it up the Texas coast and sold it for $21,500.[23]

Although these air-propelled vessels were used extensively throughout the war, the risks grew as Union cruisers increased their vigilance on the Texas coast, causing many shippers to avoid the use of these water routes. James A. Duggan's cotton lay at Columbia near the mouth of the Brazos for more than six weeks in 1863. He had the opportunity of shipping it by water to the Rio Grande at very favorable rates, but, he told his consignee, "I prefer the sure way." Others also had "but little faith in that sort of speculation."[24]

Before the introduction of the railroad, the cost and dangers

The *Rob Roy*.

of overland transportation limited cotton production to southeastern portions of the state. The developmental possibilities of the railroad were quickly recognized. In 1854 the editor of the Tyler *Telegraph* saw the railroad "built upon slave soil by slave labor, [as] the greatest creative agent in rapidly germinating the elements of a series of slave states."[25] In 1857 the editor of the Austin, *Texas State Gazette,* wrote:

> Among all suggestions to increase the populations of the State with sound and reliable Southern immigration, there are none which appeal to us with greater force than the prosecution of our railroads. If we afford the state one or two great highways of this kind we shall give a powerful impetus to the immigration of cotton planters from the surrounding states.[26]

Early in the 1850s the Texas legislature enacted provisions

which gave railroad companies sixteen sections, or 10,240 acres of land for each mile of track put into operation. However, it stipulated that they must complete twenty-five miles of track to qualify for the grant. Under these provisions ninety-nine miles of track were laid by 1857. To stimulate more rapid development, the legislature scaled down preconditions in 1858 and 1859, until a railroad company was required to build only five miles of track to begin receiving land. Also, an 1856 law permitted the railroad companies to borrow, from a Special School Fund, $6,000 for each mile of track completed. To be eligible for a loan, a company was required to have twenty-five miles of track ready for rolling stock and another twenty-five miles graded and ready for crossties and rails. With these inducements, railroad construction progressed rapidly in 1859 and 1860. When hostilities began in 1861, ten railraod companies were operating 468 miles of track in the state.[27]

Because the Texas railroad system was incomplete, it provided only limited service during the Civil War. Some 345 miles of it radiated from Houston, linking that city with Galveston, Harrisburg, Columbia, Alleyton, Brenham, Millican, Hempstead, Beaumont, and Orange. There were no connections with either the Rio Grande in the west or New Orleans in the east.[28]

The isolated Houston rail hub expedited transportation only in its immediate area and even that service was limited. The roads were all single-tracked, employed several different gauges, and were not interconnected. All cargo passing through Houston had to be transferred by wagon from one train to another. Most of the trains were powered by "American" 4-4-0 engines, capable of pulling no more than fifteen 10,000-pound boxcars at a maximum speed of twenty-five miles per hour.[29]

Outside of these Houston tentacles, the few remaining railroads were scattered, poorly equipped, ill-kept, and generally went nowhere. On the northeastern border two fingers of track jutted out from Marshall. One ran east toward Shreveport, Louisiana, and the other terminated at Swanson's Landing on the Red River about five miles northeast of Marshall. Hoping to complete the connection between Marshall and Shreveport, General Kirby Smith ordered the tearing up and repositioning of rails belonging to a neighboring Southern Pacific spur. But before the work could be completed, the Southern Pacific ran out of iron. The loss of the Southern Pacific's services was not greatly felt since its torn-up spur had run north some thirty-five miles into the countryside from Jefferson and its rolling stock included only two boxcars, one flatcar, and no locomotives. During the time of its operation, the three-car train was powered by six oxen. The animals pulled the cars up grades, and then coasted downhill riding aboard the flat car.[30]

Between 1836, when the first railroad was chartered in Texas, and 1861, at least six charters were granted to companies proposing terminals on the Rio Grande. The charters of all but one of these companies lapsed with no construction begun. Thus, in 1861, the only railroad in operation with plans to build to the Rio Grande was the San Antonio and Mexican Gulf. It operated twenty-seven miles of track between Victoria and Port Lavaca, with a short spur running to Indianola. However, in 1863 and 1864 the company's service ended when General Magruder mined its rails to strengthen the defenses of Matagorda bay.[31]

Reports of abused and broken down locomotives were received during the first year of the war, and by 1863 all of Texas's railroads were in disrepair. With their services largely committed to an army which was unable to pay, the companies could not afford the cost of repairs. And even if they could have, it was impossible to obtain engines, rails, and spare parts, all of which had to be imported. Because of heavy use and poor maintenance, the roadbeds were settling, the light rails were compressing and spreading, ties and joints were splitting, cars were falling apart, and locomotives were rapidly deteriorating. The decrepit engines of the Buffalo Bayou, Brazos and Colorado line, pulling only two cars, had to approach one steep grade by descending the facing hillside at full throttle, racing across a rickety trestle, and up the incline, hoping that the combination of steam power, momentum, and luck could overcome the slope.[32]

In spite of efforts to expand the railroads west to Austin and east to New Orleans, the milage of track in service decreased during the war. The Confederate army tore up 167.19 miles of the Texas railroad system for defensive purposes. When the struggle ended in 1865, only 309.81 miles of railroad remained in the state, and most of that was inoperative.[33] Shortly after the termination of hostilities, a newspaper correspondent reported that nothing in the state was "so sadly out of joint [and] out of repair" as the railroads. "A trip on one of them is like riding an ox-wagon over hog-wallow prairie," he warned, and one should not take "passage on a Texas Railroad without first getting his life insured, saying his prayers, and then writing to some friendly freighter to meet him halfway along the track, and transport him to the depot."[34]

Profiteers and Swindlers

After the civil conflict in Tamaulipas was settled in the spring of 1862, commerce thrived. Quintero reported that the "trade is *immense* . . . [and] it grows larger every day."[35] The American consul at Monterrey warned that it had reached "enormous proportions [and that] large trains [carrying] goods of all kinds" were departing for Texas daily.[36] The road from Matamoros was "one vast and almost unbroken line of wagons and carts carrying cotton to the Gulf."[37] Offshore some 70 to 200 ships waited "constantly at anchor [as] their cotton cargoes [were] being brought to them . . . by two small steamers."[38] Foreign consuls advised Quintero that their governments would pay "any amount of specie" for cotton, and they were ready to provide 500 wagons to haul the commodity from the South.[39]

The growing trade attracted a number of merchants who sought large profits but contributed little to the securing of military supplies. From its beginning the Confederate Rio Grande commerce suffered from waste, inefficiency, speculation, and compeition among the Southerners. The "multiplicity of purchasers, speculators . . . competition and confusion," insisted Quintero, was "detrimental to the interests of the government," causing some articles to rise critically in price within a two-month span.[40] Therefore, in an effort to control the cotton trade, the Confederate military authorities in the Trans-Mississippi Department began issuing export permits. In June 1862, having difficulties in getting supplies for his troops in Brownsville, Colonel Philip N. Luckett imposed a tax of five dollars on each bale of cotton exported, and thereby initiated a program that was to evolve into the export certificate system. Later, Confederate Texas commander, General Paul O. Hébert, ordered General Bee to restrict further the cotton trade. Bee responded by limiting export permits to government agents and those merchants engaged in importing army supplies. By these permits the merchants could export cotton at 100-percent profit on the value of their imports.

Early in 1863, General John B. Magruder replaced General Hébert in command of the Texas Department. Magruder issued General Order Number 28, allowing anyone to export cotton for war supplies provided they received permits from Major Simeon Hart, Confederate quartermaster at San Antonio. Planters could also obtain permits if they made affidavit that the cotton to be exported was to be used to purchase necessary supplies.[41]

This rapidly growing trade soon attracted a large number of profiteering merchants who established a hegemony over the market. Having large capital resources, they bought many export permits issued by the military to the planters. These contractors received payment in cotton, but whenever the government had a shortage of cotton, they accepted permits and exemptions for the cotton they held independently of their government contracts as part payment. Because government contractors could use conscript teamsters, they never lacked for transportation. Further, by offering higher prices and payment in specie, they could outbid planters, small operators and government agents for independent teamsters. These advantages could not be matched by state and Confederate agents, who were restricted by price limitations and the use of a depreciating Confederate currency. Early in 1862, Quintero summed up these difficulties for Richmond: "The waste, inefficiency, and lack of unity had provided dishonest cotton borders to monopolize the trade in a way that was detrimental to the interests of the government."[42] Although the Confederate government tried to organize the Matamoros trade for its own maximum benefit, it was unsuccessful. Private profiteers, having arrived first with the most, dominated the trade throughout the war, making enormous profits from it.

In its efforts to gain control of the trade, the Confederate government sent out agents, including Major Andrew W. McKee for the Treasury Department and Major Simeon Hart for the War Department. At the same time military commanders on the border, anxious to supply their units, began negotiating contracts in competition with McKee and Hart. In their haste to get the badly needed supplies, they often signed vague and carelessly drawn agreements giving excessive profits to the contractors. Profits usually amounted to about 150 percent, and in some instances ran as high as 300 to 400 percent. Usually these unfavorable contracts gave the merchants an advance of 2,000 bales of cotton prior to the delivery of supplies. Occasionally the Confederates received no goods in return for these cotton advances as merchants pocketed the cash from their sales instead of fulfilling their contracts.[43]

During the first eighteen months of the war the merchants in Matamoros received almost all of the government contracts. These contracts generally stipulated an advance of 100 percent on the cost of the goods and their shipment to Matamoros. Payments would be made in cotton at thirty cents a pound upon delivery of the goods. Confederate agents became disenchanted, however, when they discovered that, by the time the contracts were completed, the prices were three to four times those of the open market in Matamoros. This preplexing situation caused Quintero, in the fall of 1862, to complain to Benjamin that "speculators are running up the prices to exorbitant rates."[44]

Among the leading merchants engaged in the Confederate cotton were Droege, Oetling and Company, and Patricio Milmo and Company. One British visitor in the area wrote that "Mr. Oetling is supposed to have made a million of dollars for his firm by bold speculations" by 1863.[45] Milmo became a multimillionaire from his speculative dealing during the war and by the time of his death in 1899 was reportedly worth from $10 million to $15 million.[46] Other merchants in Monterrey garnered profits that became the economic foundation of that financial capital of northern Mexico.[47]

Disillusioned by experiences with these Mexican-based merchants, Major General Magruder, in June 1863, recommended that the army purchase supplies from companies based in the Confederacy which were subject to its authority and control.[48] With this decision, and because of the favorable contracts offered, King, Kenedy, and Stillman of Brownsville and Ball Hutchings of Houston soon dominated the trade, moving more cotton than all other individuals and agencies in Texas combined.[49]

Magruder's decision did not end financial deception and profiteering, it merely placed these opportunities in Confederate hands. King, Kenedy, and Stillman had already demonstrated their tendencies for financial deception in the fall of 1862, by making a profit of 131 percent on two lots of cotton totaling 636 bales. Early in 1863, the same partnership agreed to provide assorted military supplies for General Bee's troops at

Fort Brown, in exchange for 500 bales of cotton per month for six months. From this arrangement each member of the triumvirate made about $60,000 in specie. A year later, Stillman, using the name of José Morell, sent 530 bales to New York, netting, after all expenses, more than $15,000 in specie.[50]

Much to the chagrin of Confederate officials, profiteering became the norm in the Matamoros trade. Although it was reported that "the government had thousands of bales on wheels" to the Rio Grande, it was "noted as a little singular that nearly all the cotton arriving [was] on *private* account." At the river, teamsters reported their loads as destined for the government, but "presently some citizen [came] forward to claim the consignment."[51] "Can it be possible," asked the editor of a Houston newspaper, "that men have been furnished with public funds to purchase cotton for the public service and ship it to this market, and who finding the article suddenly advanced in price, have transferred their purchases to other parties? It is no longer whispered that such may be."[52] Gilbert Kingsbury advised his brother that if he wished "to make a speculation take as many boots and shoes as convenient get on a schooner and sale [sic] to Matamoros."[53] We have often heard that 'cotton is King,'" cried the Houston *Tri-Weekly Telegraph,* "but we begin to believe that 'mammon' is king."[54]

Texas accused the profiteers of being Yankee sympathizers. "Those who opposed disunion now are the loudest voices against a controlled cotton trade with the Rio Grande," claimed the *San Antonio Herald*. "These are the speculators [profiteers] . . . [who] reap a golden harvest by selling to the community calicoes and worthless rags at immense profits; invest the proceeds in cotton and sell the cotton for coin, reserving a small portion to repeat the same process."[55]

Although Quintero was convinced that government regulation could end profiteering, it continued until the end of the war. Many of these schemes involved cotton sales in northern markets. Early in 1864 it was estimated that a contractor could buy 2,000 bales of cotton at $100 per bale in Confederate money, and ship it to New Orleans or New York, where it would sell for $400 per bale, a total of $800,000 in United States currency. With a contract that guaranteed him a 65-percent profit on goods supplied at the Rio Grande, he could purchase $1,320,000 worth of materials for which he would receive, upon delivery at Matamoros, an additional 13,200 bales of cotton. By returning this cotton to the same American markets, he could reap a profit of $5,280,000. Thus, of 15,200 bales of cotton exported from the Confederacy the "army would receive the benefit of only 2,000 bales."[56]

Swindlers also proved to be a problem. Various illegal schemes were hatched, including a plot to dump $50,000 in counterfeit Confederate notes on Texas.[57] More perplexing and difficult to control were those acts of duplicity that took legal advantage of the trade and were often aided by Mexican officials. For example, Major Simeon Hart, the Confederate quartermaster at San Antonio, was swindled by a very simple method. He bought a wagon train with 114 mules and 5 horses from G. F. Justiniani, a Mexican citizen who had brought the train into Texas. Because it was loaded with goods, Justiniani paid a bond totalling $272 to leave Mexico. After selling the train to Hart, he returned to Piedras Negras, where the custom collector returned his bond money to him. When Hart loaded the train with cotton and tried to cross the border, he was forced to pay the bond, although it was a government train. Hart's pleas to Governor Vidaurri for restitution apparently met with little success. However, when a Confederate officer collaborated with a swindler who got 600-percent profit on one of his shipments, Hart took his complaint to the Confederate authorities, who investigated and dismissed the officer.[58]

Cotton Prices and Tariffs

The Matamoros trade brought an influx of specie that contributed to a general increase in cotton prices at Matamoros. However, local conditions, especially the availability of cotton and shipping, had greater influence on cotton prices.[59]

In the summer of 1862, when no ships were in port to move the cotton, the build-up of stocks at Bagdad and Matamoros caused prices for the commodity to slip to 12½ cents per pound from an earlier figure of 30 cents per pound in specie. The arrival of ships in August caused the demand to firm and the price to begin rising until late October, when it once more reached 28 to 30 cents per pound. When high winds and rough seas in November and December greatly restricted the loading of ships, prices slumped again.[60] During the first half of 1863, ample supplies of cotton again reduced prices. Through the first seven months of the year the commodity brought from 18 to 23 cents per pound at the Mexican port. But by August, the demand exceeded the supply and quotations rose to 50 to 60 cents a pound. Cotton prices continued to climb until they peaked at 90 cents per pound during the Federal incursion of November 1863. As cotton began arriving from upstream crossings, the price fell and stabilized at around 33 to 38 cents per pound for most of 1864. In the early months of 1865, the average price of cotton at Matamoros fell to 28 to 29 cents per pound.[61]

The interior markets in Texas showed little price fluctuation with cotton selling at between 7 and 10 cents per pound, the same as before the war. This consistency was prompted by two factors. First, specie was scarce and those who bought with it found ample supplies of cotton with little competition to force the prices upward. The lack of readily available transportation was another factor in holding down cotton prices in the interior. Having to pay for the long haul to Matamoros in specie, merchants could not afford to buy cotton at higher rates and compete on the world market.[62]

After the Federal blockade of Brazos Santiago in February 1862, merchants were forced to export cotton through Matamoros. It was an expensive proposition. Along with the Confederate export tax of one-eighth of a cent per pound and a vexing ferry fee, an exorbitant Mexican import duty had to be paid. As the trade began, this duty was two cents per pound, or $10 per bale of cotton, which hurt the competitiveness of cotton shipped through Matamoros on the European market. Hence the tariff became the special target of Quintero who was determined "to make the ports of entry on this river, free."[63]

Quintero quickly convinced Governor Vidaurri of the advantages of a lower tariff. Lower duties would result in increased import revenues for the governor. Further, Vidaurri had an added interest through his son-in-law, Patricio Milmo, who headed the largest export firm in northern Mexico and was in a position to reap huge profits from favorable trade agreements with the Confederates. On April 5, 1862, the governor decreed that in response to the "heavy expense incurred by merchants who introduce cotton for re-exportation . . . and [to the letter] addressed to me [by] the American citizen J. A. Quintero that in the future all cotton introduced for re-exportation shall pay one dollar per quintal (one cent per pound) as a total duty."[64]

This happy arrangement appeared to be short-lived. Less than two weeks later, Vidaurri suddenly announced a return to the prohibitive rates. Quintero immediately requested an interview to discuss the matter. The governor, engaged in a civil war with Juan Carvajal for the control of Tamaulipas, had been angered by the apparent aid that his opponent had received from friends in Texas. He casually told Quintero that the duty was necessary to maintain his 7,000 troops. Quintero, accurately sensing the governor's intentions, dashed off a note to the Confederate State Department "that had it not been for the attacks made on his [Vidaurri] states by parties from Texas, he would not have thrown obstacles in our way by the imposition of duties."[65] Remaining "hopeful of having them repealed soon," Quintero demanded, with a threat of resignation, that the Confederate military at Fort Brown be ordered to change its complacent attitude toward Carvajal. Orders to this effect were immediately sent from Richmond, and the issues were quickly resolved. Vidaurri once more lowered the duty to one cent per pound, and declared Monterrey to be a free deposit station for cotton in transit.[66]

This satisfactory arrangement continued with but slight interruption for the remainder of the war. In October 1862, the military governor, Juan B. Traconis, imposed a one-and-one-half-cent duty on cotton, but his act was reversed a month later by his successor, Albino López. At times, greedy warlords seized power and exacted excessive tolls. General José Cobos levied a tax of $20 per bale, and General Juan Cortina sometimes expropriated more than one-fourth of a convoy of cotton. On at least one occasion Mexican President Benito Juárez ordered Vidaurri to close the border to all Confederate traffic. However, the independent-minded *caudillo* declared that he would "not . . . tear down what he had built," and the trade continued.[67]

On goods from Europe entering Texas through Matamoros, both import and export duties were charged, greatly increasing the cost of the items. At first, the Confederates sought special concessions on specific shipments. In August 1862, Juan A. Zambrano, a native of Bexar County, Texas, became customs inspector at Matamoros. With the blessings of Governor Vidaurri, he reduced the rates on goods passing into Texas to one-fourth of the scheduled rates, bringing the prohibitive duty of $5 a barrel on flour down to $1.50. After he had some difficulties with Governor Traconis, Zambrano was removed from office in October, and his successor restored the high rates. When Albino López became governor of Tamaulipas the following month, the lower rates were restored and continued.[68]

The Texas Military Board vs. The Confederate Cotton Bureau

The high costs of war caused the Texas Secession Convention and its Committee of Public Safety to devote much of their time to finance. Early in 1861, the financial committee estimated an immediate need of $400,000. The efforts of the Secession Convention to raise the needed funds were disappointing as only $81,500 was obtained. It was also unsuccessful in obtaining arms and other military supplies. Colonel Ben McCulloch negotiated a contract for Colt pistols, but the Federal government intervened and prevented delivery. Frustrated, the convention passed these problems on to the legislature.[69]

By the fall of 1861, the Texas legislature felt the need for additional government machinery to deal with these, and other developing economic perplexities. The simple business system of the community was upset by the war and blockade. Supplying the people and the armies had been left to private enterprise, which was forced to develop new, expensive, and tortuous channels of contact with the outside world. The results were disappointing. Numerous private agents and speculators flooded the Rio Grande and Mexican markets. Seeking contracts for their own benefit, they often worked at cross purposes and to the disadvantage of the government. The state's deficit continued to climb as revenues lagged behind expenditures. With no market for her bonds, the state was unable to borrow.

To cope with the crises the legislature created the Texas State Military Board on January 11, 1862. Its membership included Governor Francis R. Lubbock as chairman, and two other state officials, Comptroller Clement R. Johns and Treasurer Cyrus H. Randolph. With minor personnel changes, this Military Board operated until April 12, 1864, when it was reorganized and called the "New Board."[70]

The board hoped to raise money by selling bonds and cotton.

After the Compromise of 1850, the United States government had paid Texas $10 million in indemnity bonds for giving up its claims to the lands west of the boundary between Texas and Mexico. The state had 634 uncashed bonds remaining, valued at $1,000 each. A greater asset was Texas's 1861 bumper cotton crop of more than 300,000 bales. Unwilling to acquiesce to Richmond's cotton embargo, the board planned to export it through Matamoros.[71]

A cooperative plan was drawn up between the board and the Confederate government by which the letter would redeem the United States bonds, bearing 5 percent interest, with Confederate 8-percent bonds. Several agents, including John M. Swisher, George H. Giddings, and James T. D. Wilson, were authorized to sell the bonds abroad. But when the United States repudiated the indemnity bonds, the Texas agents met with little success, and at least a portion of Swisher's transactions brought on an international law suit in the English Court of Chancery.[72]

Unsuccessful in selling the bonds on the international market, the board desperately turned to the Confederate government. In January 1863, the newly elected Texas Governor, Pendleton Murrah, exchanged forty-four of the United States indemnity bonds at 80 to 85 percent of their face value, for Confederate treasury notes. The deal proved to be disadvantageous to both parties. The Texans had surrendered the bonds at less than their face value, and the Confederacy was never able to redeem them.[73]

In the meantime, the Texas Military Board began to organize the cotton trade. Early in February 1862, it issued an "Address to the People of Texas" in which it proposed exchanging 8-percent Confederate bonds for cotton at fair prices. Planters and merchants were assured that these bonds would be superior to those of any other government, because they were backed by an annual tax, payable only in specie, and a sinking fund. Agents were commissioned throughout the state to take subscriptions of cotton in exchange for the bonds.[74]

One of the first agents appointed was Pryor Lea, a prominent attorney and judge from Goliad, who had served in the Secession Convention. He was instructed to find a "responsible, reliable man in Matamoros, English or French, to receive the cotton when it arrives." To prevent "seizure by the Lincoln government," all cotton was to be shipped as the personal property of the agent.[75]

From the beginning, the Texas Military Board duplicated the efforts of the Confederate Treasury and War departments, and it was evident that conflict would result. Both of the contending governmental agents accused the other of shipping cotton illegally. "There are probably six hundred bales of cotton on the road from here to Victoria, which has been thrown off the wagons," lamented a San Antonio newspaper editor, "because some Receiver or other officers thought it was being improperly sent out of the country," he said.[76] The honesty and intent of both state and national governments were questioned by many planters. But the editor concluded that the main problem was "stupid officers" and "ill-advised and improper proceedings. Many thousands of dollars worth of property has thus been lost to the owners and to the country by this stupidity," he charged.[77]

The board also contributed to its own failure by at least two regulations that it established for its agents. Agents could be reimbursed for any excessive expenses incurred, but they received no salary for their work. Nor were they permitted to pay more than ten cents per pound for the best grade of cotton. By the first restriction the board prevented itself from getting an adequate number of good agents. By the second, it allowed those which did go into the field to be easily outbid by private merchants who offered the growers from 7 to 30 cents in specie per pound of cotton. Further, few planters were inclined to exchange their cotton for nonnegotiable state bonds when other buyers paid in cash, and often in specie.[78]

In recruiting teamsters the board ran into increasing competition with private contractors and Confederate agents. Pryor Lea thought that one cent per pound in specie for every one hundred miles would be a fair price to offer the teamsters. In August 1862, Richard King wrote the board that two and one-half cents per pound in specie was the best rate by which he could have freight hauled from his ranch to Brownsville. By the spring of 1863, private shippers were paying conscript teamsters one and one-half cents in specie plus three and one-half cents in Confederate money per one hundred miles on the roads north of the King ranch. To haul goods across the dangerous "Sands" between the ranch and Brownsville, conscript teamsters received three cents in specie and three cents in Confederate paper notes. Agents of the Military Board could not meet these high rates. Teamsters were critically scarce throughout Texas anyway, and the inability of the board to bid competitively for their services left that agency almost entirely without transportation.[79]

Teamsters might have been induced by military deferment, but the board could not totally guarantee it. The best that it could offer was exemption from the state militia. It could offer no guarantees against Confederate conscription. Because Richmond agents could give such assurance, they held the advantage. Confederate agents enjoyed an additional advantage in that they could impose lower freight rates on both conscripted teamsters and those desiring exemption from conscription.[80]

As 1863 drew to a close, the board showed clear evidence of succumbing to competition and internal difficulties. Operating costs were rising and there appeared to be no way of offsetting them. It exercised no effective supervision over its agents, especially those on the Rio Grande, because mails were slow and uncertain and the agents made tardy and incomplete reports. Often orders were disregarded and much mischief done before the board had any knowledge of the facts. Despite these shortcomings, agents were seldom discharged because suitable successors could not be found. In November 1863, one board member complained that "only those who have engaged in the business can have any idea of the difficulties which the Board has had to contend with."[81]

By this time the board was the subject of widespread criticism. Few understood its operations, or appreciated its difficulties. A legislative committee appointed to investigate it in the winter of 1862–1863 showed little enthusiasm for its accomplishments, but did acknowledge that, in the face of many difficulties, it had improved the defenses of Texas.[82]

Because of the increasingly heavy duties of the state treasurer and the comptroller, the board recommended its own reorganization. Acting upon this recommendation, the legislature voted in December 1863 to reconstitute the board so that it consisted of the governor, as president ex officio, and two persons appointed by him. On April 12, 1864, Governor Murrah appointed James S. Holman and N. B. Pearce to replace the treasurer and the comptroller. With this reorganization it became known as the "New Board."[83]

Meanwhile, the Confederacy's commander of the Trans-Mississippi Department, General Edmund Kirby Smith, had moved to centralize control of the cotton trade under his authority. In June 1863, three months after assuming his command, he grumbled that he had no army and no means and that "all had to be done from the beginning."[84] Because he needed a "judicious system to effect [these] objects of the highest necessity," he determined to organize "a cotton office" to control the cotton trade.[85] On August 3, 1863, the Trans-Mississippi Cotton Bureau, headed by Colonel William A. Broadwell, was created to purchase, collect, and dispose of cotton. The bureau's headquarters was located in Shreveport, Louisiana, but practically all of its business was conducted through a branch office in Houston, designated the Texas Cotton Office. Lieutenant Colonel William J. Hutchins was placed in charge of the Houston office, with a group of Texas businessmen as his assistants. All Confederate officials engaged in the cotton business in Texas were ordered to operate directly under them. Kirby Smith gave his assurance that he was their only superior and promised not to overrule the Texas Cotton Office without prior conference with them.[86]

Early in December, Hutchins announced the policies of the Texas Cotton Office in a statement addressed "To the Cotton Planters of Texas." The office proposed to buy one-half of the planters' cotton for certificates redeemable in bonds or whatever equivalent the Confederate Congress might provide. It would give exemptions from military impressment for the other half. The cotton-growing regions of the state were divided into districts and depots set up to receive the staple.[87]

Planters generally accepted the bureau, and some improvement in the cotton commerce occurred. However, agents of the Cotton Office still contended with private merchants and state purchasers. In some areas the competition caused the price of cotton to soar to seventy-five cents a pound, and in one section $1.00 to $1.25 per pound was demanded. Many speculators obtained contracts giving them independent authority to purchase and export cotton and import military supplies. While they realized enormous profits from their cotton exports, the speculators often failed to furnish the material which they had agreed to deliver.[88]

By the end of 1863, a conflict developed between the Texas Cotton Office and the Texas Military Board. Governor Murrah conceived the so-called State Plan, which seemed designed to defeat the competition of the Confederate agency. Under this plan the state Military Board was given control of all cotton purchasing for the state. It was authorized to contract for all of a planter's cotton, who would then transport it to the Rio Grande at his own expense. Because it belonged to the government, this cotton was protected from impressment while in transit. Upon reaching the river, one-half of the cotton was returned to the owner and he was given interest-bearing bonds for the other half. These were Confederate 8-percent bonds which Richmond had exchanged with Texas for 634 of the United States Indemnity bonds. This empowered the agents of the Texas Military Board to offer about three times as much as the Confederate Cotton Office could pay. Murrah and his associates also practically monopolized the services of the teamsters by offering them superior contracts, and by forcing anti-impressment laws through the Texas legislature which enabled the board to offer the teamsters and their teams and wagons protection that other drivers did not have. Furthermore, the board's agents circulated rumors that the Cotton Office was not authorized by Congress, and was organized only for private gain. Under these circumstances the Cotton Office found it difficult to compete, which became a source of great concern for Kirby Smith and Quintero.[89]

The conflict soon broke into the open as each side accused the other of illegal acts. Governor Murrah protested that the Confederate Cotton Office was guilty of impressment and "stoppage of state cotton at the [border]."[90] Denouncing it as "a power [acting] entirely independent of the commander of the district," he threatened to place its agents "under arrest very soon if they didn't mind."[91] On the other side, William P. Ballenger, legal advisor for the Cotton Bureau, questioned the honesty of both Murrah and his chief agent, Ebenezer B. Nichols of Galveston. Ballenger accused Murrah of having a personal financial interest in cotton speculation because a close friend of the governor was a subagent of Nichols. While his attack on the governor's integrity apparently was unfounded, there seems to have been justification for his suspicions of Nichols. That agent's report indicated that he had personally purchased 8,102 bales of cotton, which when sold, yielded $211,655.87, of which, according to other records, the state government received only $80,213.05.[92]

The issue rapidly developed toward a Texas-Confederate confrontation. Ballanger advised Kirby Smith that the governor was "undertaking to vindicate State rights, or state might, rather, in a perilous manner for these times."[93] Both Broadwell and Hutchins implored Kirby Smith to impress whatever cotton the military needed, regardless of ownership. Broadwell even recommended that, if Murrah continued to obstruct Confederate attempts to regulate the trade through Matamoros, the Trans-Mississippi Department should remove all Confederate troops from Texas soil, leaving the state's defense to the governor and his state militia.[94]

Hoping to settle their differences quietly and quickly, General Kirby Smith addressed a temperate direct appeal to Governor Murrah, asking him either to modify the state plan or restrain its execution. Granting that "the former management of the Government business on the Rio Grande was properly and severely criticised,"[95] The general explained that the Cotton Office had been established for the purpose of bringing order to the trade, but it could not fulfill this function unless Texas ceased impeding its performance. He then listed the various ways in which "the system inaugurated by [Murrah's] agents [had] already completely paralyzed the efforts of [his] officers" in procuring the cotton needed to sustain the department.[96]

Exchanges between Shreveport and Austin continued until early July. In often strongly worded notes, Governor Murrah protested that the general's innovations subverted Texas sovereignty and the rights of its citizens, while Kirby Smith insisted that the state plan threatened the interests of the Confederacy, disarmed many soldiers, and destroyed the Trans-Mississippi's capacity to defend itself. In view of the ease with which the Federals were taking areas of Louisiana, Arkansas, and Texas, some of the state's newspapers rallied behind the general and began to implore Murrah to cooperate with the Cotton Office.[97]

Responding to public pressure and Kirby Smith's entreaties, Murrah invited the general to meet him at Hempstead, Texas, to discuss the cotton problem. No transcript of the conference survives, but Kirby Smith's arguments appear to have been effective for the governor capitulated without reservation to the general's demands.[98]

On July 19, shortly after the conference ended, Murrah published an address to the people of Texas calling for their complete support of the Cotton Bureau and the Texas Cotton Office. The survival of the army, of the Department, and of Texas itself, he told the people, depended upon the unobstructed importation of military supplies. To procure these supplies the army needed cotton which could be obtained only from the people. It was, therefore, the patriotic duty of every loyal Texan to deliver his cotton to the army's agents in return for whatever compensation the army might consider just. Murrah then abandoned his state plan, and ended state protection to shipments of privately owned cotton. While cotton previously purchased under the state plan continued to arrive at the Rio Grande during the winter of 1864–1865, the Texas State Military Board came to an end.[99]

It is difficult to determine the amount of cotton exported by the Texas State Military Board. The "Old Board" sold 5,551 bales during its twenty-six months existence, an average of 213.5 bales per month. Records do not show how much cotton was contracted for under the state plan. But, in May 1864, barely a month after its organization, the New Board's chief agent, E. B. Nichols, stated that it had exported 8,102 bales, realizing a profit of $10 million for the state. Nevertheless, it is evident that the board purchased but a small part of the Texas cotton crops harvested during its operations. Its average export of about 500 bales per month was no more than 12 percent of the total cotton exported monthly through Matamoros during the war.[100]

Army Purchasing Conflicts and Impressment

In their efforts to gain badly needed supplies, local commanders often exercised independent authority over the Rio Grande cotton trade. They often worked at cross purposes, which resulted in continued confusion, mistrust, and scandals.

On November 21, 1862, Brigadier General Paul O. Hébert, Confederate commander of the Department of Texas, New Mexico, and Arizona, ordered the prohibition of cotton export except by agents of the Confederate government or by individuals "known to the commanding general to be engaged . . . in supplying the actual necessities of the people and the army."[101] He directed Brigadier General Hamilton P. Bee to enforce this order along the lower Rio Grande. From his headquarters at Fort Brown, Bee issued regulations permitting those engaged in supplying the army to export cotton at 100-percent profit on the costs of their imports. Planters could also obtain permits provided they would make affidavit that the cotton exported was for necessary supplies rather than speculation.[102]

When General John B. Magruder replaced General Hébert, early in 1863, he modified the plan. He gave orders allowing anyone, private merchants as well as government agents, to export cotton to Mexico under the regulations set up by General Bee. All private contracts had to be approved by one of three officers, Brigadier General William R. Scurry at Houston, Colonel S. P. Bankhead at San Antonio, or Lieutenant Augustus Buchel at Brownsville. With each contract a permit would be granted specifying the amount of cotton to be exported. The only military contracts that would be honored were those made by Major Simeon Hart.[103]

These military controls on the cotton trade aroused the criticism and opposition of planters, politicians, and newspaper editors. They regarded them as a conspiracy between the military leaders and the profiteers to monopolize the Rio Grande commerce.[104] Confederate Senator William S. Oldham, one of the most bitter and outspoken critics of the military regulations, later recalled:

> The people were literally robbed of their property by speculators and sharpers, under military usurpation, converted into a fund for enriching speculators and swindlers . . . corrupting subordinate officers of the army, demoralising the private soldiers and the people, crushing out their spirits and subjugating the country. That which might have been made an invaluable blessing was perverted into an unmitigated evil and a curse.[105]

Generals Magruder and Bee especially came under severe criticism. Oldham called Magruder "the absolute dictator, the pro-consul of Texas," who had favored particular speculators by detailing some 6,000 conscripts to drive their wagons.[106] Others labeled him "Prince John . . . the Burgomaster [who enjoyed] parading with music up and down the streets" and accomplishing very little else.[107] "The enemy," Oldham claimed, "had blockaded the Gulf ports and General Bee blockaded the Rio Grande."[108] One of his own rangers accused Bee of speculating in cotton and issuing permits only to those who were his own "creatures."[109] "What a field for corruption," exclaimed Oldham. With "Bee [sitting] at the gates of the Rio Grande, and Magruder at those of the ports of the Gulf."[110]

Protests against military restrictions on the Rio Grande cotton trade brought an immediate response from Richmond. In January 1863, Secretary of War James A. Seddon issued a special order removing the objectionable restrictions on the commerce. The result was a rise in cotton prices on the border from twenty-five cents to sixty cents per pound.[111]

Many planters refused to sell their cotton for the Confederate currency offered by the military agents. Instead, they preferred to export it themselves in exchange for specie. Hundreds of bales of cotton falsely marked as government property were carried to the Rio Grande by impressed teams and wagons. Once the river was reached, the government marks were removed and the cotton claimed by individuals. Major Hart found it difficult to obtain enough cotton to fulfill his contracts.[112] "We do not hesitate to say," wrote the editor of the Corpus Christi *Ranchero,* "that it appears that there is something rotten in the state of Texas. . . . One thing we know . . . there is no cotton belonging to the C.S.A. govt. in Brownsville."[113]

On May 22, 1863, the powerful British steamer *Sea Queen,* having made the passage from London in twenty-six days, dropped anchor at the mouth of the Rio Grande. For its cargo of arms and munitions Major Hart had contracted to deliver nearly 2,000 bales of cotton.[114] However, he had only seventy-five bales at Brownsville at that time and he was unable to close the deal. General Magruder strongly criticized him for showing a great want of "energy . . . foresight . . . and ability in the management of his department."[115]

The reports of Major Charles Russell, General Bee's quartermaster at Brownsville, contributed to Magruder's lack of confidence in Hart. Russell blamed Hart for the shortage of government cotton at Brownsville. On June 10, 1863, he wrote a lengthy letter to Magruder claiming that because of Hart's failure to supply cotton the local troops as well as those in the interior had received provisions for the last six months only on the credit of the Brownsville merchants.[116] The supplies were furnished on the promise that payment in cotton would begin in April. Russell complained that although thousands of bales of cotton belonging to speculators arrived daily, the merchants had not received any. He was even more concerned about foreign contracts. He reported that two large English steamers had brought army supplies to the Rio Grande, but after waiting four weeks and finding "no one authorized to receive the shipments and not one bale of cotton to meet the payment," they left to sell their cargoes in Nassau.[117] He bitterly closed his report that "the result of this . . . deception upon the part of Govt. agents, is too apparent to render an expression of opinion from me . . . , four other ships . . . are hourly expected, and unless something is done, they too will have to return with cargoes . . . , *all of which we need.*"[118]

Russell also lodged a strong complaint with General Bee concerning Hart's failures to deliver promised cotton. Charging that Hart was deliberately withholding 500 bales of cotton per month due on a contract with King, Kenedy, and Stillman, he requested that Bee call a board of inquiry to investigate all of the quartermaster's transactions. Bee forwarded the complaint to Magruder with a request for further action.[119]

Learning of the accusations, Hart issued a strong defense of himself and brought countercharges against Russell. He claimed to have fulfilled his obligations in the King, Kenedy, and Stillman contract "strictly and in a more liberal spirit toward them [than] the letter of the contract required."[120] Only once had there been a slight delay while cotton was collected from the remote areas, and this had been sanctioned by the contractors. On the other hand, Russell had only turned over $20,000 of money allocated to Hart for the purchase of the cotton. Hart also claimed that he had not received any receipts from Russell for the cotton he had shipped to Brownsville.[121]

The controversy finally led General Edmund Kirby Smith to order impressment to meet the needs of the Trans-Mississippi army. On June 23, he ordered General Magruder to impress enough cotton to buy the cargo of the *Sea Queen.*[122] In a subsequent order, Kirby Smith directed Magruder to continue to impress cotton to meet the increasing demand for supplies. Assuming full responsibility for the acts, the general granted exemptions only for state cotton, that belonging to Major Hart, and for associations aiding the families of soldiers. Also planters were allowed to export thirty bales of cotton for every 100 slaves they owned.[123]

General Bee neglected Smith's impressment orders and instituted an alternate plan designed to pacify the disgruntled Brownsville merchants. By the agreement, the merchants would advance 20 percent of their cotton, for which payment would be made in Confederate Treasury notes. The remaining cotton could be exported by the owners for private profit.[124] At that time there were some 11,000 bales in the vicinity of Brownsville, of which about 3,000 belonged to the state, to the Association for the Benefit of the Soldiers' Families, or to plant-

Cotton being pressed at Piedras Negras. *(Courtesy of the Texas State Historical Association)*

Brownsville from the Matamoros wharf. *(Courtesy of the Texas State Historical Association)*

ers expecting to buy supplies. Of the 8,000 bales remaining, Bee would receive only 20 percent, which would be scarcely enough to meet the obligation for the *Sea Queen* cargo. In July, the *Gladiator* and the *Sir William Peel* had arrived, expecting to receive cotton in exchange for their goods.[125]

When Magruder learned of Bee's 20-percent policy, he emphatically instructed him to carry out the impressment orders. "You appear to be influenced by the debts due at Brownsville and Matamoros," Magruder wrote, "but we have decided that the cargoes from abroad in ships named in the orders shall be taken care of by impressment, and that is final, however hard it may operate on individuals."[126]

Despite these explicit orders, Bee continued to violate Kirby Smith's decree's by seizing the cotton shipped to Brownsville by Major Hart. At the same time he denounced the foreign contracts which Hart was attempting to complete. Authorized by Richmond, these agreements called for an advance payment of 100 percent of the contract for the same goods that were available in Matamoros for only 25-percent advance. He was especially critical of the contract with Bellot and Company, owners of the cargo on the *Sea Queen*. Bee wrote:

> In my opinion the Bellot contract has not a spark of vitality; it has been dead for months; and no liberal, impartial arbiter would say that our public faith is in any way involved. It is on proof that the contract was hawked around Paris and London for months, and finally invested in as lottery. The agents of the house of Bellot owe thousands of dollars to our own citizens . . . on drafts drawn by them on Bellot in Paris. There was no such house, and in a garret in Bordeaux Bellot was found, who protested, of course, the drafts. Would not our own citizens . . . have a just and legal right to stop this cotton in my hands before it leaves the State? I think they would, and hope they will do so.[127]

Bee then reiterated his claim that his 20-percent policy was the only one of "justice and right." However, if impressment must be followed, he asked "that no more exceptions be allowed."[128] His pleas were ignored by Magruder, and Kirby Smith's impressment orders were continued.

Impressment was unpopular with the planters who felt swindled by government agents and all too often had legitimate complaints. At times large amounts of cotton were illegally seized. At Eagle Pass the inspector of customs claimed that the government demanded a "duty" of "*one bale for each bale that went out of the country to Mexico.*[129] These and other similar practices were attacked by the editor of the Austin *Texas State Gazette* as being designed to "rob the planter of the only means he has to supply his family with the necessities of life."[130]

When some planters travelled to Mexico to reclaim impressed cotton, Confederate relations with Governor Vidaurri seemed threatened. One Texan followed his impressed cotton to Matamoros, where he produced the bill of sale which the Confederate officer had neglected to confiscate. The Mexican official, after checking the document, declared that the cotton belonged to the planter. The latter then politely thanked the Confederate officer for helping him across the river with the produce, and left for the market to sell his cotton. The tense situation was relieved when Quintero received assurance from Vidaurri that "should any parties come here to claim [cotton] as their property, the authorities of Texas will be fully sustained by this government."[131]

As the impressment controversy continued, the rivalry and animosity between Russell and Hart came to a head. Although Hart, as the agent of the War Department, was to receive all impressed cotton, he had no authority to impress on his own. Thus, when Hart's cotton arrived at the border, Russell, as Bee's quartermaster, impounded it and used it to meet his obligations.[132] Never a modest man, Russell, having purchased the cargo of the *Sea Queen* with cotton seized from Major Hart's shipments, took sole credit for saving the Confederacy $300,000. And although the cargoes of the *Sir William Peel*, the *Gladiator*, and the *Colt* were contracted by Hart, Russell said he was "standing by with cotton if needed."[133]

Early in July, Major Hart protested to General Magruder against Russell's actions. Quoting the appropriate clause in General Kirby Smith's original impressment orders, he reminded Magruder of the superior authority of the War Department in the contractual arrangements of the trade. He added that "any interference with or diversion of . . . cotton from its proper purpose would disgrace and dishonor me and the government, and could not possibly be contemplated when the facts . . . are appreciated."[134] But Magruder, having heard Russell's complaints and believing that Hart was involved in private speculation, did not respond to the quartermaster's protest.[135]

In the fall of 1863, General Kirby Smith initiated an investigation of the Hart-Russell controversy. He sent Major George Williamson and Captain Felix Ducayet to examine Hart's records at San Antonio. Turning over all of his records to the two officers, Hart requested that his duties be suspended as soon as he met his unfulfilled obligations.[136] It was found that the quartermaster's difficulties arose primarily from preemption of his cotton by Bee and Russell, and the failure of Magruder to give him proper support. A number of influential people voiced confidence in Hart. William P. Ballanger, the attorney for the Cotton Bureau, wrote that he was "a nice old fellow . . . [and] I don't think he has been judiciously dealt with or that it is right to relieve him."[137] From Monterrey, Quintero wrote to Secretary Benjamin that "Major Hart . . . has been sadly abused. . . . He has invariably been interfered with, by orders from the military authorities of Texas."[138] In Matamoros, Richard Fitzpatrick observed that the problem was not Hart's fault because "his subordinates have not aided him as they should have done . . . [but] I have no doubt that [he] will come out all right."[139]

While the findings of the investigation supported Major Hart, a cloud formed over the character and integrity of Russell. It was discovered that in the summer of 1863, the Mexican firm of Droege, Oetling and Company secured Russell's backing of a plan to give them a monopoly of government cotton export at a price far below market value. This plan guaranteed Russell large personal profits for assisting the company in getting the contract. It was vetoed by Quintero, who felt that better deals were available. Russell also purchased goods from Mexican firms at inflated prices, even after Hart had refused the deals as being too expensive.[140] Two months later, when the Federal forces under General Nathaniel P. Banks seized Brownsville, Russell fled to Matamoros and went into hiding; as much from his fellow agents as from the enemy.[141]

The Milmo Affair

Russell became involved in one of the most controversial episodes of the wartime trade along the Rio Grande. On November 6, 1863, a few days after the Union forces had chased the Confederates from Brownsville, Clarence C. Thayer, a Confederate treasury agent, arrived in Matamoros with seven cases containing $16 million in Confederate treasury notes. His mission was to relieve the money shortage in the Trans-Mississippi Department and to restore confidence in the government. After some effort, he found Major Russell, who claimed to be the ranking officer on the frontier with authority over all Confederate personnel there. The treasury agent explained that the public funds in his possession had to be delivered to San Antonio and Shreveport, but that Union occupation forces in Brownsville blocked his route.

For several reasons, Matamoros did not appear to be a safe place to keep the money. The bandit general Juan Cortina had taken advantage of the confusion resulting from the Federal invasion to capture Matamoros in the name of the Juárez government. Furthermore, the town was a gathering spot for Texas renegades, Mexican bandits, Yankee agents, and unpaid creditors. Russell instructed Thayer to place the money in the hands of Milmo and Company with the assurance that it would be shipped through Monterrey to Eagle Pass and turned over to Confederate officials there. Russell, conspiring with Milmo, told him of the contents of the chests.[142]

Because he was the son-in-law of Governor Vidaurri, Milmo had become the assignee of other large Mexican merchant houses along the border, including Attrill and Lacoste and Droege, Oetling and Company. Using Confederate indebtedness to these firms as an excuse, Milmo notified Hart on December 11, 1863, that he was confiscating the funds, and all Confederate cotton at Piedras Negras and in transit on the Mexican side of the border. Nearly a week later he notified Thayer of his actions.[143]

Quintero endeavored to get the funds released. When Milmo refused, Quintero conferred with Vidaurri, requesting that he intervene in the interest of preserving the close commercial ties between the two countries. The governor promised to talk to Milmo, but later informed Quintero that his son-in-law was determined to keep the money and to continue confiscating cotton until the debts were paid in full.

When Quintero interviewed Milmo, he listed a number of reasons for his actions. Starting with his first deal with the South, he cited instances where he had suffered losses by being paid in depreciating Confederate notes, and by failing to receive cotton promised to him.[144]

Attacking Vidaurri for his "blind obstinacy" in refusing "to lend ear to [his] just reclamations," Quintero recommended that Richmond take "prompt action . . . in order to obtain a satisfactory arrangement of the difficulties."[145] "Vidaurri promises all things to all parties . . . and carries out none," he added. "His policy has been to cultivate friendly relations with all . . . and let the course of events decide as to his future action."[146] Quintero was fully convinced that similar Mexican seizures would continue to occur unless the Confederate government enforced strong counter measures against them. He suggested that the Confederates stop the "passing . . . of all cotton both public and private" into Vidaurri's domains and increase their commerce through Laredo in Tamaulipas. In this way Vidaurri, deriving "his main revenue from the cotton trade at Piedras Negras," would be compelled to come to terms.[147]

Apparently the suggestion was accepted by Richmond because on January 12, 1864, General Kirby Smith issued Special Order Number 8 closing the border to any further shipment of cotton to Mexico. The general also improved upon Quintero's suggestion by stipulating that all Mexican assets in Texas should be frozen until the controversy could be settled. Then, in a wise and conciliatory move, he tempered his action by appointing a commission consisting of Colonel Thomas F. McKinney, Judge Thomas J. Devine, and Captain Felix Ducayet, to go to Monterrey to negotiate a settlement.[148]

The general gave explicit instructions to his commissioners. First, he wanted them to "fully explain to Governor Vidaurri the precise nature of the steps" he had taken regarding "Mexican property and the exportation of cotton." They were then to give assurance that the Confederacy would pay the debts owed the Mexican firms. Yet, they were also to "demand firmly the release and delivery" of the funds that Milmo held. Finally, as "fully authorized" representatives of the government, they were empowered to conclude a peaceful settlement.[149]

Kirby Smith's cotton embargo brought considerable pressure on Vidaurri who was "surrounded by many difficulties and complications."[150] Almost entirely dependent upon the Rio Grande customs revenue for revenue he stood to lose an estimated $50,000 to $175,000 monthly because of the embargo. Politically he was alienated from the Juárez regime and not yet committed to the Conservative Church party, which favored a monarchy. Therefore, he saw no immediate alternative to reestablishing friendly relations with the South. When a large shipment of cotton consigned to Milmo and Company was seized at Eagle Pass by the Confederates, the governor capitulated.[151]

The settlement was quickly drawn up and on February 24, 1864, Judge Devine notified General Kirby Smith of the terms. Milmo was to get 500 bales of cotton at Eagle Pass in payment of his substantiated claim that the Confederacy owed him 500 to 600 bales at twenty cents per pound. For interest on his claim, Milmo was awarded an additional 200 bales delivered in San Antonio. His partner, Evaristo Madero, received 1,500 bales in three installments. On his part, Milmo was to release the confiscated $16 million in Confederate notes. The issue settled, Quintero recommended that everyone "put aside their pride, revenge or passion, and set themselves about the work of securing for the cause and country the greatest advantages possible to be obtained."[152]

An investigation indicated that Major Russell had, on a number of occasions, accepted bribes from Mexican firms, and conspired with Milmo in the seizure of the funds. He reportedly received $10,000 for buying goods from Attrill and Lacoste at inflated prices. After reviewing the mounting evidence against Russell, Quintero wrote, "It is a misfortune for our Confederacy to have so many fools or scoundrels in charge of her interests."[153] The Confederate commercial agent at Matamoros, Richard Fitzpatrick, recommended that "no military man ought to be entrusted with any duty of a commercial nature, but should be kept in the army where he belongs and there made to do his duty."[154] As a result of the findings, Russell was relieved from duty by order of President Davis in April 1864.[155]

With the border reopened, the trade immediately surged again. On at least two occasions in 1864, a satisfied Quintero reported that "the commerce between Texas and Mexico is quite brisk."[156] One observer noted that "upwards of ten thousand bales of cotton have been ferried over the river at Eagle Pass alone within the past four or five weeks . . . [and] hauled down . . . to [Matamoros] . . . for shipment."[157] In exchange for the cotton, a "great . . . quantity of clothing, ammunition, material of war, and other supplies from Europe [were] ran into Texas via the Rio Grande."[158] In the summer of 1864, the correspondent for the London *Times* wrote "that General Kirby Smith calculates on unmistakable data, that if not another ship were to run the blockade he would have *sufficient stores of all kinds to supply the wants of his army for two years.*"[159]

From Monterrey, Quintero sent a dispatch to Kirby Smith endorsing the Cotton Bureau.

> I am gratified [he wrote] to see the commercial business of the Confederacy in this country will hereafter be controlled by the cotton bureau. By these means the multiplicity of agents and private speculators who have always created a competition detrimental to the interests of the Government will be done away with, *and* the supplies needed will no doubt be obtained much cheaper.[160]

The End of the Cotton Bureau

Shortly after the trade was reopened and while optimism was developing along the Rio Grande for the success of the Cotton Bureau, decisions in Richmond doomed Kirby Smith's program. In the spring of 1864, President Davis issued orders governing the control of cotton and other essential items. These regulations stipulated that half of all the exports named had to be exchanged for incoming consignments of strategic goods, and that permits to trade would be issued to any merchant who agreed to import his allotment of war material. Making large-scale impressment illegal, the orders struck at the very heart of the Cotton Bureau.[161]

Opposition to impressment had forged a protest coalition of planters, speculators, private citizens, and state agents. Because the military had impressed cotton to purchase only supplies to equip and sustain the army, a scarcity of goods for domestic consumption developed. In April 1864, a group of San Antonio ladies appealed to Major Hart for an allotment of government cotton to meet their needs:

> We the undersigned, mothers, wives, and sisters of absent soldiers in the field would most respectfully represent to you that we have wheels and cards and they are dull for the want of cotton, for we have been unable to purchase a pound from the merchants and speculators in the city, and we cannot furnish our husbands and sons that is [sic] now in the army with cloths [sic] that we could manufacture at home, for the want of cotton; many of our husbands and sons are even without socks at this time, and we are sorry that we are under the necessity of calling on you to furnish us with this article of prime necessity. If it be in your power to do so, as we must have it in some way or other, we hope that you will give this request your earnest attention without delay.[162]

Texas citizens were also dissatisfied with the inadequate prices paid for cotton impressed. The impressment act required the commissioners to publish revised price schedules every two months in harmony with market-price fluctuations. But, according to one protest addressed to Governor Murrah, "in scarcely a single instance does the price fixed by them reach 50 percent of the fair average market value: in many instances it is not 25 percent."[163] Early in 1864, when the market price for a barrel of flour was $60, the impressment schedule was $14. In June, a horse valued from $1,500 to $6,000 could be seized for $675.[164]

Both civil and military authorities received countless complaints about illegal seizures of cotton, slaves, animals, firearms, and other property. In March 1864, an irate homesteader wrote the governor that a contingent of enlisted men had stripped his farm of forage and equipment, and had ridden off with everything he owned, without leaving as much as an expression of gratitude.[165] Receiving little response from their letters and petitions, some angered citizens took matters into their own hands. In May, three self-appointed impressment officers were hanged after illegally seizing property and threatening uncooperative victims in Lavaca County.[166]

On April 28, 1864, President Davis informed General Kirby Smith that major revisions were necessary in the Trans-Mississippi commercial structure. After remaining silent about the operations of the Cotton Bureau for almost nine months, he wrote the general that "there is no authority in law for the impressment of cotton for the purpose designed by you."[167] Kirby Smith responded in two letters to Davis dated May 12 and June 6. Reminding the president of the southwest's isolation and unique difficulties, he advised that the central government legalize the Cotton Bureau and redeem its outstanding obligations. He also recommended the transfer of its jurisdiction to the Trans-Mississippi Treasury Agency, which had been created by the Confederate Congress in January.[168]

Apparently Richmond accepted Kirby Smith's suggestion, for on July 1, 1864, the Treasury Agency opened its Trans-Mississippi office at Marshall, Texas, under the direction of Assistant Secretary of the Treasury P. W. Gray. Although Kirby Smith continued to operate the Cotton Bureau, the proceeds were turned over to Gray. These funds were used to meet contracts for army supplies made by agents of the War Department.[169]

On August 3, 1864, exactly one year after its creation, the Cotton Bureau was reconstituted as a branch of the Treasury Agency. Kirby Smith ordered the officers and agents of the Cotton Bureau to act under the instruction of the new agency. Impressment, however, continued with Gray's sanction, and newspapers continued to publish passionate denunciations of the usurpations.[170]

The Cotton Bureau terminated its activities as scheduled on February 1, 1865, and the Treasury Agency assumed complete control of all government transactions.[171] Available records indicate that the Texas Cotton Office, which purchased almost all of the Trans-Mississippi Cotton Bureau's cotton, contracted for about 47,000 bales. Although severely criticized, the leaders of the bureau were proud of their accomplishments. Colonel Hutchins recalled that "the entire supply of the army in this Department with articles from abroad has been through this agency, and many . . . have been paid for, almost totally without expenditure of money by the Government."[172] Captain C. G. Wells remarked, "I think the day will come when the people will sigh for the rules of the Cotton Bureau as the Hebrews did for the fleshpots of Egypt."[173]

The consolidation of the trans-Mississippi cotton and commercial activities under the Treasury Agency came too late. By February 1865, the South was crumbling, Confederate credit was gone, and Richmond could not provide Gray with operating funds. Texans, always independent in spirit, saw no need to subject themselves further to the unpopular impressment practices of an outside authority; especially of one that was rapidly collapsing. They refused the agency's offers of credits and sold their cotton to private merchants who paid in specie and were exempt from impressment. Thus, the final attempt in the Confederate government's three-year effort to control the cotton trade on the Rio Grande failed.[174]

Although about 320,000 bales of cotton were exported through Matamoros during the war, the government handled only a minor portion of the total.[175] "If the government handled the cotton *only* and honestly," Colonel Broadwell wrote bitterly, "there never would have been the slightest difficulty."[176] But government success required widespread impressment, which the public rejected as a usurpation of their civil rights. Forced to turn to the contract system for military supplies, government agents were constantly outbid by private merchants and victimized by speculators. With contracts that provided excessive profits, and monopolizing much of the cotton exports, speculators were the chief beneficiaries of the Rio Grande cotton trade.

Notes

1. Pierce to Seward, March 1, 1862, Consular Dispatches, Matamoros; Brone to Wallace, January 13, 1865, *Official Records of the Union and Confederate Armies* [ORA], Ser. I Vol. 47, Pt. 1, pp. 512–13.

2. Quintero to Hunter, November 4, 6, 1861, Confederate State Papers, Vol. 58.

3. Kerby, pp. 84–85.

4. Tyler, *Vidaurri*, pp. 104–05; Ramsdell, *Southwestern Historical Quarterly* 27: 265.

5. Tyler, *Southwestern Historical Quarterly* 63: 461; *San Antonio Herald*, January 4, 1862.

6. *San Antonio Herald*, September 21, 1861, March 18, 1862.

7. Fremantle, *Diary*, p. 49.

8. Tyler, *SWHQ* 73: 461.

9. August Santleben, *A Texas Pioneer: Early Staging and Overland Freighting Days on the Frontiers of Texas and Mexico*, I. D. Affleck, editor (New York: Neale Publishing Company, 1910), pp. 107–08; *Cincinnati Gazette*, April 16, 1865, in Kirby Smith Papers, 3: 4.

10. Fremantle, *Diary*, pp. 38–39; Ford, Memoirs, 6: p. 1092; Irby, pp. 70–71; Tyler, *SWHQ* 73: 462.

11. Tyler, *SWHQ* 73: 461.

12. Santleben, *A Texas Pioneer*, pp. 22, 32, 33: Cowling, pp. 89–90; Kerby, p. 179.

13. Santleben, pp. 107–08; Cowling, p. 82–83.

14. Santleben, pp. 107–08; Cowling, pp. 81–83.

15. Anderson to Magruder, June 26, 1863, Pendleton to Quartermaster, July 6, 1863, *ORA*, Ser. I, Vol. 26, Pt. 2. pp. 85–86, pp. 104–05; Ramsdell, *SWHQ* 27: 264.

16. *Tri-Weekly Telegraph* [Houston], March 27, 1862, August 10, 1863, January 26, 1864; *San Antonio Herald*, June 27, 1863. See random selections of *Austin Gazette*, *Fort Brown Flag* [Brownsville], *Texas Republican* [Marshall], *Patriot* [LaGrange]; San Román Papers, March 25, 1863, May 30, 1863, 2G 63–67, 71.

17. *San Antonio Herald*, September 6, 1982.

18. *Tri-Weekly Telegraph*, [Houston], February 23, 1863.

19. Ramsdell, *SWHQ* 27: 264; San Román Papers, January 31, 1863, 2G 63–67, 71.

20. Cowling, p. 77; Kleiber to Reed and Company, February 6, 1862, Kingsbury Papers, p. 117; Windham, *Journal of Southern History* 27: 162.

21. Ramsdell, SWHQ 27: 265; *LaBandera* [Brownsville], September 25, 1863.

22. McCulloch to Cooper, October 17, 1861, *ORA*, Ser. I, Vol. 4, p. 122; Dunnell to Seward, December 20, 1861, June 2, 1863, Lamson to Welles, November 18, 1863, *Official Records of the Union and Confederate Navies* [ORN], Ser. I, Vol. 17, pp. 38–39, Vol. 19, p. 169, Vol. 20, pp. 285, 688; Shearns to San Román, February 7, 1863, Ingalls and Company to San Román, March 26, 1863, Leary to Clark, February 28, 1863, San Román Papers, 2G 63; Hamilton Cochran, *Blockade Runners of the Confederacy* (Indianapolis: Bobbs-Merrill Company, 1958), p. 216; Ellis, *Southwestern Historical Quarterly* 77: 184–89.

23. Cochran, pp. 216, 217; Bidwell to San Román, May 26, 1863, San Román Papers, 2G 64; Ellis, *SWHQ* 77: 189.

24. Duggan to San Román, June 21, 1863, San Román Papers, 2G 65; Woody to Thomas, October 24, 1862, Ballinger Papers 2A 183; Ellis, *SWHQ* 77: 189.

25. Lee Van Zant, "Early Economic Policies of the Government of Texas," *Southwestern Studies* 4, No. 2 (1966): 23–24.

26. Ibid., p. 24.

27. Ibid., pp. 25–28; S. G. A. Reed, *A History of the Texas Railroads* (Houston: St. Clair Publishing Company, 1941), p. 125.

28. Kirby, pp. 81–82.

29. Ibid., p. 83.

30. Ibid., p. 82.

31. Bradford to Turner, November 26, 1863, Boggs to Magruder, December 22, 1863, *ORA*, Ser. I, Vol. 26, Pt. 2, pp. 446–47, 524, Kerby, p. 81; Reed, pp. 122, 123–24, 257–58.

32. Gentry to Hébert, December 12, 1861, *ORA*, Ser. I, Vol. 4, p. 158; Kerby, p. 83; R. S. Cotterill, "Southern Railroads, 1850–1860," *Mississippi Valley Historical Review* 10: (1924): 404.

33. Van Zant, *SWS* 4, No. 2: 47; *Texas State Gazette* [Austin], April 27, 1861, May 3, 1862.

34. *Tri-Weekly Herald* [San Antonio], November 14, 1865.

35. Quintero to Benjamin, September 24, October 19, 1862. Confederate State Papers, Vol. 8.

36. Kimmey to Seward, October 29, 1862, Consular Dispatches, Monterrey, in Tyler, *SWHQ* 73: 466.

37. Pierce to Seward, March 1, 1862, Consular Dispatches, Matamoros; Kimmey to Seward, November 21, 1862. Consular Dispatches, Monterrey, in Tyler, *SWHQ* 73: 466.

38. Fremantle, *Diary*, p. 6; Bailey to Welles, April 2, 1863, *ORN*, Ser. I, Vol. 17, p. 403.

39. Quintero to Benjamin, October 18, 1862, Confederate State Papers, Vol. 8.

40. Quintero to Benjamin, January 30, 1863, Quintero to Browne, March 4, 1862, Confederate State Papers, Vol. 8.

41. Seddon to Holmes, January 28, 1863, Magruder General Orders No. 28, February 22, 1863, *ORA*, Ser. I, Vol. 53, pp. 845–46; Vol. 15, pp. 986–88; Hébert, General Order No. 8, November 21, 1862, Bee, General Orders No. 25, November 25, 1862, Cotton Bureau Records, Record Group 365, Envelope 3903; Irby, pp. 105–07.

42. Irby, p. 18; James L. Nichols, *The Confederate Quartermaster in the Trans-Mississippi* (Austin: University of Texas Press, 1964), p. 65; *Tri-Weekly Telegraph* [Houston], February 23, 1863. Quintero to Hunter, February 1, 1862, Quintero to Browne, March 4, 1862, Quintero to Benjamin, January 30, 1863, Confederate State Paper, Vols. 8, 58.

43. Hébert to Benjamin, October 24, 1861, Russell to Johnson, January 1, 1864, Broadwell to Memminger, January 28, 1864, *ORA*, Ser. I, Vol. 4, pp. 126–27, Vol. 26, pp. 566–70, Vol. 53, pp. 955–59; Quintero to Hunter, November 18, 1861, Confederate State Papers, Vol. 8.

44. Russell to Johnson, January 1, 1864, *ORA*, Ser. I, Vol. 26, Pt. 2, pp. 568–69; Quintero to Benjamin, October 19, 1862, Confederate State Papers, Vol. 8.

45. Fremantle, *Diary*, p. 12.

46. Tyler, *Vidaurri*, p. 152.

47. Ibid.

48. Magruder to Cooper, June 8, 1863, *ORA*, Ser. I, Vol. 15, pp. 1073–74.

49. *Tri-Weekly News* [Galveston], September 28, 1864.

50. Irby, pp. 18–19

51. *Tri-Weekly Telegraph* [Houston], June 15, 1863.

52. Ibid.

53. G. Kingsbury to M. Kingsbury, undated, 1860's, Kingsbury Papers, Vol. I, p. 80.

54. *Tri-Weekly Telegraph* [Houston], August 27, 1862.

55. *San Antonio Herald,* May 23, 1863.

56. Burton to Holmes, January 4, 1864, *ORA,* Ser. I, Vol. 24, Pt. 2, pp. 824–25.

57. Tyler, *SWHQ* 63: 474–75.

58. Hart to Quintero, November 4, 1863, Quintero to Vidaurri, November 20, 1863, Silva to Castro, October 27, 1863, Expediente 343, Correspondencia de Vidaurri, as cited in Tyler, *Vidaurri,* pp. 117–18.

59. Irby, p. 94.

60. San Román to Kaylor, July 3, 1862, San Román to Joseph Railton and Son, August 14, 1862, San Román to Levi and Schwartz, October 7, 1862, San Román to Edmundson and Culwell, October 28, 1862, San Román to Kleiber, November 13, 1862, San Román Papers, 2G 120; *Tri-Weekly Telegraph* [Houston], December 5, 15, 1862; Quintero to Browne, May 17, 1862, Quintero to Benjamin, October 13, 1862, Confederate State Papers, Vols. 8, 58: *Texas Almanac Extra* [Austin], October 16, December 9, 23, 1862.

61. San Román to Levi and Schwartz, June 2, 1863, San Román to Sanborn, April 22, 1864, San Román Papers, 2G 121; *Ranchero* [Corpus Christi], July 9, 1862; Kleiber to San Román, August 25, 1863, Kleiber Letter Press, cited in Irby, p. 95; *Tri-Weekly Telegraph* [Houston], February 1, December 12, 16, 30, 1864; Cowling, p. 140.

62. *Semi-Weekly News* [San Antonio], October 25, 1862;

63. Quintero to Benjamin, April 4, 1862, August 30, 1862, Confederate State Papers, Vols. 8, 58; Kerby, p. 180.

64. Russell to Johnson, January 1, 1864, *ORA,* Ser. I, Vol. 26, Pt. 2, p. 566; French to Pierce, September 12, 1862, *ORN,* Ser. I, Vol. 19, pp. 193–94; Vidaurri: Order to Collector of Customs, Matamoros, April 5, 1862, Confederate State Papers, Vol. 8.

65. Quintero to Browne, April 17, 1862, Confederate State Papers, Vol. 58.

66. Quintero to Browne, April 17, 1862, Confederate State Papers, Vol. 58.

67. Irby, p. 80; Kerby, p. 180; Quintero to Benjamin, July 5, 1862, Confederate State Papers, Vol. 8.

68. Quintero to Benjamin, August 12, 1862, October 12, 1862, Confederate State Papers, 8: 58; Pierce to French, September 16, 1862, *ORN,* Ser. I, Vol. 19, p. 195.

69. Ramsdell, *SWHQ* 27: 255; Irby, pp. 64–65.

70. Ramsdell, *SWHQ* 27: 261, 168, 173–74; Irby, pp. 66, 67.

71. Ramsdell, *SWHQ* 27: 257–62; Smith, *SWR* 37: 319–24; Irby, p. 67.

72. Ramsdell, *SWHQ* 27: 261; Irby, p. 76.

73. Ramsdell, *SWHQ* 27: 261–62; Irby, p. 68; Kerby, pp. 168, 169.

74. Military Board to Pryor Lea, March 8, 1862, quoted in Irby, p. 68, and Ramsdell, *SWHQ* 27: 263.

75. *Semi-Weekly News,* [San Antonio], July 17, 1862.

76. Ibid.

77. Ramsdell, *SWHQ* 27: 263–65; Kerby, p. 169.

78. Lea to King, June 17, 1862, King to Cordova, August 7, 1862, Correspondence of the State Military Board, cited in Irby, p. 76–77.

79. Lea to Gray, June 19, 1862, Correspondence of the State Military Board, cited in Irby, p. 77.

80. Ramsdell, *SWHQ* 27: 266.

81. *Report of the Joint Committee on the Report of the Military Board to the Tenth Legislature, etc.,* December 14, 1863, cited in Ramsdell, *SWHQ,* 27: 269.

82. Ramsdell, *SWHQ* 27: 269.

83. Kirby Smith to Johnston, June 4, 1863, Kirby Smith Papers.

84. Kirby Smith to Murrah, July 5, 1864, *ORA,* Ser. I, Vol. 53, pp. 1010–11.

85. Kirby Smith, General Orders No. 35, August 3, 1863, *ORA*, Ser. I, Vol. 22, Pt. 2, p. 953; Kirby Smith, Special Orders No. 198, November 22, 1863, in Joseph H. Parks, *General Edmund Kirby Smith C.S.A.* (Baton Rouge: Louisiana State University Press, 1954), pp. 437–38.

86. Hutchins and associates, December 4, 1863, *ORA*, Ser. I, Vol. 21, Pt. 2, pp. 480–82.

87. Parham to Broadwell, March 31, 1864, Oldham to Davis, January 4, 1864, Broadwell to Johnson, January 19, 1864, *ORA*, Ser. I, Vol. 34, Pt. 2, pp. 820, 1105, Vol. 36, Pt. 2, p. 577; *Daily Telegraph* [Houston], May 22, 1864; Ballanger Papers, 2Q4 27, p. 152.

88. Ramsdell, *SWHQ* 27: 253–61, 270; Parham to Broadwell, April 5, 1864, Kirby Smith to Murrah, July 5, 1864, Trenholm to Seddon, July 21, 1864, *ORA*, Ser. I, Vol. 53, pp. 1010–15, 1016; Quintero to Kirby Smith, October 21, 1864, Confederate State Papers, Vol. 58.

89. Ballanger Papers, 2Q422, p. 160.

90. Ibid., pp. 134–35, Magruder to Boggs, January 6, 1864, *ORA*, Ser. I, Vol. 34, Pt. 2, p. 835.

91. Ballanger Papers, 2Q422, p. 153, 163; Irby, p. 87.

92. Ballanger Papers, 2Q422, pp. 163–64.

93. Kerby, p. 200.

94. Kirby Smith to Murrah, April 5, 1864, *ORA*, Ser. I, Vol. 34, Pt. 3, p. 734.

95. Ibid.

96. Murrah to Kirby Smith, June 17, 21, 24, 25, 28, 1864. referred to in Kerby p. 202; Kirby Smith to Murrah, April 5, July 4, 5, 1864, *ORA*, Ser. I, Vol. 34, p. 734, Vol. 53, pp. 1008–10, 1010–15; *Tri-Weekly News* [Galveston], January 13, 1865, *Daily Telegraph* [Houston], July 6, 20, 1864.

97. Kirby Smith to Murrah, August 25, 1863, *ORA*, Ser. I, Vol. 41, Pt. 2, pp. 1082–84; Kerby, p. 202.

98. Murrah, Address to the People of the State of Texas, July 19, 1864, Executive Record Book, No. 280, as cited in Kerby, p. 202; Kirby Smith to Murrah, August 25, 1864, *ORA*, Ser. I, Vol. 41, Pt. 2, pp. 1083–84; Ramsdell, *SWHQ* 27: 271.

99. Miscellaneous Papers, Correspondence of the State Military Board, MSS., Texas State Archives, Austin, cited in Irby, p. 87; Report of E. M. Pease and Swante Palm to Governor A. J. Hamilton; October 30, 1865, *Executive Record* Book, No. 281, pp. 95–111, cited in Ramsdell, *SWHQ 27: 267; Irby, pp. 88–89; Daily Telegraph* [Houston], May 24, 1864.

100. Hébert, General Order No. 8, November 21, 1862, Confederate Treasury Department, Correspondence of the Trans-Mississippi Cotton Bureau, Record Group 365 (unpublished), National Archives, Washington, D.C., Envelope 3903, hereafter cited as Cotton Bureau Correspondence.

101. Bee, General Orders No. 25, November 25, 1862, Cotton Bureau Correspondence, Envelope 3903; *Tri-Weekly Telegraph* [Houston], December 19 1862.

102. Magruder, General Orders No. 28, February 22, 1863. *ORA*, Ser. I, Vol. 15, pp. 986–88.

103. *The Texas Almanac Extra* [Austin], March 17, 24, 31, 1863; *Tri-Weekly Telegraph* [Houston], May 22, 1863; *Ranchero* [Corpus Christi], May 2, June 11, July 2, 30, 1863.

104. William S. Oldham, Memoirs (unpublished), Eugene C. Barker Library of Texas History, University of Texas, Austin, p. 439.

105. Ibid., p. 447.

106. Sarasin to Guenther, May 19, 1863, Oscar Haas Manuscript (unpublished), Eugene C. Barker Library of Texas History, University of Texas, Austin.

107. Oldham, Memoirs, p. 444.

108. R. H. Williams, *With the Border Ruffians: Memoirs of the Far West,* 1852–1863, E. W. Williams, editor (New York: E. P. Dutton and Company, 1907), pp. 277, 285.

109. Oldham, Memoirs, p. 455.

110. Seddon to Holmes, January 28, 1863, *ORA,* Ser. I, Vol. 53, pp. 845–46; *Ranchero* [Corpus Christi], June 11, 1863.

111. Magruder to Cooper, June 8, 1863, Hart to Myers, June 8, 1863, *ORA,* Ser. I, Vol. 26, Pt. 2, pp. 57–65; Vol. 53, pp. 882–83. *Ranchero* [Corpus Christi], May 21, 1863.

112. Magruder to Cooper, June 8, 1863, *ORA,* Ser. I, Vol. 26, Pt. 2, p. 62; Oldham, Memoirs, p. 449–50; *Ranchero* [Corpus Christi], May 7, July 2, 30, 1863.

113. Quintero to Benjamin, December 30, 1863, Confederate State Papers, Vol. 8; Bennett to Hart, May 30, 1863, *ORA,* Ser. I, Vol. 26, Pt. 2, p. 78.

114. Magruder to Cooper, June 8, 1863, Magruder to Boggs June 25, 1863, *ORA,* Ser. I, Vol. 26, Pt. 2, pp. 63, 88–89; Bee to Magruder, May 22, 1863, *ORN,* Ser. I, Vol. 20, p. 827,

115. Russell to Magruder, June 10, 1863, Cotton Bureau Correspondence, Record Group 365, Envelope 3940.

116. Ibid.

117. Ibid.

118. Magruder, General Orders No. 131, May 5, 1863, Russell to Bee, June 30, 1863, Cotton Bureau Correspondence, Record Group 2, Envelopes 4002, 3940.

119. Hart to Turner, August 25, 1863, Cotton Bureau Correspondence, Record Group 2, Envelope 3936.

120. Ibid.

121. Kirby Smith to Magruder, June 23, 1863, *ORA,* Ser. I, Vol. 26, Pt. 2, p. 78.

122. Kirby Smith to Magruder, June 27, July 27, 1863, *ORA,* Ser. I, Vol. 26, Pt. 2, pp. 94–95, Vol. 53, pp. 885–86; *Tri-Weekly News* [Galveston], September 9, 1863.

123. Oldham, Memoirs, pp. 448–49; *Tri-Weekly Telegraph* [Houston], July 31, 1863.

124. Bee to Turner, July 16, 1863, Turner to Bee, July 29, 1863, Magruder to Bee, August 4, 1863, *ORA,* Ser. I, Vol. 26, Pt. 2, pp. 113–14, 122–25; 137–39.

125. Macgruder to Bee, August 4, 1863, *ORA,* Ser. I, Vol. 26, Pt. 2, pp. 137–39.

126. Bee to Turner, August 27, 1863, *ORA,* Ser. I, Vol. 26, Pt. 2, pp. 184–86.

127. Ibid.

128. Tyler, *Vidaurri,* p. 113.

129. *Texas State Gazette* [Austin], August 12, 1863.

130. Quintero to Benjamin, September 11, 16, 1863, Confederate State Papers, Vol. 58; Watson, pp. 28–30.

131. Russell to Turner, August 15, 1863, Cotton Bureau Correspondence, Record Group 365, Envelope, 3940.

132. Hart to Magruder, July 6, 1863, Cotton Bureau Correspondence, Record Group 365, Envelope 3940.

133. Hart to Magruder, July 10, 1863, Cotton Bureau Correspondence, Record Group 365, Envelope 3940; Magruder to Cooper, June 8, 1863, *ORA,* Ser. I, Vol. 26, Pt. 2, p. 63; Fitzpatrick to Benjamin, October 22, 1863, Confederate State Papers, Vol. 8.

134. Fremantle, *Diary,* p. 25; *Patriot* [LaGrange], August 27, 1863; *Ranchero* [Corpus Christi], August 13, September 17, 1863; *San Antonio News,* October 8, 1863; Fitzpatrick to Benjamin, October 22, 1863, *ORA,* Ser. I, Vol. 34, Pt. 2, pp. 827–28, and Confederate State Papers, Vol. 8.

135. Hart to Kirby Smith, November 25, 1863, Ballanger Papers, 2Q422, Ballanger, Diary, pp. 151–52; *Tri-Weekly Telegraph* [Houston], November 18, 1863.

136. Ballanger, Diary, 2Q422, pp. 154, 157.
137. Quintero to Benjamin, December 30, 1863, Confederate State Papers, Vol. 58.
138. Fitzpatrick to Benjamin, July 15, October 22, 1863, Confederate State Papers, Vols. 8, 59, *ORA,* Ser. I, Vol. 34, Pt. 2, pp. 817–28.
139. Quintero to Benjamin, September 16, 1863, Confederate State Papers, Vol. 58.
140. Bee to Turner, Thayer to Hart, December 20, 1863, *ORA,* Ser. I, Vol. 26, Pt. 2, p. 396, Vol. 53, p. 942; Owsley, *King Cotton Diplomacy,* p. 126.
141. Quintero to Benjamin, December 23, 1863, Confederate State Papers, Vol. 58; Thayer to Kirby Smith, December 20, 1863, Thayer to Hart, December 20, 1863, *ORA,* Ser. I, Vol. 53, pp. 931–32, 942.
142. Quintero to Benjamin, December 23, 1863, Quintero to Hart, December 20, 1863, Confederate State Papers, Vol. 58; Thayer to Kirby Smith, December 20, 1863, Milmo to Thayer, December 17, 1863, *ORA,* Ser. I, Vol. 53, pp. 931–33.
143. Quintero to Benjamin, December 23, 1863, January 25, 1864, Confederate State Papers, Vol. 58; Milmo to Thayer, December 17, 1863, *ORA,* Ser. I, Vol. 53, 933; Tyler, *Vidaurri,* pp. 124–25.
144. Quintero to Benjamin, January 25, 1864, Confederate State Papers, Vol. 8.
145. Ibid.
146. Quintero to Benjamin, January 21, 25, 1864, Confederate State Papers, Vols. 8, 58.
147. Kirby Smith to Vidaurri, January 12, 1864, Quintero to Benjamin, January 25, 1864, Kirby Smith, Special Orders Number 8, in Quintero to Benjamin, February 1, 1864, Confederate State Papers, Vol. 58; Kirby Smith to Devine, January 12, 1864, Devine Papers, 2Q496, 1738, 1739.
148. Kirby Smith to [selected commissioners], January 12, 1864, *ORA,* Ser. I, Vol. 53, 949–50.
149. Quintero to Benjamin, February 1, 1863, Confederate State Papers, Vol. 58.
150. Quintero to Benjamin, January 25, 1863, Vidaurri to Kirby Smith, February 2, 1864, Confederate State Papers, Vol. 58; Kerby, p. 180; Tyler, *Vidaurri,* p. 126.
151. Devine to Kirby Smith, February 24, 1864, Devine Papers, 2Q496; Quintero to Benjamin, February 28, 1864, Confederate State Papers, Vol. 58.
152. Quintero to Benjamin, February 3, 1864, Confederate State Papers, Vol. 58; Fitzpatrick to Benjamin, March 8, 1864, *ORA,* March 8, 1864, Ser. I, Vol. 34, Pt. 2, p. 1031.
153. Fitzpatrick to Benjamin, March 8, 1864, Confederate State Papers, Vol. 59, *ORA,* Ser. I, Vol. 34, Pt. 2 pp. 1031–32.
154. Davis to Seddon, notations and endorsements, April 15, 1864, on the back of a letter from Kirby Smith to Davis, January 10, 1864, *ORA,* Ser. I, Vol. 53, pp. 930–31.
155. Quintero to Benjamin, June 1, 1864, December 7, 1864, Confederate State Papers, Vol. 58.
156. *New York Herald,* April 15, 1864.
157. *The Times* [London], May 23, 1864, in miscellaneous news clippings, Kirby Smith Papers, 3: 3.
158. Ibid.
159. Quintero to Kirby Smith, October 21, 1864, Confederate State Papers, Vol. 58.
160. Kerby, p. 201.
161. Julia A. Thomas, et. al. to Hart, April 11, 1864. Bexar County Court Records, County Court House, San Antonio, in Kerby, p. 203.
162. Epperson to Murrah, June 14, 1864, Governors' Letters, in Kerby, p. 203.
163. Kerby, p. 204.

164. Harcourt to Murrah, March [?], 1864, Governors' Letters, in Kerby, p. 204.

165. Kerby, p. 204.

166. Ibid., p. 206.

167. Kirby Smith to Davis, May 12, June 6, 1864, *ORA*, Ser. I, Vol. 34, Pt. 3, p. 821, Pt. 4, pp. 645–46.

168. Kirby Smith to Gray, October 6, 1864, *ORA*, Ser. I, Vol. 41, Pt. 3, p. 984.

169. Seddon to Kirby Smith, August 3, 1864, *ORA*, Ser. I, Vol. 53, pp. 1016–18; Kirby Smith, General Orders Number 84, October 24, 1869, Cotton Bureau Correspondence, Record Group 365, Envelope 2032; Kirby Smith to Gray, August 11, 1864, Kirby Smith to Walker, October 11, 1864, Kirby Smith Papers, Vol. 4, *Tri-Weekly Telegraph* [Houston], November 18, 1864, January 18, February 3, March 7, 1865; *Daily State Gazette* [Austin], August 24, December 7, 1864, *Tri-Weekly News* [Galveston], January 30, 1865.

170. Kirby Smith, General Orders Number 101, December 20, 1864, *ORA*, Ser. I, Vol. 44, Pt. 4, p. 1133.

171. "Cotton Sold to the Confederate States," *United States Senate Documents*, 62nd Congress, 3rd Session, Number 8, pp. 261–307; Samuel B. Thompson, *Confederate Purchasing Operations Abroad* (Chapel Hill: University of North Carolina Press, 1935), p. 117.

172. Wells to Broadwell, September 24, 1864, Cotton Bureau Correspondence, Record Group 365, Envelope 1358.

173. Kirby Smith to Gray, February 11, 1865, *ORA*, Ser. I, Vol. 48, Pt. 3, pp. 1383–84.

174. Thompson, pp. 117–18.

175. Maguire to Cracroft, November 27, 1863, Foreign Office Papers, F.O. 50/378; *Weekly Texas State Gazette* [Austin], March 22, 1865, *New York Times*, September 6, 1865.

176. Broadwell to Wells, October 10, 1864, Cotton Bureau Correspondence, Record Group 365, Envelope 1679.

5
THE TRADE AT SEA

The Blockade Established

By two proclamations in April 1861, President Abraham Lincoln gave notice that the seceded states were under blockade. The blockade covered 3,549 miles of coastline, including 189 rivers, bays, and inlets between the Potomac and the Rio Grande. At its initiation the United States Navy had only forty steamers and fifty sailing vessels. The sailing vessels were useless against the swift steam-powered ships used as blockade runners. And most of the steamers were either on foreign stations or in drydock, only three steamers were available for blockade duty.[1]

Under Secretary of the Navy Gideon Welles's skillful guidance, the Federal government bought and built ships rapidly. By the end of 1861, it had seventy-nine steamers, ranging from 800 tons to ferry boats, and eighty-one sailing vessels. By October 1861, the navy had 256 ships of all kinds, and by the end of the war it had 600. When Lincoln first declared the blockade, he had only one vessel for each sixty-six miles of blockaded coast; by the end of the war he had one ship for each six miles of coast.[2]

Only the major ports were blockaded during the first year of the war, and the rest of the coast was irregularly patrolled by cruisers. Until February 1862, the Rio Grande was only occasionally visited by the blockaders of the West Gulf squadron that cruised along the coast south of Corpus Christi. However, on February 1, the twenty-two-gun Federal screw-steamer *Portsmouth* took up a blockading station "to look after contraband runners" at the mouth of the Rio Grande and the Texas port at Brazos Santiago, seven miles to the north.[3]

The U.S.S. *Portsmouth. (Courtesy of the National Archives)*

Before the appearance of this Union ship, the Confederates had conducted trade through Brazos Santiago on the Texas side of the Rio Grande. Now, to give their operations a neutral disguise, they transferred them to the Mexican side. Article V of the 1848 Treaty of Guadelupe Hidalgo set the international boundaryline at the center of the Rio Grande and extended the line three leagues into the gulf, but because international law recognized national boundaries as extending only one league from land, this provision "only affect[ed] the rights of Mexico and the United States . . . [and was] never intended . . . to question the rights which Great Britain or any other power may possess under the law of nations."[4]

On its arrival at the river, the crew of the *Portsmouth* counted ten merchant vessels, several of which were British, discharging cargoes and taking on cotton. Captain Samuel Swarthout seized those he found to be anchored north of the international boundary with contraband on board. London immediately protested the seizures on the grounds that "there had been no warning, notification or interruption of the trade of Matamoros or the Rio Grande."[5]

To the British, Lincoln's blockade of the Confederacy marked a reversal of the traditional American stand on neutral commerce during time of war and violated international law regarding blockades. From 1793 to 1861 America had tried to induce foreign powers, and especially England, to recognize the doctrines of maritime neutral rights adopted by the League of Armed Neutrality of 1780 and 1800 concerning contraband, visit and search of merchant vessels, enemy goods on neutral ships, neutral goods on enemy ships, and, most importantly of all, the legal requirements to make a blockade effective and binding.[6]

Internationally recognized blockades are those of notification or de facto. The former is established by public announcement simultaneously with the presence of force before the blockaded port and becomes effective after sufficient warning time has elapsed following notification without seizure of the neutral vessel on its arrival at the blockaded port. Under these circumstances, neutrals have a right to be warned until the establishment of the blockade is known. However, the Union had an insufficient number of ships to fulfill these requirements of international law, and its blockade of the Southern coast remained merely a paper one for most of the war.[7]

Nevertheless, both the British government and press accepted the illegal American paper blockade. The measures and methods used to enforce it were those which England had used in the past, but had agreed to give up in signing the Declaration of Paris of 1856. The people in England who were inclined to be impatient or resentful of the illegal blockade were reminded by other Englishmen that the role of their country was usually that of the belligerent and that it was to her ultimate, though not immediate, interest to have America extend belligerent rights as far as possible at the expense of neutral rights on the sea. America, whose usual role was that of the neutral and the leading champion of neutral rights, should be allowed to set precedents in the employment of naval power that could be used against itself in the future. An editorial in the London *Times* reflected that a "blockade is by far the most formidable weapon of offense we possess. Surely we ought not to be over-ready to blunt its edge or injure its temper."[8] Later declaring that America had pushed the doctrine of ultimate destination of contraband "beyond anything that has ever been claimed" by Britain, the *Times* reminded its readers that, "if the Americans are determined to rivet this patch upon the hard old international law, we of all people in the world are the least interested in opposing the innovation."[9]

Although pleased by the stance taken by the United States, the British were at times exasperated and aroused at the zeal with which Union naval officers executed the blockade. They assured the Lincoln government that the blockade would be respected and neutrality maintained, but throughout the war registered both official and public protests at the methods by which the paper blockade and the doctrine of ultimate destination of contraband were enforced.

English officials saw the Matamoros trade as a loophole permitting British merchants to carry on a lucrative commerce with the Confederates. For that reason Lord Lyons, the British minister in Washington, was instructed to inform Secretary of State William H. Seward that Her Majesty's government viewed "the trade to Matamoros . . . [as] a perfectly legitimate trade" And, "while submitting to the most severe interpretation of the Law of Nations, she cannot allow that, under pretext of that law, hostilities should be carried on against a lawful branch of her commerce."[10]

Once it attracted British merchants, the Matamoros trade grew rapidly. In mid-February, 1862, thirteen vessels, six or seven of which were British, were lying off the mouth of the river. In September, twenty ships were counted, including eight English, six Spanish, two Danish, and one each of American, Bremen, and Prussian registries. A British visitor soon observed "seventy vessels . . . constantly at anchor outside."[11] Early in 1863, 180 to 200 ships of all nations lay at anchor at the mouth of the Rio Grande. A northern newspaper correspondent at Matamoros, in late 1864, described the trade as having "flourished ever since the blockade of the ports of the Gulf."[12] An eyewitness counted from 200 to 300 merchantmen trading with Matamoros during the closing weeks of 1864 and the beginning of 1865.

These ships, with their manifests drawn up to disguise their contraband cargoes as noncontraband, ignored the Union navy as they hovered off Bagdad, Mexico, awaiting their turn to trade. "They all come for cotton," reported the commander of a Federal blockader, "and there are hundreds of bales brought out of the river every day in a Mexican steamer and in small

Mexican lighters." There was "also piled up on the Mexican side . . . a very large number of bales, distinctly visible from [the] deck" of his ship. Although "fully convinced that the trade with Matamoros [was] most, if not all illegal," the captain did not know how it could "be interfered with . . . as the papers of all the vessels [were] so well authenticated."[13]

The British customs records in the Public Record Office in London indicate a growth of commerce through Matamoros that corresponds with the accounts of the eyewitnesses. There is no record of cotton being imported into England from that port in 1860. Cotton exports to England from Matamoros began during the second half of 1861, and by the end of 1862 totaled more than three million pounds. In the following year these shipments increased more than sixfold, totalling 22½ million pounds. The 1864 records indicate an additional 75-percent increase, and the commerce continued to grow, reaching its climax in the first half of 1865. British records show that by the end of the war more than 84½ million pounds of cotton were exported to England from Matamoros.[14] Sizable commercial dealings were also carried on between Matamoros and the European continent, the West Indies, Cuba, and Union ports, especially New York.

The Illicit Trade with New York

New York customhouse records show that in 1861 only one ship arrived from Matamoros. In 1862, there were twenty such arrivals, in 1863, seventy-two, and in the less than three months from January 1 to March 18, 1864, thirty-two ships. Before the Civil War, requests for clearance from New York to Matamoros were made about once a year. From August 1861 to March 1864, 152 vessels, with aggregate capacity of 35,000 tons, sailed to the Rio Grande. Continuing throughout the war, this New York–Matamoros trade was described, late in 1864, as "heavy and profitable."[15]

Included in cargoes from New York were large quantities of munitions and war supplies destined for the Confederate army. A sizable number of harnesses and wagons as well as thousands of pistols, carbines, uniforms, shoes, blankets, and other materials from the Northern states found their way from New York into the Confederacy through Matamoros.[16]

Northern civilian goods were also shipped. Early in 1862, the schooner *Hannah M. Johnson* cleared from New York for Matamoros with $18,000 worth of dry goods, provisions, spirits, wines, silks, cutlery, and assorted other cargo. Texas newspapers openly advertised items such as "garden seeds fresh from New York via Matamoros,"[17] and openly discussed the commerce with New York in their editorials:

> Reader, the paper before you . . . we are certain . . . came from New York from the fact that it is a style of paper made nowhere else. . . . Some of the shoes worn by our men were made by these Massachusetts men long after the War began. It is a curious fact, that some of the gold brought back into the State by patriotic citizens, in exchange for cotton, and which is too good to pay debts with, bears the Philadelphia mint mark.[18]

Records indicate that most of the Rio Grande merchants including the respectable José San Román and the Federal informant D. G. Kingsbury, were adept at "turning a dollar" in this illicit trade with the North.[19] Exchanging their goods on the Rio Grande for cotton at 20 to 25 cents per pound, these speculators realized as much as 300-percent profit by selling it in New York at 75 to 80 cents per pound. "This is a splendid business," exclaimed one Matamoros merchant to his New York contact. "If we carry out what I have undertaken there is a fortune."[20]

Matamoros and New York merchants used both the direct and broken-voyage systems in shipping between the two ports. Direct shipments were protected by "fronts" utilizing "strawmen" in Mexico and reliable brokers in New York to handle exports and imports. The broken-voyage system was used when clearance could not be obtained for direct shipments and to avoid suspicion of trading with the enemy. Vessels destined for either Matamoros or New York would use St. Thomas, Nassau, Havana, or Halifax as the intermediary point. With papers drawn up for only the first leg of the journey, the ships would put in at one of these neutral ports and secure papers to cover the second half of the voyage.[21]

One of the Rio Grande merchants most deeply involved in the New York trade was Charles Stillman. Born in Connecticut, he had moved to Durango, Mexico, in 1827, at the age of seventeen to manage a store for his father. A year later his father sent him to the lower Rio Grande to sell merchandise, and Charles made it his home. Shrewd, self-reliant, a master of trade and politics, he became known along the river as Don Carlos. He married a New England girl who, not being able to tolerate the Rio Grande climate, returned to New York with their children in 1853. Stillman joined his family in New York during the summers, but always felt himself an alien there, and regarded the Yankees as "haughty and domineering."[22] By 1861, he was a converted Confederate, stating, "My sympathy is with the South, in fact, I never desire to go north again."[23]

He maintained connections in New York with the commission agency that later became Smith and Dunning, and also built a riverboat monopoly with Mifflin Kenedy and Richard King on the Rio Grande. Thus, when the Civil War began, his location and business interests put him in position to reap great profits from the trade.[24]

Stillman appointed John H. Donahue his agent in New York to purchase goods to be sent to Matamoros and to receive and sell the cotton shipped to New York. But, having some reservations about Donahue's drinking habits, Stillman placed the handling of his money in the firm headed by his trusted friend, James Smith. Like Stillman, Smith had gained much of his business experience on the Rio Grande and had Confederate sympathies. To conceal his Confederate interests, Stillman appointed Jeremiah Galvan, José Morell, and Santiago Yturria as strawmen in Matamoros and Monterrey to handle his mail and contracts.[25]

In the fall of 1861 Stillman developed close ties with George W. Brackenridge of the Texana, Texas, firm of Brackenridge and Bates. This company became one of Stillman's largest cotton suppliers. Early in 1863, however, Brackenridge dissolved his cotton firm, and defected to the Federals. After traveling to Washington, where he was appointed the assistant special agent for controlling trade in occupied Texas, he returned to the Rio Grande frontier with General Banks's invasion force in November 1863. Locating Stillman in Matamoros, he persuaded him to take the oath of allegiance to the United States and took him across the river to meet the Union commander at Brownsville. The partnership was recemented, ostensibly in the interest of the Federal government, and the cotton trade with New York continued.[26]

Constantly operating a fleet of at least three ships, the *Emma Dean*, the *Alice Tainter*, and the *Banshee*, between New York and Matamoros, Stillman and his associates realized large financial returns. On two shipments, the Smith and Dunning ledgers show profits of $152,681.43 and $132,874.68. Near the end of the war James Smith reportedly boasted of making "a million dollars" for Stillman and "bouncing commissions" for himself.[27]

Stillman's New York operation was facilitated by Federal blockade policies. Southern cotton was needed to manufacture uniforms for the Northern army. Blockade instructions, carefully worded to avoid antagonizing the British, legalized the Matamoros trade for those shippers obtaining permits from the United States government. The wartime trade promised immense profits to persons in positions to obtain permits and to exert political pressure.[28] New York merchants, utilizing their contacts in Washington, took full advantage of the opportunity. Thus, from the beginning Union naval commanders were restricted in their efforts to curb this "illegal, dishonorable, and traitorous" trade between Matamoros and New York.[29]

The British were aware of the Northern trade with Matamoros. They noted "large stocks of goods at Matamoros, constantly replenished by direct shipments from New York and Boston, for use in the Rebel States."[30] The British foreign office received a growing list of complaints from British commercial houses about ships trading unmolested between New York and the Rio Grande while their own were seized.

In the spring of 1863, British Foreign Minister Russell instructed Lord Lyons to protest strongly the illicit trade. In stating that Britain saw "the trade to Matamoros [as] . . . a perfectly legitimate trade," the minister was told to emphasize that it was impossible to say

> before hand that certain goods will be consumed in Mexico, and certain other goods will be carried into the so-called Confederate States. It might be used in Mexico, and all the goods sent from New York might be transported by land to Texas. This is a matter beyond the scope and destination of the sea voyage."[31]

Lyons concluded his talks with Secretary of State Seward by reminding him that any further "hostilities" against "a British vessel bound to Matamoros" would be regarded "as little less than a calamity."[32]

Stillman and the New York trade came under congressional investigation in 1864. Federal naval officers had long been suspicious of Stillman's activities. The attention of the congressional committee focused on him when the *Banshee* put in to

New York harbor in the spring of 1864, ostensibly loaded with Mexican cotton consigned to Smith and Dunning by Jeremiah Galvan. The committee suspected the cotton to be Confederate property shipped by Stillman.[33]

No papers linked Stillman with the *Banshee,* and the congressmen sought to prove their suspicions through testimony. Under oath, James Smith admitted his former friendship with Stillman, and acknowledged that Stillman had once had a desk in the office of Smith and Dunning. But he professed complete ignorance of certain large cash transactions on the agency books, and he denied receiving any money from Stillman since Texas's secession. Smith, stating that he was the agent for Jeremiah Galvan of Matamoros and José Morell of Monterrey, swore that John Donahue was Stillman's agent with the firm. But Donahue was not available to testify because he had fled to Canada months earlier.[34]

Without Donahue's testimony, the congressmen could not establish that Smith and Dunning were engaged with Stillman in illicit trade. However, their suspicions were not allayed. "It is impossible to read the testimony . . . and not entertain strong convictions of the nature of that trade," they concluded. "The sworn ignorance of an active member of the house, as to, with whom and for whom, large cash entries were made in the company books, if credible, is realy wonderful."[35]

The Size of the Matamoros Trade

Establishing the precise size of the Matamoros trade is difficult since neither the Brownsville nor the Matamoros customhouse records have survived. In July 1862, Lord Lyons wrote to Foreign Minister Russell that Secretary of State Seward had received a report that the South had "exported, chiefly through Mexican ports, . . . two or three hundred thousand bales" of cotton.[36] Nearly all of the cotton shipped from the lower Rio Grande to England was cleared through Matamoros.[37] According to Frank Owsley, Southern cotton shipments to New York exceeded 800,000 bales during the war, more than the total shipped to England or Europe. Most of this cotton came from the blockaded Gulf ports, and after 1862, as more Southern Gulf ports were closed by Union capture or blockade, much of it was exported through Matamoros.[38]

In the second half of 1863, Captain Rochfort Maguire of the British Gulf squadron reported that Matamoros cotton statistics showed that 150,000 bales of cotton had been exported from there since the beginning of the war. Early in 1865, as the conflict neared its end, the Austin, *Weekly State Gazette* reported that "prior . . . to November, 1863, over 200,000 bales of cotton had passed out of Texas across the Rio Grande."[39] These records indicate that during the first twenty-seven months of the Matamoros cotton trade, an average of 6,000 to 7,000 bales was exported each month.

Between January 1863 and February 1864, nearly 85,000 bales were shipped from Matamoros. During a four- or five-week period in March and April 1864, about 10,000 bales crossed into Mexico from Eagle Pass alone. These figures suggest that the monthly average of nearly 7,000 bales exported through Matamoros held firm through the first quarter of 1864.[40]

A study of a partial list of cotton shipments by one Matamoros merchant, José San Román, between February 1863 and December 1864 indicated that during that period Román shipped at least 29,508 bales for an average of 1,405 bales per month. The Román Papers suggest a steadily growing market during 1863 and 1864. And from the reports available, the size of his exports remained consistent at about 150 to 250 bales each in 1865.[41] Others, such as Droege, Oetling, Attrill and Lacoste, and Milmo and Company were much larger exporters of cotton.

These statistics are supported by those of the British customs office which show large cotton imports from the Rio Grande between 1862 and 1865. Using British standards of 112 pounds for the hundredweight, and 400 pounds per cotton bale, it appears that more than 213,000 bales of cotton were imported into England from the Rio Grande during the Civil War.[42] The cotton shipped from Matamoros to the European continent, the Bahamas, Cuba, New York and other Northern ports could total another 100,000 to 150,000 bales.[43]

At least during the three-year period from 1862 to 1865, the cotton trade was growing. During the forty-six months of the war, the average monthly export was nearly 7,000 bales, for a total of about 320,000 bales. Frank Owsley estimated that 1,250,000 bales of cotton were exported through the blockade, excluding that from Mexico.[44] If so, the 320,000 bales shipped through Matamoros represents more than 20 percent of the total Confederate cotton exports making the Rio Grande port one of the largest single outlets for Confederate cotton during the war.[45]

Interdiction and International Law

During the months immediately following the beginning of the trade, American consuls in the Caribbean notified Washington of its growth. From Havana the American consul R. W. Shufeldt wrote that supplies of every description were being exchanged at the Rio Grande for cotton, and suggested that "the mere appearance of a man of war" would effectively curtail the trade.[46]

After Washington ordered the U.S.S. *Portsmouth* to take up permanent station on the Rio Grande, the first of "the Matamoros seizures" was made.[47] Captain Samuel Swarthout first captured the Confederate schooner *Wave,* then, hoisting the French flag, he ran the *Portsmouth* close in to the 1,200-ton British screw-steamer *Labuan.* The British merchantman, anchored about three miles off the mouth of the river at 25°55′ north latitude, was very close to American territorial waters taking on cotton. Swarthout went aboard only to discover that the captain had gone ashore with the ship's papers, but he noticed that the logbook registered the ship's position as "off Barra Santiago." He concluded that the vessel was in American waters, and returning to the deck he saw the small steamer *Matamoros,* flying the Mexican flag, coming from the river with cotton. When it sighted the *Portsmouth,* it turned back, but Swarthout, assuming that the *Matamoros* belonged to Texans and was loaded with Confederate cotton for the *Labuan,* declared the *Labuan* in violation of the blockade and seized it as a "legal prize." He sent it to New York for adjudication with 490 bales of cotton on board, most of which belonged to Droege, Oetling and Company.[48]

The British vice-consul at Matamoros called the seizure of the *Labaun* an "outrage to the British flag and requested that a British man-of-war be sent to the Rio Grande.[49] On the other hand, the American consul at Matamoros defended Swarthout's action, claiming that the *Labuan* had "landed her entire cargo in Brownsville . . . and her return cargo, consisting of cotton, hides and specie, was placed on rebel steamboats at

Brownsville for conveyance down the river." The duplicity was made easier, he said, because "the Matamoros Custom House was located in Brownsville at the time, the collector having moved his office over for safety during the seige [in Matamoros]."[50]

To Whitehall the *Labuan* had been seized without "the slightest prima facie justification." On May 8, Lyons told Seward that he had "conclusive evidence that the capture had taken place in Mexican waters." And even if the facts regarding the cargo were as the American secretary had stated, they did not justify, he maintained, "the proceedings of the United States cruisers."[51]

Meanwhile, Confederate authorities urged British, French, and Spanish merchants to seek protection for the commerce from their governments. British consuls in the Caribbean area made growing complaints against American seizures. From Havana, British Consul J. T. Crawford wrote, "They board everything they fall in with, no matter how distant from the blockaded coast, and send them on suspicion."[52]

The Royal navy responded by sending the heavily armed H.M.S. *Phaeton,* which arrived at the Rio Grande on March 16. The following day the French corvette H.I.M. *Berthollet* dropped anchor off the mouth of the river. Two days later, Captain Edward Tatham of the *Phaeton* received a note of gratitude from Droege, Oetling and Company, stating that since his arrival "no more difficulties were put in our way to lighter."[53]

The American and British naval commanders exchanged notes on the controversy. The British claimed that the *Portsmouth*'s seizures had caused "a stagnation to the legal trade of neutrals with Matamoros, and . . . serious injury to British interests." Swarthout replied that he had no intention of interfering with the free navigation of the Rio Grande by neutrals, nor would he "interdict their legal commerce with Matamoros," but he did intend to prevent, as far as possible, "illicite trade" by the enemies of the United States.[54]

When Swarthout boarded and searched the French merchantman *LeTage,* Captain Jean Philippe Ernest de Jonquieres of the *Berthollet* joined the debate, raising a new point. In a strongly worded note, he demanded that Swarthout explain why he felt he had "the right of visiting a neutral merchant vessel, even in places where such a visit is generally permitted, when a man-of-war of that neutral nation is present?" When the American captain replied that no insult was intended, and that the entire matter of visit and search would be reviewed by higher military and diplomatic officials, Jonquieres seemed mollified.[55]

Swarthout sent copies of the correspendence with Tatham and Jonquieres to Admiral David G. Farragut, commander of the West Gulf Blockading Squadron, and recommended that the blockade of the Rio Grande be ended. He was satisfied, he said, that it was "impossible to prevent illicit trade on the Rio Grande unless we can take possession of Brownsville and the American side of the Rio Grande from there to its mouth." He suggested that the blockade not be extended south of Brazos Santiago so as to "prevent the possibility of a breach with England and France, growing out of the rights of neutrals."[56] After reviewing the matters, Secretary of the Navy Gideon Welles instructed Farragut that in the future no vessels were to be captured off the Rio Grande unless on their "way to a port of Texas, after having been properly warned of the existence of the Blockade."[57]

On May 21, 1862, Judge George F. Betts of the United States District Court for the Southern District of New York, declaring that the *Labuan* had been illegally seized in neutral waters, ordered the immediate release of the ship and its cargo. However, it was detained for a time because of its "great speed, [and being] destined for the same part of the world, . . . lest she should carry information respecting General [Nathaniel P.] Banks' expedition to New Orleans.[58] The delay was brief and by September it was back at the Rio Grande, loading cotton for New York.[59] Thus, the Matamoros trade continued in spite of troublesome delays caused by the Federal seizures.

There was also much blockade running from the broken Texas coast to Matamoros in small ships that could operate in shallow coastal waters where large warships could not venture. Slipping out of Texas ports, they dashed south and "come up close in to the Mexican coast and slip in over the bar, where their cotton would be transferred to lighters, taken out over the bar again, and shipped in some vessel bound to Europe or New York."[60]

After the stationing of Union warships in the western Gulf, these blockade runners were put under foreign registry, usually British. Under British navigational law a shipowner could make such a change quite easily by simply registering his vessel with a British consular agent. As the war progressed almost every British consul in the Caribbean area placed rebel ships under British registry. From Havana the American consul reported that "transfers to the English flag are getting to be of frequent occurance [sic]," and some of the changes are "for fraudulent and treasonable purposes."[61] Franklin Chase, the United States consul at Tampico, advised the State Department in 1863 that "this system of Consular Agency blended with the capital of British merchants is rapidly undermining" American interests and lessening the nation's power abroad. Before the war was over, hundreds of ships took this cover, and Chase concluded that "the British flag now covers and controls every thing in this Gulf connected with Secession."[62]

The blockade runners preferred dark nights, particularly rainy or foggy ones. The cover of darkness or bad weather helped the low-hulled vessels, often "painted a dirty white," to elude Union warships. According to Admiral Farragut, forty loaded vessels waited in Texas ports in September 1864 for bad weather or a dark night to try to slip through the blockade. To prevent the runners' success, he doubled the number of ships on watch.[63]

In late May 1863, Commodore H. H. Bell, aboard the U.S.S. *Brooklyn,* cruised along the Texas coast to ascertain the extent of the intercoastal trade and to inquire about privateers reportedly being fitted out at the Rio Grande. At San Luis Pass he saw a schooner and two river steamboats, and at Lavaca one sloop, a riverboat, and one schooner. On May 27, he captured the sloop *Blazer* south of Velasco. Manned by a master and three crewmen, the seventeen-ton ship was on course from Houston to Matamoros with thirty-nine bales of cotton. Sending the prize to the bar off Galveston, Bell continued south and anchored near the mouth of the Rio Grande that night. The next morning he counted sixty-eight sails outside the bar "and a forest of smaller craft" inside the river.[64]

Soon Bell sighted the masts of the *Kate,* a sloop of near seven-ton capacity, as it approached the Rio Grande from the north. Getting underway, he quickly closed on the craft and found it to be loaded with eighteen bales of cotton from Houston. Since the sloop was too small for distant sailing at sea, he took the prize's cargo aboard the *Brooklyn.*[65]

On his return to the Rio Grande, he noticed two sloops and two schooners inside of Brazos Santiago. Dropping anchor off the bar of that Texas port at midnight on the thirteenth, the commodore sent an expedition of eighty-seven men in four boats to capture the vessels. The boarding party brought out the 100-ton schooner *Star* and a fishing sloop *Victoria,* of Jamaican registry, but it grounded on the way out and was burned. Another schooner was fired by local citizens when they saw the expedition approaching.[66]

On June 1, the *Brooklyn* returned to her watch off Galveston. In six days she had captured or destroyed five blockade runners. Although Union warships maintained a vigilance against these small sailing vessels throughout the war, they met with varying degress of success.[67]

Among the reasons for Bell's visit to the Rio Grande were reports that Confederate privateers were fitting out at Brazos Santiago. He found none, but records reveal that continuing Federal suspicions were justified. On June 22, 1863, the 1,535-ton British screw-steamer *Sir William Peel* dropped anchor off the Rio Grande and began discharging "valuable cargoes for the Confederacy."[68] Six days later General Kirby Smith dispatched a Confederate naval officer to the Rio Grande to inspect and advise upon its purchase as a cruiser.[69]

At Matamoros United States consul Leonard Pierce became suspicious of the Confederate interests in the *Sir William Peel* and notified Commander M. B. Woolsey of the U.S.S. *Princess Royal.* Upon boarding and inspecting the suspect vessel, Woolsey observed that she was "an old vessel, broken-backed, and represented as being slow," with exposed machinery. After a forty-eight-hour delay, he released the ship and her cargo was "landed safely in Texas."[70]

When Captain Henry Rolando arrived a few days later with the U.S.S. *Seminole,* he seized the *Peel* on suspicion of trading with the enemy, and being a potential privateer. Reportedly it had landed contraband of war, machinery, and blankets and had taken on board 904 bales of cotton with another 300 expected. Rolando found two 18-pound guns mounted on her deck and "munitions of war intended to be used to convert her to a privateer." Built for a man-of-war, she was 347 feet long, and "in all her strengthenings and machinery adapted for one," he reported. "Her engines [were] below the water line and her capacity for coal very great." He concluded that if he had not seized her, "we should have had another Confederate cruiser on the high seas, second to none that are there."[71]

Rolando sent the *Peel* to the prize court at New Orleans. On the voyage, its crewmen, being held as prisoners, refused to assist the prize crew in the operation of the vessel. Consequently, through their ignorance of English steamers, the captors damaged its boilers, steering mechanism, and caused a major leak that required "the steam pumps to be kept going day and night." By the time the ship reached New Orleans, it was "in a sinking condition." The necessary repairs cost the United States nearly $6,000.[72]

The capture of the *Peel* touched off one of the most tangled maritime incidents of the Civil War. The governor of Tamaulipas, claiming that the ship was in Mexican waters, said that Rolando was wrong and demanded the ship's release. Milmo and Company, consignees of the *Peel*'s cargo, took the same position, as did her British owners. Captain A. W. A. Hood, who observed the capture from the British warship *Pylades,* accused Rolando of intoxication and abuse of the *Peel*'s crew, and demanded its immediate release. In Washington, Lord Lyons protested that the ship was "in Mexican waters near Matamoros," when it was seized. He also told Secretary of State Seward that "her Majesty's Government objects that this officer considers what he terms 'Confederate Cotton' to be contraband of war, and . . . if the search is to justify a seizure it ought, by international law, to proceed and not to follow the act of taking possession."[73]

Meanwhile, the Confederates intercepted a personal letter from Captain Rolando to G. V. Fox, the assistant secretary of the navy, in which he wrote of the British and Mexicans in uncomplimentary terms. Noting the "immense value" of the Rio Grande to the South, he mentioned that "steamers are constantly landing cargoes—contraband—which go to Texas . . . [for] cargoes of Confederate cotton." This trade, he said, was carried on by "the hocus-pocus of those Englishmen there . . . with the convenience of the miserable Mexicans . . . [who] hourly violate their neutrality by assisting and giving aid and comfort to the enemy." "It gaulled [sic] me," he continued, "to have a scoundrel of an Englishman crying out 'neutrality' when he knew as well as I did that he had been trafficking in the blood of my countrymen and making money out of our misfortunes."[74] The letter, printed in American and English newspapers, caused the British to step up their demand for "the immediate restitution of the vessel with proper indemnification to the owners, and . . . a proper rebuke to be administered to the Captor."[75] Nearly three weeks later, Seward told Lyons that Rolando was on his way north and would be questioned as to the authenticity of the letter when he arrived.[76]

At first Seward was ready to order the release of the *Peel* because it was seized in Mexican waters. His views were opposed by Secretary of the Navy Welles, who felt that if the ship was "captured in Mexican waters, no power but Mexico could make the claim." Lyons, however, hesitated to ask the Mexican minister to intervene in the case, since he represented the Juárez government, which was trying to maintain the sympathy and assistance of the Washington government. But Seward remained determined and Welles was "fearful he will make a misfire on this question. He has never looked into maritime law, and will make any sacrifice of national or individual rights to keep in with England."[77]

The prize court handed down its decision on the *Peel* in the spring of 1864. It restored the ship and its cargo to their owners. But having "grave doubts as to the object of the voyage," the court denied the claimants request for damages.[78]

As the war continued, the lists of Matamoros seizures grew. The *Will o' the Wisp*, the *Science*, the *Volante*, the *Dashing Wave*, the *Matamoros*, and the *Teresita*, were among the many taken at the Rio Grande. All were charged with engaging in contraband trade while anchored in American waters. In every case, however, the prize courts, finding it difficult to establish a violation of neutrality and American waters, released the ships. Even Secretary of State Seward admitted that "our right to blockade the mouth of the Rio Grande, for the purpose of preventing this commerce, may be considered as at least questionable."[79] Nevertheless, Vice-Admiral Sir Alexander Milne, commander of the British Gulf squadron, hoping to avoid future difficulties, directed that every British ship make more precise bearings and notations of its anchorage in Mexican waters.[80]

A sample of the cargoes confiscated by the Federal warships at the Rio Grande suggested the variety of goods shipped through Matamoros. Seized after one-third of its cargo was landed, the *Will o' the Wisp* contained 24 barrels and 46 kegs of gunpowder and 89,000 percussion caps. The *Love Bird* yielded 14,200 Enfield rifles, 156 revolvers, 2 million cartridges, and 5 million rifle caps. From the *Gladiator* and the *Sea Queen* was taken 20,000 pounds of gunpowder, while the *Sea Drift* yielded

1,048 pounds of lead, boots, spurs, percussion caps, gunpowder, and bird shot. The cargo of the *Volante* included 11,943 pairs of boots, 2,570 pairs of socks, and a large quantity of cloth and blankets. The *Flying Scud* was found to be carrying 65,000 rounds of gunpowder, 7 tons of horseshoes, and $4,000 to $5,000 worth of medical supplies. The blockaders also captured wagons, caissons, harnesses, saddles, artillery, Confederate uniforms, buttons, and buckles marked "C.S.A.," steel, and bar-iron. Great Britain was the chief supplier of these goods.[81]

Not all of the seizures of the ships in the Matamoros trade took place at the Rio Grande. On February 25, 1863, the 1,200-ton, English screw-steamer *Peterhoff* was captured about four miles from St. Thomas in the Virgin Islands by the U.S.S. *Vanderbilt* and sent to New York for adjudication. Having cleared from London on January 5, she was en route to Matamoros with the royal mails and an assorted cargo including harnesses, boots, blankets, horseshoes, medicines, shovels, and spades. On board were three gentlemen who were part owners of the cargo and who planned to open a mercantile house at Matamoros. All were British born; two were British subjects and the third, Mr. Samuel J. Redgate, was a naturalized American and recent resident of Texas.[82]

The seizure, directed by Admiral Charles Wilkes, brought British public opinion close to the war pitch it had reached when he had captured the Confederate agents James Mason and John Slidell from the *Trent* fifteen months earlier. The debates it precipitated in Parliament lasted for several weeks. In Commons, Seymour Fitzgerald accused the United States of trying to drive British commerce from Matamoros. The London *Times* said the Americans were deliberately attacking British commerce to gain the carrying trade of the world, and the *London Economist* declared the *Peterhoff* seizure to be a more flagrant violation of international law than was the *Trent* episode.[83]

When Lyons learned that royal mail had been taken from the *Peterhoff*, he asked Seward to restore them immediately. The secretary of state, considering the interference with the mail a more serious matter than the capture of merchant vessels, urged its release. Secretary Welles, however, insisted that the seizure of mail was not covered by international law and that the right to seize it should be insisted on as a means of obtaining evidence regarding the true character and destination of

The U.S.S. *Vanderbilt*. *(Courtesy of the National Archives)*

captured vessels. He therefore refused to release the mail. Seward, sensing serious diplomatic consequences, laid the case before President Lincoln. The president sustained Seward, and Welles was informed that the mails of the *Peterhoff* were to be forwarded to their destination, but as a concession and not as a right.[84]

Meanwhile, the case went through the prize court and the *Peterhoff* was condemned. The decision, handed down by Judge Samuel R. Betts of the District Prize Court for the Southern District of New York on July 31, 1863, was on the grounds that it was carrying contraband ultimately destined for the Confederacy by way of Matamoros. Of course, this ruling upheld the doctrine of continuous voyage, against which America had made many protests in earlier days when it was neutral and England was at war.[85]

Theh decision was appealed and, in 1867, came before the United States Supreme Court. In reviewing the case, the court closely inspected the ship's cargo, a very large portion of which was found to be particularly adapted to army use. Because the search of the vessel revealed this contraband, the court held that it was the duty of the officer of the *Vanderbilt* to bring the *Peterhoff* in for adjudication.[86]

The court then reviewed the doctrine of continuous voyage as it related to both contraband and noncontraband goods. Noting that inland commerce with a blockaded country was accepted by international law, the court declared that trade "with a neutral port in immediate proximity to the territory of one belligerent is certainly inconvenient for the other."[87] However, noncontraband goods shipped from London to Matamoros, although destined for Texas, violated no blockade. On the other hand, the court declared:

> Contraband is subject to a different rule in respect to ulterior destination than that which applies to merchandise not contraband. The latter is liable to capture only when a violation of blockade is intended; the former when destined to the hostile country, or to the actual military or naval use of the enemy, whether blockaded or not.[88]

The pronouncement thus held that while the doctrine of continuous voyage could not be applied to noncontraband articles, it could be invoked to justify seizure of contraband goods.

Finally, the court condemned its contraband cargo along with portions "infected with contraband," but ordered the ship and the noncontraband portion of its cargo released. Because the *Peterhoff* had been taken into service by the United States Navy, and had sunk following a collision with another ship off the coast of North Carolina, the court awarded its owners $67,672.33 in compensation.[89]

The American prize courts carefully studied earlier admiralty decisions for precedents, especially the British decisions handed down during the Napoleonic Wars. They concluded that the United States squadron lying in wait for merchantmen bringing contraband to Matamoros, or using the Mexican port as a blockade-running base, was conducting a legitimate blockade. England, or any other neutral whose commerce was injured, had no legal grounds on which to protest the actual blockading of the neutral port of Matamoros. However, when the Americans seized the *Magicienne*, the *Peterhoff*, and the *Dolphin* on the high seas on the suspicion that they were carrying contraband to Matamoros, and the American minister in London, Charles Francis Adams, granted immunity from capture to parties shipping arms to Matamoros for the Juárez faction, the British had grounds upon which to base a first-class controversy. Matamoros became the focal point of as sharp a public controversy as grew out of America's exercise of belligerent rights on the seas.[90]

British confidence that the Matamoros trade was legitimate was displayed in part by the type of vessel they generally employed in the voyage. Those attempting to run the blockade illegally customarily broke the trip from England and used two different types of ships. Large commercial vessels carried the goods to neutral *entrepôts* in the Caribbean area. There the cargoes were transferred to low, swift blockade runners for the dash into a blockaded port. No such stratagem was used by the British in their trade with the Rio Grande port. British records show that nearly all of their goods were hauled directly from English ports, such as Liverpool and London, in large steam-powered merchantmen.[91]

As the Matamoros seizures continued, the British became concerned at what they considered to be attempts to introduce new principles into international law. These new doctrines were that a neutral vessel could be seized in neutral waters after it had discharged contraband in a neutral port, that it could be seized for carrying contraband away from a neutral port, that capture could be made on suspicion without search in the hopes of uncovering evidence to incriminate the vessel, and that conducting trade with a belligerent was sufficient grounds for capture without reference to blockade or contraband. Palmerston instructed Russell to have Lyons raise these points with Seward.

Throughout the war the British were given no reason to doubt the fairness and independence of the American courts and no grounds for complaint concerning American prize judgments. Palmerston later expressed appreciation for the manner in which the Union government had "invariably received our representations in a spirit of respect, equity, and justice."[92]

The British government, in turn, sought to prevent the dispute from escalating into war. In a letter to the English owners of a vessel seized by the Union navy, Foreign Minister Russell said that Her Majesty's government could not "deny in this war the exercise of those rights which, in all wars in which Great Britain had been concerned, she has claimed herself to exercise."[93] When he thought that the war fever was on the rise in England and America, he told Lyons: "May both nations cool down from this insane fury before it is too late!" Declaring that he would do what he could in England, he directed Lyons to work with Seward and Lincoln for Anglo-American peace.[94]

The admiralty seconded the views of the foreign office and followed Foreign Minister Russell's recommendations. Instructions of February 1864 issued to the commander of British warships on the North American and West Indian Station illustrated the moderate attitude of the admiralty. The commander was ordered to be "extremely careful to maintain on all occasions a perfect neutrality." He was to be certain that his subordinates should in no way give "countenance to vessels under the British Flag which may be employed in a manner inconsistent with the Neutrality which Her Majesty has enjoined all Her Subjects to maintain during the Contest." In difficult times he was to exercise forbearance, referring all serious problems to the home government for settlement.[95]

The orders issued to the British fleet cruising the Atlantic and American waters directed that Her Majesty's Navy avoid a conflict with the United States at all costs. This should not be interpreted that Whitehall had neither the interest in nor serious intentions of intervention in the American conflict; both of which it demonstrated in 1862 and early 1863 when the cabinet proposed and Parliament debated intervention. However, they do underscore the determination of the London government to keep its options open and not to allow its military to dictate policy.

Perhaps the man most responsible for preventing a naval confrontation between the two countries was Vice-Admiral Sir Alexander Milne, who commanded the British squadron on the North American and West Indian Station for most of the war. He always exhibited tact, impartiality, sound judgment, and legal knowledge. His admirable qualities were recognized by all who dealt with him, including President Lincoln and Secretaries Seward and Welles. In October 1863, Lyons wrote that the Northern government recognized that "to nothing more than to the excellent judgement and to the firm but temperate conciliatory conduct of the Admiral is owing to the maintenance of harmonious relations between the two Countries."[96]

Milne kept a tight reign on his subordinates, many of whom displayed pro-Confederate sympathies, and he influenced and shaped policy as circumstances developed. When English shippers demanded naval convoys to protect their merchant ships, he refused because he felt that convoys would only increase the chances of Anglo-American collisions. He ordered his officers to abstain from any act likely to involve England in hostilities with the United States. Although irritated by the ways in which the Americans exercised belligerent rights, he wrote: "If we change positions with Adm. Wilkes, I dare say we would feel annoyed to see several steamers full of contraband of war in a harbour of a neutral port ready to break *our* blockade."[97]

Notes

1. Frank Owsley, "America and the Freedom of the Seas, 1861–1865," *Essays in Honor of William E. Dodd,* Avery O. Craven, editor (Chicago: 1935), pp. 196, 197; hereafter cited as Owsley, *Dodd Essays;* Lyons to Russell, January 2, 1862, Foreign Office Papers, F.O. 5/823.

2. Owsley, *Dodd Essays,* 197; *The Times* [London], December 4, 1861.

3. Bell to Gillis, December 23, 1863, Stations of Vessels composing the Gulf Blockading Squadron, January 23, 1862, Swarthout to McKean, February 3, 1862, *Official Records of the Union and Confederate Navies* [ORN], Ser. I, Vol. 17, pp. 71, 101; Blacker to Crawford, February 9, 1862, Lyons to Russell, March 28, 1862, Foreign Office Papers, Case of "Labuan," F.O. 97/42; *Tri-Weekly Telegraph* [Austin], February 14, 1862.

4. Buchanan to Crampton, August 19, 1848, Seward to Welles, September 3, 1863, *ORN,* Ser. I, Vol. 20, pp. 503, 504; Lyons to Russell, January 12, 1864, Foreign Office Papers, F.O 5/1181.

5. Blacker to Crawford, February 9, 1862, Crawford to Russell, March 1, 1862, Lyons to Russell, March 28, 1862, Foreign Office Papers, F.O. 97/42.

6. Owsley, *Dodd Essays,* p. 194.

7. James R. Soley, *The Blockade and the Cruiser* (New York: Charles Scribner's Sons, 1885), p. 33; Owsley, *Dodd Essays,* p. 195.

8. Palmerston to Russell, October 18, 1861, Earl Russell Papers, P.R.O. 30/22/14B; Owsley, *Dodd Essays,* pp. 195, 202; *The Times* [London], February 10, August 9, 1862.

9. *The Times* [London], June 30, 1863; *The London Herald,* May 3, 1861, expressed the opposition view of Lord Derby's Tory party, attacking the Union blockade and holding the cabinet accountable for the consequences.

10. Russell to Lyons, April 24, 1863, Parliamentary Papers, 1863, Vol. 72, p. 507; Lyons to Seward, August 4, 1864, Foreign Office Papers, F.O. 5/1007.

11. Quintero to Benjamin, September 24, 1862, January 25, 1864, Confederate State Papers, Vols. 8, 58; Fremantle, *Diary,* p. 6.

12. Read to Angel, November 27, 1863, Foreign Office Papers, F.O. 5/1187; Seward to Lyons, May 12, 1863, Parliamentary Papers, 1863, Vol. 72, pp. 509–10; Bailey to Welles, April 2, 1863, *ORN,* Ser. I, Vol. 17, p. 403; Irby, p. 42; Ellis, *Southwestern Historical Quarterly* 77: 209–10; *New York Herald,* January 9, 1865.

13. French to Farragut, September 18, 1862, *ORN,* Ser. I, Vol. 19, p. 291.

14. Cotton Imports into Britain from Mexico, 1860 to 1865, Great Britain, Customs Office, Ledgers for Imports, 1860–1865, Cus. 4/55–60, 5/62, 64, 66, 68, 72, 74; *Cotton*

Supply Reporter [Manchester], April 1, September 1, 1863, March 1, September 1, 1864, March 1, September 1, 1865; Parliamentary Papers, 1862, Vol. 65, p. 60, 1863, Vol. 65, p. 358, 1864, Vol. 30, p. 331, 1865, Vol. 27, p. 9.

15. United States Congress, *House Committee Reports,* 38th Congress, 1st Session, Number 111; Delaney, *Southwestern Historical Quarterly* 58: 479–80; *Era* [New Orleans], November 1, 1864, as quoted to Delaney, p. 480; Quintero to Benjamin, August 14, 1862, Fitzpatrick to Benjamin, March 12, 1863, Confederate State Papers, Vols. 58, 59.

16. Quintero to Hunter, October 18, 1861, Quintero to Benjamin, March 1, 1863, Confederate State Papers, Vol. 8; J. Marks to Dear Marks, January 22, 1863, Magruder to Cooper, March 3, 1863, Bee to Dickinson, March 11, 1863, *Official Records of the Union and Confederate Armies* [ORA], Ser. I, Vol. 15, pp. 660–61, 1004, 1014; Strong to Bell, *ORN,* Ser. I, Vol. 20, pp. 741–42; *Weekly State Gazette* [Austin], March 22, 1865.

17. Couthey to McKean, March 19, 1862, *ORN,* Ser. I, Vol. 17, p. 191; *Tri-Weekly Telegraph* [Houston], November 24, 1862; *Tri-Weekly News* [Galveston], March 8, 1862; *Daily Telegraph,* March 7, 1865. Kingsbury (F. F. Fenn) to Editor, *New York Herald,* March 1, 1864, Kingsbury Papers.

18. Kingsbury [F. F. Fenn] to Editor, *New York Herald,* March 1, 1864, Kingsbury Papers.

19. Farragut to Denison, December 10, 1862, *ORN,* Ser. I, Vol. 19, p. 400; Quintero to Hunter, October 18, 1861; Quintero to Benjamin, August 14, 1862, March 1, 1863; McGrath Tweed and Col. to San Román, June 24, 1861, Spearwater to San Román, September 2, 1864, San Román Papers, 2G 61, 63–67, 71; *New York Herald,* September 17, 1863; Kingsbury to Milton Kingsbury, October 20, 1862, Kingsbury Papers.

20. J. Marks to Dear Marks, January 22, 1863, *ORA,* Ser. I, Vol. 15, pp. 660–61; Marilyn McAdams Sibley, "Charles Stillman; A Case of Entrepreneurship on the Rio Grande, 1861–1865," *Southwestern Historical Quarterly* 77 (October 1973): 236.

21. Donahue to Stillman, June 26, July 30, August 12, September 1, November 9, December 9, 1861, January 7, 1862, Stillman Papers, as cited in Ellis, *SWHQ* 77: 208–09.

22. Chauncey D. Stillman, *Charles Stillman, 1810–1875* (New York: Privately published, 1956), pp. 14, 26.

23. Ibid., pp. 32–33.

24. Sibley, *Southwestern Historical Quarterly* 77: 230–31.

25. Ibid., pp. 231–32.

26. Ibid., pp. 232–36; Duff to Tarver, November 11, 1863, Dana to Stone, December 11, 1863, *ORA,* Ser. I, Vol. 26, Pt. 1, pp. 439–43, 842–44.

27. Shipment No. 142, Account sale of 530 bales of cotton ex. "Carioca," and Account sale of 465 bales of cotton ex. "Banshee," Stillman Papers, in Sibley, *SWHQ* 77: 236.

28. Seward to Lyons, February 23, 1864, Foreign Office Papers, F.O. 5/1007; Sibley, *SWHQ* 77: 228–29; see A. Sellow Roberts, "The Federal Government and Confederate Cotton," *American Historical Review* 32 (January 1927): 262–75.

29. Couthouy to McKean, March 19, 1862, *ORN,* Ser. I, Vol. 17, p. 192.

30. Bennett to Russell, April 25, 1863, Cunard to Archibald, February 26, 1864, Foreign Office Papers, F.O. 5/1007, 12356.

31. Russell to Lyons, April 24, 1863, Parliamentary Papers, 1863, 72: 507.

32. Lyons to Russell, May 8, 1863, Parliamentary Papers 1863, 72: 508.

33. Couthouy to McKean, March 19, 1862, *ORN,* Ser. I, Vol. 17, p. 192; Sibley, SWHQ 77: 227.

34. *House Executive Documents,* 38th Congress, 1st Session, No. 25, pp. 18–38.

35. Ibid., p. 1.

36. Lyons to Russell, July 25, 1862, Foreign Office Papers, F.O. 5/834.

37. Extracts from British Customs Ledgers Showing Cotton Imports from Mexico, 1861–1865, British Customs Records, Cus. 4/55–60, 5/62–74; *Cotton Supply Reporter* [Manchester], April, 1863–September, 1865; Parliamentary Papers, 1862, 65: 60, 1863, 65: 364, 1864, 30: 331.

38. Owsley, *King Cotton Diplomacy*, pp. 264–66; Owsley, *Dodd Essays*, p. 201.

39. Maguire to Cracroft, November 27, 1863, Foreign Office Papers, F.O. 50/378; *Weekly State Gazette* [Austin], March 22, 1865.

40. *New York Herald*, February 18, April 15, 1864; Kerby, p. 180, suggests that throughout 1863, at least 21,875 bales and perhaps as many as 29,167 bales of cotton crossed the Rio Grande into Mexico at Reynosa and Piedras Negras. The *New York Herald*, September 6, 1862, reports that cotton went from Texas to Monterrey, Mexico, at the rate of 2,000 bales each month. The dispatches of José Quintero to Judah Benjamin between March 1862 and August 1864, Confederate State Papers, Vols. 8, 58, show that while most of the cotton went directly to Matamoros, that portion going to Monterrey was also carried to Matamoros for export.

41. Compilations from Partial Listings of Cotton Exports of José San Román, February 1863–December 1864, San Román Papers, 2G62–66, 69, 70, 72.

42. Extracts from British Customs Ledgers Showing Cotton Imports from Mexico, 1861–1865, British Customs Records, Cus. 4/55–60, 5/62–74; Randolph to Dunlop, January 1, 1863, Foreign Office Papers, F.O. 50/378, reports that in January, 1863, some thirty ships were waiting for approximately 10,000 bales of cotton to be loaded at the Rio Grande.

43. Owsley, *King Cotton Diplomacy*, p. 263.

44. *Ibid.*, p. 266; Owsley's estimates were substantiated by figures published in the Manchester *Cotton Supply Reporter*, October 2, 1865.

45. *New York Times*, January 12, 1863, *Tri-Weekly Telegraph* [Houston], January 28, 1864.

46. Shufeldt to Seward, January 16, 1862, Consular Dispatches, Havana, as quoted in Ellis, *SWHQ* 77: 204.

47. Owsley, *Dodd Essays*, pp. 220–21. The seizure of merchant vessels at the mouth of the Rio Grande, known in diplomatic history as "the Matamoros seizures," in fact belongs in the same category as the blockade of St. Thomas, Havana, Nassau, Madeira, or other neutral ports. The United States squadron which lay in wait for merchantmen bringing contraband to Matamoros or using the Mexican port as a blockade-running base was at the same time carrying on a legitimate blockade of the Texas coast and, for the reason that the American cruisers on the Texan station had legitimate business here and an unchallenged right to lie near Matamoros, England—or any other neutral whose commerce was injured—had no legal grounds on which to protest the actual blockading of the neutral port of Matamoros. However, the blockading squadron at this point soon furnished other grounds on which to base a first-class controversy.

48. *New York Herald*, February 25, 1862, clipping in the Foreign Office Papers, Case of the "Labuan," F.O. 97/42; Crawford to Russell, March 1, 1862, Deposition of Charles Hargill, March 5, 1862; Statement of William Leetham and John Atkinson, March 15, 1862, Bailey and Leetham to Russell, March 15, 1862, Lyons to Russell, March 28, 1862, Foreign Office Papers, Case of the "Labuan," F.O. 97/42; Swarthout to McKean, February 3, 18, 1862, Swarthout to Tatham, March 17, 1862, *ORN*, Ser. I, Vol. 17, pp. 101, 106–07, Vol. 18, p. 81.

49. Blacker to Crawford, February 9, 1862, *ORN*, Ser. I, Vol. 18, pp. 109–10.

50. Quintero to Browne, March 4, 1862, Confederate State Papers, Vol. 58, *ORN*,

Ser. I, Vol. 18, p. 831; Pierce to Seward, March 21, 1862, Foreign Office Papers, Case of the "Labuan," F.O. 97/42, Consular Dispatches, Matamoros; Ellis, *SWHQ* 77: 204–05.

51. Lyons to Russell, May 8, 1862, Stuart to Seward, October 19, 1862, Foreign Office Papers, Case of the "Labuan," F.O. 97/42, 43.

52. Crawford to Lyons, March 11, 1862, Foreign Office Papers, Case of the "Labuan," F.O. 97/42.

53. Dunlap to Farragut, March 19, 1862, Droege, Oetling and Company to Tatham, March 19, 1862, Admiralty to Foreign Office, March 31, 1862, Dunlop to Lyongs, April 3, 1862, Russell to Lyons, March 29, 1862, Foreign Office Papers, F.O. 5/818; Quintero to Browne, March 22, 1862, Confederate State Papers, Vol. 58.

54. Tatham to Swarthout, March 16, 18, 1862, Swarthout to Tatham, March 17, 1862, *ORN*, Ser. I., Vol. 18, pp. 80–82.

55. Jonquieres to [Swarthout], March 18, 1862, Swarthout to Jonquieres, March 18, 1862, *ORN*, Ser. I, Vol. 18, pp. 83–85.

56. Swarthout to Farragut, March 18, 1862, *ORN*, Ser. I, Vol. 18, pp. 79–80.

57. Welles to Farragut, March 14, 1862, *ORN*, Ser. I, Vol. 18, p. 66.

58. Lyons to Russell, May 22, 23, 1862, Lyons to Archibald, December 13, 1862, Foreign Office Papers, Case of the "Labuan," F.O. 97/42, 43; *Richmond Enquirer*, July 29, 1862.

59. Pierce to Seward, September 21, 1862, Consular Dispatches, Matamoros.

60. Report of United States Consul Pierce at Matamoros, August 31, 1864, *ORN*, Ser. I, Vol. 21, p. 653.

61. Deposition of T. C. Haggart, October 4, 1863, Foreign Office Papers, F.O. 5/1181; Hammond to the President of the Manchester Chamber of Commerce, January 19, 1861, *Cotton Supply Reporter* [Manchester], February 1, 1861, Shufeldt to Seward, June 18, 1861, Consular Dispatches, Havana, quoted in Ellis, *SWHQ* 77: 179.

62. Registration and Trade Returns for Tampico and Vera Cruz, Foreign Office Papers, F.O. 207/43; Adams to Russell, May 12, 1862, Foreign Office Papers, Case of the "Labuan," F.O. 97/42; Adams to Dupont, April 9, 1863, Foreign Office Papers, F.O. 5/1235b; Chase to Seward, May 14, 27, October 13, 1863, Consular Dispatches, Tampico, quoted in Ellis, *SWHQ* 77: 179–80.

63. Farragut to Welles, September 15, November 16, 1864, *ORN*, Ser. I, Vol. 21, p. 644; Ellis, *SWHQ* 77: 194.

64. Bell to Farragut, June 2, 1863, Bell to Welles, June 2, 1863, *ORN*, Ser. I, Vol. 20, pp. 285–86, 287–88.

65. Ibid., Bell to Beardsley, June 1, 1863, *ORN*, Ser. I, Vol. 20, pp. 280–81.

66. Excerpts from Bell's Diary, May 29, 1863, Bell to Farragut, June 2, 1863, *ORN*, Ser. I, Vol. 20, pp. 757–58, 285–86.

67. Ibid.

68. Quintero to Benjamin, September 16, 1863, Confederate State Papers, Vol. 8; Statement of Jesse Thornham, Master of the *Sir William Peel* before the British Consulate General at New Orleans, September 29, 1863, Certificate of British Registry, Foreign Office Papers, F.O. 5/1181, 1183.

69. Kirby Smith to Magruder, June 28, 1863, Kirby Smith to Cooper, June 29, 1863, Bee to Turner, September 14, 1863, *ORN*, Ser. I, Vol. 20, p. 832; Vol. 26, Pt. 2, p. 229.

70. Woolsey to Bell, September 5, 1863, *ORN*, Ser. I, Vol. 20, p. 511; Quintero to Benjamin, September 16, 1863, Confederate State Papers, Vol. 58.

71. Rolando to Hood, September 15, 1863, Milne to Lyons, October 20, 1863, Deposition of Robert Clark, September 29, 1863, Deposition of Charles Pycraft, October 1, 1863, Foreign Office Papers, F.O. 5/1181, 1183; Rolando to Bell, September 11, 1863, Rolando to Welles, September 11, 1863, *ORN*, Ser. I, Vol. 20, pp. 568–69, 569–70;

Depositions of Robert Clark, September 29, 1863, and James Garety, January 7, 1864, Foreign Office Papers, F.O. 5/1182, 1183, stated that the *Peel* was loaded with cotton directly from Texas, and was going to Havana to be fitted out as a privateer.

72. Rolando to Bell, September 18, 1863, Shock to Bell, November 24, 1863, *ORN*, Ser. I, Vol. 20, pp. 570, 578–79.

73. Ruiz to Bell, September 18, 1863, Milmo and Company to Ruiz, September 14, 1863, *ORN*, Ser. I, Vol. 20, pp. 574–81; Rolando to Hood, September 15, 1863, Lyons to Russell, December 7, 1863, Foreign Office Papers, F.O. 5/1181.

74. Rolando to Fox, October 3, 1863, *ORN*, Ser. I, Vol. 20, pp. 579–81; Lyons to Russell, December 7, 1863, Foreign Office Papers, F.O. 5/1181; Magruder to Boggs, October 17, 1863, *ORA*, Ser. I, Vol. 26, Pt. 2, p. 332.

75. Lyons to Seward, March 1, 1864, Foreign Office Papers, F.O. 5/1182.

76. Lyons to Russell, March 22, 1864, Foreign Office Papers, F.O. 5/1183.

77. Lyons to Russell, December 21, 1863, Foreign Office Papers, F.O. 5/1181; Welles, *Diary*, 2: 4.

78. Lyons to Russell, June 20, 1864, Coppell to Russell, June 20, 1864, Order of the Prize Court, June 3, 1865, Foreign Office Papers, F.O. 5/1183, 1184.

79. Lyons to Russell, March 11, June 20, 28, 1864, Foreign Office Papers, F.O. 5/1183; Seward to Stanton, March 13, 1862, quoted in Abbey, *Journal of Southern History* 11: 223.

80. Milne to Zurn, December 22, 1863, Foreign Office Papers, F.O. 5/1182.

81. Blacker to Jonson, June 9, 1862, Jonson to Russell, June 20, 1862, Parliamentary Papers, 1863, 72: 515–516; Lyons to Russell, January 12, 1864, Document Number 9, Trial of the "Valante," Foreign Office Papers, F.O. 5/1181, 1183; Tyler, *Vidaurri*, pp. 150–51.

82. Log of the *Peterhoff*, February 20, 1863, Butterfield to Archibald, March 10, 1863, Archibald to Russell, March 30, 1863, Archibald to Lyons, April 6, 1863, Foreign Office Papers, Case of "Springbok" and "Peterhoff," F.O. 5/1235a; Redgate to Halstead, March [?], 1863, *The Seizure of the Peterhoff*, (London: Effingham Wilson, 1863), p. 6; *The Times* [London], December 12, 24, 1862.

83. *The Times* [London], April 2, 1863; *London Economist*, April 4, 1863.

84. Archibald to Lyons, April 6, 1863, Seward to Lyons April 17, 1863, Lyons to Russell, April 13, 27, 1863, Foreign Office Papers, Cases of "Springbok" and "Peterhoff," F.O. 5/1235a; Seward to Welles, April 20, 1863, Notations of Welles, April 22, 1863, Welles, Diary, 2: 282–84. Although Welles surrendered the mails, he did not retreat from his position. "It is a great error," he noted in his diary, "which has its origin in the meddlesome disposition and loose and inconsiderate action of Mr. Seward. Having in a weak moment conceded away an incontestable national right, he has sought to extricate himself, not by retracing his steps, but by involving the President, who confides in him and oven whom he has, at times, an unfortunate influence."

85. United States vs. Steamer Peterhoff and Cargo, July 31, 1863, Foreign Office Papers, Cases of "Springbok" and "Peterhoff," F.O. 5/1235b. The decision of Judge Betts made a strong case for seizures on the grounds of ultimate destination of goods and was based primarily upon British precedents. See the Appendix for an excerpt of the decision.

86. Edward D. Smith, *The Peterhoff*, An argument addressed to the Court by Edward Delafield Smith (New York: John W. Amerman, 1863), p. 9; Herbert W. Briggs, *The Doctrine of Continuous Voyage* (Baltimore: The Johns Hopkins Press, 1929) p. 55.

87. Montague Bernard, *A Historical Account of the Neutrality of Great Britain During the American Civil War* (London: Longsmen, Green, Reeder, and Dyer, 1870), p. 315.

88. Briggs, p. 55.

89. Archibald to Stuart, August 20, 1863, Memorandum: "Peterhoff" and Cargo, February 20, 1868, Foreign Office Papers, Cases of "Springbok" and "Peterhoff," F.O. 5/1235b, 1235c; Briggs, p. 56.

90. Owsley, *Dodd Essays*, pp. 220, 21

91. *Journal of Commerce and Daily Shipping and Mercantile Advertiser* [Liverpool], tabulations from issues, 1861–1864.

92. Lyons to Russell, January 12, 1864, Russell to Lyons, February 5, 1864, Foreign Office Papers, F.O. 5/1181.

93. Russell to Stuart, September 18, 1863, Russell Papers, P.R.O. 30/22/97.

94. Russell to Lyons, April 25, June 13, 20, 1863, Russell Papers, P.R.O. 30/22/97.

95. Somerset and Grey to Rodney, February 3, 1864, Great Britain, Admiralty Papers, Public Record Office, London, Adm. 13/5, hereafter cited as Admiralty Papers.

96. Lyons to Russell, October 16, 1863, Foreign Office Papers, F.O. 5/894; Welles, *Diary*, 1: 468.

97. Standing Orders for British squadron on North American and West Indian Station, July 1, 1862, Admiralty Papers, 13/184; Milne Memo, September 9, 1862, Admiralty Papers, Adm. 128/56; Supplemental Instructions for Cruisers employed on the Coast of America, November 12, 1861, Milne to Watson, August 8, 1862, Admiralty Papers, Adm. 128/56, 58.

6
THE TRADE DIES

The French Assist the Confederates

On July 30, 1864, Confederate Colonel John Ford and his mounted riflemen retook Brownsville. Although sick and confined to bed, Ford continued to issue orders with the aid of his adjutant, Captain James H. Fry. He sent Colonel Dan Showalter's regiment to reconnoiter the Union forces which had retreated downriver. Advancing to within six miles of Brazos Santiago, they found the Federals strongly entrenched there and outnumbering Ford's troops nearly three to one. They also reported that the Federals had the services of the steamboats *Matamoros* and *Mustang* seized from King, Kenedy, and Stillman. Ordered to maintain their observations of the enemy, they dug into positions from which they engaged in daily skirmishes.[1]

Across the river General Juan Cortina held Matamoros for President Juárez with 1,200 men and eighteen cannons. Once the Federals retreated from Brownsville, Cortina became friendly with the Confederates and opened a correspondence with them. Cortina assured Ford that both he and Juárez desired to reestablish "pleasant and mutually advantageous" commercial relations between Matamoros and Brownsville.[2]

On August 22, Ford received news that 400 French sailors had landed on the Mexican side of the river and taken possession of Bagdad. This action marked a departure from earlier French policy, which was torn between aiding the Confederates to secure their independence, fear of goods reaching the forces of Mexican President Benito Juárez through Matamoros, and their own designs on Texas. Thus, the appearance of the French on the Rio Grande may have caused the Confederates some apprehension.

Two years earlier, the French consul in Texas, Benjamin Theron, had addressed a letter to then Texas Governor Francis Lubbock, in which he offered his country's protection for an independent Texas. At the same time the French vice-consul in Richmond approached Texas Senator William S. Oldham with the proposal. A protectorate over Texas would have guaranteed a consistent and independent cotton supply, and placed a buffer state between its Mexican colony and the Confederacy. Confederate Secretary of State Judah Benjamin, long suspicious of Louis Napoleon's desires for empire, believed that a French coup in Texas would undermine the "cornerstone of Confederate foreign policy." Therefore, on October 17, 1862, he ordered Theron to leave the country.[3] These aggressive attitudes of Paris disturbed Prince Maximilian, who feared United States's intervention in Mexico, and, therefore, constantly sought a modus vivendi with Washington. With the Federals holding Brazos Santiago, Ford dispatched two envoys to Bagdad to discuss the maintenance of the Rio Grande trade with "the officer in command of the French forces." They were instructed to conclude an agreement "by which our supplies can be passed over the Rio Grande, within [French] lines, and transported to Fort Brown" on the Texas side.[4] The following day the commander of the French contingent, Captain A. Vernon, replied that Ford would "not suffer in anything on account of my presence here." And "if the exigencies of war should take me to Matamoros," he continued, "you may rest assured that I shall see that all persons and property covered by the flag of your nation are respected."[5]

However, the agreement between the French and the Confederates angered Cortina. Accusing the Confederates of aiding the French, he encouraged his soldiers to snipe at Confederate pickets across the river. By the end of the month, Confederates were returning the fire. Cortina then stopped trade across the river and planted his artillery along the riverbanks with the muzzles pointing toward Bronsville. To Colonel Henry M. Day, the Union commander at Brazos Santiago, he suggested a joint operation against Fort Brown. Cortina "hates Americans, particularly Texans," Ford reported. "He has an old and deep-seated grudge against Brownsville. He knows his career is nearly closed. If he could force his way through our lines, plunder our people, and get within the Yankee lines, it would be a finale he would delight in."[6]

On the morning of September 6, Cortina divided his command, sending 600 men and two field pieces upriver to cross above Brownsville, and took the remainder some fourteen miles below the town. Under the cover of a heavy rainfall and an artillery barrage on the positions held by Colonel Showalter's Fourth Arizona Cavalry, he crossed the river near Palmito Ranch with 800 men. Apparently, he hoped to draw the bulk of Ford's brigade downriver, leaving Brownsville open to attack by his troops above the town. However, Showalter, "as chivalrous a man who ever drew a sword [when] not under the influence of liquor,"[7] had "recourse to the bottle" during the engagement and lost control of his regiment, which broke and retreated to Brownsville, thereby incidentally foiling Cortina's strategy. Showalter followed his troops "in a maudlin condition," and erroneously reported that a strong Federal column from Brazos Santiago was advancing on the fort.[8]

Anticipating that both "Cortina and the Federals would be on [him] early the next day," Ford took defensive measures.[9] He sent an urgent request to the French for assistance and he resorted to the military theatrics that had been used so successively against Union General George McClellan by General Magruder before the gates of Richmond in the summer of 1862. He had only 300 men in the city, but Ford constantly marched them from place to place and had them change uniforms often. As he had learned that they were delaying their attack until he had left for Palmito Ranch, he also made himself highly visible to the Mexicans across the river. The rain continued throughout the day and evening.[10]

The expected attack did not come. High water and a near mutiny among Cortina's staff prevented the Mexicans from crossing the river. The mutiny centered around four officers, including Colonel Servando Canales, a longtime friend of Ford's, who refused to attack the Texans. Ford seized the opportunity to write Cortina asking whether a state "of war exists between your government and that of the Confederate States."[11]

As Cortina hesitated, Ford moved against the Federals encamped at San Martin Ranch near Palmito. In the early afternoon of September 9, 370 Texas troopers under Lieutenant Colonel George H. Giddings charged the Union positions. Although outnumbered almost two to one, they quickly turned in the Federal pickets and drove their main body back to the mouth of the Rio Grande. Among the prisoners taken were twelve Mexicans, who revealed that about 300 Cortinists had joined forces with the Federals.[12]

Although he made no further attempt to attack Brownsville, Cortina kept his guns trained on the Confederates for another week. After he removed them, negotiations were opened which culminated in the reestablishment of"peaceable relations" on September 22. But Ford, suspicious of Cortina's motives, reported that "until the French forces . . . take possession of Matamoros, we shall not relax our preparations."[13]

On September 26, 1864, French forces under General Thomas Mejia occupied Matamoros, and Cortina fled into the interior. The French and Confederates exchanged notes and visits and "peace and repose [prevailed] upon both banks of the Rio Grande."[14] Meanwhile, a Union evacuation from the Rio Grande left only a 950-man garrison on Brazos Island. The Confederates quickly took control of the Texas side of the river to Point Isabel. The border became so peaceful that, when General James Slaughter assumed command in the autumn of 1864, he transferred or furloughed two-thirds of Ford's brigade. By the beginning of 1865, only Colonel Giddings's battalion and a few units of home guards remained at Fort Brown.[15]

During the closing months of 1864, the cotton trade flowed smoothly through Matamoros. The streets of Brownsville were churned to dust as hundreds of cotton wagons rolled toward the river. Visiting Matamoros near the end of August, Colonel Ford found it to be

> a city of strange denizens, a motely [sic] crowd. There were millions of dollars of merchandise in the place. Every room, every niche capable of being occupied and of holding a man was rented at a large price. Never was a place of the same size crowded with more people, and made a display of more goods.[16]

At the same time United States Consul Leonard Pierce at Matamoros complained that "large quantities of merchandise now cross the river daily for the interior of Texas."[17] In October and November more than 600,000 pounds of ordinance were transported from Matamoros through Brownsville and into the interior of Texas. From Monterrey José Quintero wrote, "We have never before been in such a favorable condition as we are at present in regard to our intercourse with Mexico. There will be no difficulty to export (in a quiet way) any arms and ammunition we may purchase in this country." And in his last dispatch to Richmond Quintero observed, "Goods come in as fast as possible."[18]

In the first weeks of 1865, the trade was slowed by rains that caused many cotton trains on the trails to Brownsville to become mud-bound. By late February, however, a correspondent for the Houston *Tri-Weekly Telegraph* noted that cotton stocks in Matamoros were large and growing. He predicted that cotton prices would soon drop. As peace rumors spread, merchants rushed to sell their cotton before the war ended, reopening all the Southern ports.[19] Nevertheless, prices held at thirty-two to thirty-four cents per pound with the approach of spring. As the risk in the Matamoros trade declined, shipping charges to Liverpool fell from four cents to one and one-half cents and two cents per pound and large quantities of cotton were shipped to England. In mid-March United States General Lew Wallace counted "at least 100 vessels of all kinds lying off Bagdad." He added that "neither the port of New Orleans nor that of Baltimore can present to-day such a promise of commercial activity."[20]

During the winter of 1864–1865, friction grew between Colonel Ford and his colleague, General James E. Slaughter, recently appointed commander of Confederate forces in the Western Sub-District of Texas. Slaughter outranked Ford, who appeared to resent having to give up his prerogatives to him.[21]

Some excitement was created in the Confederate camp when E. Dorsey Etchison, who replaced Leonard Pierce as United States consul in Matamoros, was expelled by the French. Reportedly he was handed his passports because of his personal confrontations with Confederates in town and because he raised the United States flag over the consulate in celebration of the capture of Fort Fisher at Wilmington, North Carolina. The consul's conduct embarrassed Washington. General Wallace, describing him as "a humbug, a drunkard, and a fool," reported:

> His official conduct was unworthy of our Government. He has mutilated the books of his consulate. He charged our own citizens unwarrantable fees, and I am assured on excellent authority that it can be established that he has in his pockets several thousand dollars in gold not his own. Even his washerwoman was left unpaid.[22]

As Etchison was leaving, the captain of the U.S.S. *Seminole* found him "on shore . . . surrounded by a suspicious class of rebel refugees which, . . . he is taking out of the country with him, and so much under the influence of liquor that he came off disgusted."[23] "It is lamentable," wrote Captain George Emmons, of the U.S.S. *Lackawanna*, "that at a place of so much importance . . . and at this particular time . . . we have not a better representative on shore to look after our interests."[24]

The Confederacy Collapses

On January 14, 1865, General Lew Wallace, who commanded the Union army's Middle Department (West Virginia, Pennsylvania, and Maryland), requested permission from General-in-Chief Ulysses S. Grant to undertake a peace mission to the Rio Grande. He advised Grant that he had received reliable intelligence from a former schoolmate from Texas that "the rebel soldiery in Western Texas, particularly those at Brownsville," were ready to abandon the Confederate cause. Proposing to "invite the commandant at Brownsville to an interview on the old battle-field of Palo Alta [sic]," Wallace confidently predicated that "if the man's a soldier, I'll wager you a month's pay that I win."[25] Grant assented and Wallace was soon on his way to Matamoros.

On March 11, after a few days of preliminary negotiations, Wallace met Slaughter and Ford under a flag of truce at Point Isabel. "Very early in the interview," Wallace concluded "that both General Slaughter and Colonel Ford were not only willing but anxious to find some ground upon which they could honorably get from under what they admitted to be a failing Confederacy."[26] Exceeding their authority, the two Confederate officers joined Wallace in drafting terms for the capitulation "of the Trans-Mississippi States and Territories," and for "the re-establishment of the authority of the United States Government over all the region above designated."[27]

As soon as the conference adjourned, Slaughter sent a copy of the proposed agreement to General John Walker, the Confederate commander in Texas, requesting that he forward a copy to General Kirby Smith's office in Shreveport. Walker refused, and bitterly wrote Slaughter that he regretted "that you should have consented to entertain, or rather receive, the proposals . . . made," since to accede "to them would be the blackest treason to the Confederacy."[28] Walker then took it upon himself to address an angry reply to Wallace. He stated that the memory of anyone who accepted such terms would be rendered "infamous for all future time. Stripped of all disguise," he charged:

> Your proposition is nothing less than that we of the Trans-Mississippi States are to lay down our arms, surrender at discretion, take an oath of allegiance to the United States Government, and in return to accept such terms of amnesty, pardon, or foreign exile as our conquerors shall graciously accord us. When the States of the Trans-Mississippi united their destiny with the Confederacy of Southern States we pledged ourselves to share their good and evil fortune; and . . . it is still our unalterable purpose to share the common danger and the common fate. . . .
>
> It would be folly in me to pretend that we are not tired of a war that has sown sorrow and desolation broadcast over our land; but we will accept no other than an honorable peace. With 300,000 men yet in the field, we would be the most abject of mankind if we should now basely yield all that we have been fighting for during the last four years, namely nationality and the rights of self-government. With the blessing of God, we will yet achieve these, and extort from your own Government all that we ask.[29]

Rejection of the Wallace peace proposal prolonged the struggle in Texas for only two months. Although the troops in Texas were better fed, armed, and equipped than were their comrades east of the Mississippi, the lack of funds with which to pay them lowered their morale. By the end of April 1865, soldiers in Texas were deserting by tens and twenties every night. A general demoralization soon developed throughout the department. As early as January 7, General Kirby Smith had confided to his mother that "God in his mercy and wisdom is chastizing us with the heavy hand of misfortune."[30] A few days later he commissioned his friend General Camille J. Polignac to visit Confederate agent John Slidell in France with the appeal that "our cause has reached a crisis, which calls for foreign intervention."[31] On February 1, with hope of success rapidly fading, he asked a businessman, who was on his way to Mexico City, to convey to Maximilian the offer of his services in the event the Confederacy was overthrown.[32] Early in May 1865, Colonel Theodore H. Barrett, in temporary command of the Federals at Brazos Island, received news of General

Robert E. Lee's surrender at Appomattox on April 9, and moved upriver to secure Brownsville for the Union. On May 12, he met some resistance at Palmito Ranch, but the Confederates soon retreated through the underbrush leaving a number of horses, a few head of cattle, and some supplies. Setting fire to the ranch, the Federals pushed several miles further upriver and bivouacked at the White Ranch.[33]

The next morning, the Federals resumed their advances, but the Confederates retreated slowly, putting up strong rearguard resistance. In midafternoon, Colonel Ford arrived from Fort Brown with reinforcements and six 12-pound field guns. Immediately taking command, Ford concealed his cavalry in the chaparral, positioned the field guns in the center, and two companies of Colonel Giddings's batallion on the right. The retreating Confederates had drawn the Union skirmishers far ahead of their main body, and Ford ordered his troops on the left and right to attack and close off their retreat. In the center the field artillery did its deadly work. Quickly following up this successful ambush, he unleashed a swift and determined counterattack on the main body of Federal troops, sending them reeling back upon Brazos Santiago. As night fell and the exhausted armies crouched in the marshes near Brazos Santiago, they were unaware that they had fought the last battle of the Civil War, ironically a Confederate victory under the command of an officer who had sought to surrender.[34]

The Trans-Mississippi Department was crumbling. Even as Colonel Ford counterattacked, the governors of Louisiana and Arkansas petitioned General Kirby Smith to come to terms with the United States government, "that peace may be restored to the country."[35] Confusion and disorder soared throughout his command. A young woman who had moved from Louisiana to Tyler, Texas, wrote that "anarchy and confusion reign over all. Jayhawking is the order of the day. The soldiers are disbanding throughout the Department and seizing Government property wherever they can find it. . . . All work is over and all who can are going home."[36] At Brownsville, General Slaughter reported that "at least one half have already, or will, desert their colors," because "they say 'we are whipped, tis [sic] useless for the Trans-Mississippi Department to undertake to accomplish what the cis-Mississippi department has failed to do.' "[37] Faced with anarchy, General Edmund Kirby Smith surrendered to

Major General Edward R. S. Canby at Galveston, Texas, on June 2, 1865.[38] The Confederate Matamoros trade was dead.

The Matamoros trade had been essential to the war effort in the Trans-Mississippi Department. Almost alone, this vital artery had sustained the department during the war. Without it, the Trans-Mississippi might have collapsed before Appomattox. At the height of the conflict, Confederate Trans-Mississippi Commander General Kirby Smith called Matamoros the "only channel" through which the Confederacy could obtain many necessities.[39] Unfortunately for the Confederates, the port was thousands of miles from the most important scenes of the conflict, and serviced by inadequate overland transportation facilities. Thus isolated in a far corner of a nation dedicated to States Rights, the trade never received the control and nurturing from the Richmond government necessary for its full development.

The importance of the Matamoros trade is difficult to assess since no complete record exists of the distribution of the goods imported there. Writers have differed widely on the subject. In his monumental work on Confederate diplomacy, Frank L. Owsley indicates that the Union blockaders at the Rio Grande effectively curtailed the trade.[40] Yet the many and varied reports of those associated with the trade throughout the war provide evidence for a quite different conclusion. On the other hand, some regional historians have tended to exaggerate the importance of the trade. Tom Lea, in the *King Ranch,* implies that the only obstacle to the Matamoros trade's becoming the lifeline for the entire Confederacy was the shortsightedness of the Richmond bureaucracy.[41] Apparently Lea feels that Southern leaders, blinded by the hope of British intervention to break the blockade, refused to take the necessary steps to organize and administer the Matamoros trade efficiently from the beginning.

But had Richmond bent all of its energies to developing the route, enormous difficulties would have remained. First, the determination of Texans to organize and control the trade for their own benefit conflicted with the efforts of the Confederate agents. Almost always working at cross purposes, the two parties were unable to reach a modus vivendi that would have made the trade serve their war purposes well. Secondly, the Rio Grande lacked the port facilities necessary to handle commerce of the magnitude demanded by the Confederate cause. Thirdly, the inadequate internal transportation system, covering hundreds of perilous miles before the goods reached the nearest railroad head, could hardly be substantially improved upon by the beleaguered Confederate government under wartime conditions. Also, while the Federal blockaders were not so effective as some have represented them to be, their presence did much to discourage and slow the development of the Matamoros trade. The South did not have a navy sufficient to protect the merchantmen calling at the Rio Grande from the Federal cruisers that stopped and boarded ships at will.

Perhaps an even greater difficulty for the Confederates was the internal disorders in Mexico. The Rio Grande valley was in constant political turmoil as many Mexican factions, ranging from contending governmental parties to plundering groups of bandits, struggled to gain control of the region and the lucrative trade. These embroilments prevented the Confederates from establishing the strong and permanent diplomatic and commercial relationships so necessary for the full fruition of the trade. Having to deal with first one faction and then another, they were constantly frustrated in their attempts to get the Mexicans to reduce tariffs and curtail profiteering.

For their part the French failed to fulfill Southern expectations for cordial relations. The Maximilian regime was placed in a dilemma by the Matamoros trade. The town served as a commercial center for both the Confederates and the *Juaristas*. While eager to cash in on the lucrative Confederate trade, the Maximilian government found it difficult to distinguish between goods destined for Texas and those earmarked for the Mexican patriots. Further, the French, quietly seeking ways to normalize their relations with the United States, were not eager to offend the Washington government further by an official commercial agreement with the Confederates.

The attitude of the English was, at times, disappointing to the Confederates. London often acquiesced in the seizing of valuable cargoes destined for the Southern war effort via Matamoros. Having set the precedent for the seizure of neutral commerce, the British found it difficult to protest too strongly against the actions of the United States cruisers. Furthermore, they felt that in the future they might again have to stretch international law governing blockades to their own benefit. Orders were issued to British cruisers in the gulf not to interfere with Union seizures of British commerce. Thus, while Whitehall, in response to pressure from its shippers, lodged formal protests against the seizures, leaders in the foreign office and the admiralty took a much more restrained position.[42]

Military operations along the Rio Grande owe their significance entirely to their impact on the cotton trade. There were comparatively few rebel troops throughout Texas, and the state had a large number of Unionists who rallied behind ex-governor Sam Houston until his death in 1863, but the Federals, before General Lee's surrender, were in no position to commit the manpower and logistical support necessary to ensure the success of a major invasion of Texas from the Rio Grande. Texas and Confederate forces were stationed in the Brownsville-Matamoros area to protect the flow of trade from bandits and Federals, and Federal troops were sent there only to interrupt it.[43]

Throughout the conflict the specie profits and the commodities received in exchange for its cotton provided the state of Texas with a prosperity that few other Southern states enjoyed during the war. A Federal scout passing through the Trans-Mississippi region in the spring of 1865 found "Arkansas literally starved out" and Louisiana nearly as destitute. He noted the steady stream of refugees from those states into Texas, and reported the latter to be well stocked with the necessitites of life.[44]

The close economic ties established between Texans and Mexicans along the Rio Grande did not survive the surrender of the Trans-Mississippi Department. Economic collapse struck the valley as thousands who had swarmed into the region to take advantage of the wartime cotton boom departed overnight. The Texas-Mexican commercial links and partnerships were dissolved, and as the Mexican struggle against Maximilian continued, the restoration of prewar avenues of trade was delayed. Old tensions that had been temporarily covered over by the mutually beneficial economic arrangements resurfaced to plague border relations once again.

One of the most lasting effects of the trade was that the economic prosperity that accompanied it laid the foundation for financial empires on both sides of the river. Men in the cotton business accumulated "vast and immense fortunes," wrote John Warren Hunter.[45] In Texas, Richard King, Charles

Stillman, Mifflin Kenedy, and many others invested their earnings in cattle and other enterprises. On the Mexican side of the border also war fortunes were created, among which the most notable were those of Patricio Milmo and José Oliver. Merchants in Monterrey garnered profits that bolstered the economic foundation of present-day Monterrey, the country's third largest city and the financial capital of northern Mexico.

With the end of hostilities, the Matamoros trade fell off rapidly, although it did continue as a main supply route for Juárez as he continued his struggle against Maximilian. After the French forces withdrew from Mexico and the Maximilian regime was overthrown, economic and social conditions along the lower Rio Grande soon returned to their prewar status. Matamoros received few ships, its population diminished, and it subsided into the sleepy little town that it had been before *Los Algodones*.

Notes

1. Fry to Tobin, August 4, 1864, Ford to Kearney, August 16, 1864, *Official Records of the Union and Confederate Armies* [ORA], Ser. I, Vol. 41, Pt. 1, pp. 185–86, Pt. 2, pp. 1069–70.

2. Pierce to Seward, September 1, 1864, Consular Dispatches, Matamoros, John S. Ford, *Rip Ford's Texas*, Stephen B. Oates, editor (Austin: University of Texas Press, 1963), p. 369.

3. Pierce to Seward, September 1, 1864, Consular Dispatches, Matamoros, O. F. Aldis, "Louis Napoleon and the Southern Confederacy," *North American Review* 129 (October 1879): 344, 349–50; Elaine Carland Crook, "Benjamin, Theron and the French Designs in Texas During the Civil War," *Southwestern Historical Quarterly* 68 (1965): 434–37.

4. Ford to The Officer in Command of the French Forces on the Rio Grande, August 24, 1864, *ORA*, Ser. I, Vol. 41, p. 1089.

5. Vernon to the Colonel Commanding the Confederate Forces on the Rio Grande, August 25, 1864, *ORA*, Ser. I, Vol. 41, p. 1089.

6. Pierce to Seward, August 31, 1864, *Official Records of the Union and Confederate Navies* [ORN], Ser. I, Vol. 21, p. 652; Pierce to Seward, September 1, 1864, Consular Dispatches, Matamoros; Ford to Swyer, September 3, 1864, Ford to Slaughter, September 5, 1864, Combe to Ford, September 5, 1864, *ORA*, Ser. I, Vol. 41, pp. 909, 911, 912; Stephen B. Oates, "John S. Ford: Prudent Cavalryman, C.S.A.," *Southwestern Historical Quarterly* 64 (1961): 306; *Weekly State Gazette* [Austin], September 28, 1864.

7. Quintero to Benjamin, September 5, 1864, Confederate State Papers, Vol. 58; Combe to Ford; September 6, 1864, Pierce to Herron, September 8, 1864, *ORA*, Ser. I, Vol. 41, Pt. 3, pp. 101, 912; Kerby, p. 370.

8. Kerby, p. 370.

9. Ford to Vernon, September 6, 1864, *ORA*, Ser. I, Vol. 41, Pt. 3, p. 912; Kerby, p. 370.

10. Ford to Vernon, September 6, 1864, *ORA,* Ser. I, Vol. 41, Pt. 3, p. 912; Irby, p. 180.

11. Statement of Mexican Officers who defied Cortina, October 4, 1864, Ford Military Correspondence, cited in Irby, p. 180; Kerby, p. 370; William J. Hughes, *Rebellious Ranger: Rip Ford and the Old Southwest* (Norman: University of Oklahoma Press, 1944), p. 228.

12. Ford to Commanding Officer, U.S. Forces at Brazos Island, September 12, 1864, Day to Ford, September 13, 1864, *ORA,* Ser. I, Vol. 12, Pt. 3, pp. 931–32, 947; Skerrett to Woolsey, September 13, 1864, *ORN,* Ser. I, Vol. 21, p. 651.

13. Drayton to Walker, September 21, 26, 1864, Ford and Cortina correspondence, September 22, 23, 1864, *ORA,* Ser. I, Vol. 41, Pt. 3, pp. 957–59.

14. Fitzpatrick to Benjamin, September 27, 1864, Quintero to Benjamin, November 5, 1864, Confederate State Papers, Vols. 58, 59; Drayton and Mejia correspondence, September 28, 1864, Drayton to Walker, October 1, 1864, *ORA,* Ser. I, Vol. 41, Pt. 3, pp. 973, 74; *Dallas Times Herald,* October 15, 1864.

15. Quintero to Kirby Smith, October 21, 1864, Confederate State Papers, Vol. 58; Walker to Slaughter, October 1, 1864, ORA, Ser. I, Vol. 41, Pt. 3, pp. 972–73; Kerby, p. 371; *Weekly State Gazette* [Austin], September 28, 1864.

16. Ford, *Rip Ford's Texas,* p. 403.

17. Report of Pierce, August 31, 1864, *ORN,* Ser. I, Vol. 21, pp. 652–53; Quintero to Kirby Smith, October 21, 1864, Confederate State Papers, Vol. 58; *Dallas Times Herald,* October 15, 1864.

18. Quintero to Kirby Smith, October 21, 1864, Quintero to Benjamin, December 7, 1864, Confederate State Papers, Vol. 58.

19. *Tri-Weekly Telegraph* [Houston], December 16, 1864, January 16, February 24, March 8, 1865.

20. Wallace to Grant, March 14, 1865, *ORA,* Ser. I, Vol. 48, Pt. 1, p. 1279; *Daily News* [Galveston], February 23, 1865, *Tri-Weekly Telegraph* [Houston], February 24, March 8, 1865.

21. Oates, *Southwestern Historical Quarterly* 64: 309.

22. Wallace to Grant, March 14, 1865, ORA, Ser. I, Vol. 48, Pt. 1, p. 1279; Emmons to Palmer, February 18, 1865, Mejia to Emmons, February 19, 1865, ORN, Ser. I, Vol. 22, pp. 42, 46; *Weekly State Gazette* [Austin], March 29, 1865.

23. Emmons to Palmer, February 18, 1865, *ORN,* Ser. I, Vol. 22, p. 42.

24. Ibid.

25. Wallace to Grant, January 14, 1865, *ORA,* Ser. I, Vol. 47, Pt. 1, pp. 512–23. General Lew Wallace is better known for having written *Ben-Hur.*

26. Wallace to Grant, March 14, 1865, *ORA,* Ser. I, Vol. 48, Pt. 1, pp. 1276–77.

27. Ibid., p. 1281.

28. Walker to Slaughter, March 27, 1865, *ORA,* Ser. I, Vol. 43, Pt. 1, p. 1448.

29. Walker to Wallace, March 25, 1865, *ORA,* Ser. I, Vol. 43, Pt. 1, pp. 461–62.

30. Kirby Smith to Mother, January 7, 1865, Kirby Smith Papers; Report of C. S. Bell, [no date], Magruder to Boggs, April 29, 1865, *ORA,* Ser. I, Vol. 48, Pt. 2, pp. 398–403, 1285.

31. Kirby Smith to Slidell, January 9, 1865, Kirby Smith Papers.

32. Kirby Smith to Rose, February 1, 1865, *ORA,* Ser. I, Vol. 48, Pt. 1, p. 359.

33. Report to Theodore Barrett, August 10, 1865, *ORA,* Ser. I, Vol. 48, Pt. 1, pp. 265–66; John M. Swisher, Memoirs (unpublished), Eugene C. Barker Library of Texas History, University of Texas, Austin, p. 76; *Weekly State Gazette* [Austin], May 5, 1865; Irby, p. 207; Larios, *MidAmerica* 40: 88–89.

34. Report of Theodore Barrett, August 10, 1865, *ORA*, Ser. I, Vol. 48, Pt. 1, pp. 265–66; Swisher, Memoirs; Irby, p. 207.

35. Memorandum, May 13, 1865, Kirby Smith Papers.

36. Windham, *Journal of Southern History* 27: 168.

37. Slaughter to Magruder, May 17, 1865, Kirby Smith Papers.

38. Smith to Magruder, June 2, 1865, Kirby Smith Papers.

39. Kirby Smith to Magruder, July 17, 1863, *ORA*, Ser. I, Vol. 53, p. 885; Tyler, *Southwestern Historical Quarterly* 73: 477.

40. Owsley, King Cotton Diplomacy, pp. 258–59.

41. Lea, *King Ranch*, 1: 191, 193.

42. Somerset and Grey to Rodney, February 3, 1864, Great Britain, Admiralty Papers, Public Record Office, London, Adm. 13/5.

43. Ford, Memoirs, 5: 914–17.

44. Report of C. S. Bell, c. May, 1854, in Herron to Reynolds, May 11, 1865, *ORA*, Ser. I, Vol. 48, Pt. 2, p. 401.

45. Hunter, "The Fall of Brownsville," p. 5.

APPENDIX

Excerpts from the Decree of Condemnation by Judge Betts of the "Peterhoff" and Cargo. United States District Court. July term 1863. Taken from Great Britain Foreign Office, Cases of "Springbok" and "Peterhoff," F.O. 5/1235.

If the Peterhoff had on board goods contraband of war which were destined, when they left England, for the use of the enemy, and not for sale or consumption in Mexico, the mere destination of the vessel to Mexican waters, and even the mere intended landing of the goods at Matamoras, on their way to the enemy's country, would not exempt the vessel or her contraband cargo from lawful capture as prize of war. . . . It is equally well settled, that the ulterior destination of contraband determines the character of the trade no matter how circuitous the route by which they are to reach that destination; that, even though the Peterhoff was destined to Mexican waters, and the goods were there to be unladen, yet if they were to be transported thence, by any mode of conveyance to the enemy's country, the trade was unlawful; that the trade in contraband goods with the enemy's country, though through neutral territory, is likewise unlawful; that the goods so shipped through neutral territory, even though they may be unladen and transshipped, are liable to condemnation; that, if the voyage of the Peterhoff was of such a character, it was an attempt to carry on trade with the enemy by the circuitous route of Mexican waters or a Mexican port, which the law will not countenance; that under such circumstances her voyage was illegal at its inception; and that she and her goods were liable to seizure at the instant it commenced. . . . So also, the inception of the voyage completes the offense; and from the moment that the vessel, with the contraband articles on board, quit her port on the hostile demonstration, she may be legally captured. It is not necessary to wait until the goods are actually entering the enemy's country, but the voyage, being illegal at its commencement, the penalty immediately attaches, and continues so long as the illegality exists.

BIBLIOGRAPHY

Primary Sources

Manuscripts

Adams, Charles Francis. Diary. Microfilm Nos. 75–78. Massachusetts Historical Society, Boston.

———. Letter Books. Microfilms Nos. 178–179. Massachusetts Historical Society, Boston.

Ballanger, William P. Diary. Eugene C. Barker Library of Texas History, University of Texas, Austin, Texas.

Banks, Nathaniel P. Papers, 1862–1865. Microfilm, Eugene C. Barker Library of Texas History, University of Texas, Austin, Texas.

Confederate States of America. Confederate State Papers, Manuscript Division, Library of Congress, Washington. D.C.

———. Treasury Department. Record Groups 98, 109, & 365, Correspondence of the Trans-Mississippi Cotton Bureau, National Archives, Washington, D.C.

———. War Department. Collection of Confederate Records, Letters Received, Record Group 109, National Archives, Washington, D.C.

Devine, Thomas J. Letters, 1861–1867. Eugene C. Barker Library of Texas History, University of Texas, Austin, Texas.

Ford, John S. Collection of Military Correspondence. Daughters of the Confederacy Museum. Austin, Texas.

———. Memoirs. Eugene C. Barker Library of Texas History, University of Texas, Austin, Texas.

Great Britain, Admiralty Papers. Public Record Office, London, England.

———. Customs Office. Customs, Ledgers of Imports, 1860–1865. Cus. 4 & 5, Public Record Office, London, England.

———. Foreign Office. General Correspondence: America, United States. Series II, F.O. 5. Correspondence to and from Her Majesty's

Minister in Washington, D.C., January 1861–December 1865. Public Record Office, London, England.

———. Foreign Office. General Correspondence: America, United States. Series II, F.O. 5. Correspondence with Her Majesty's Consuls at New Orleans, Galveston, etc., 1861, 1862. Public Record Office, London, England.

———. Foreign Office. General Correspondence: America, United States. Series II, F.O. 5. Case of the "Peterhoff," Trade between Neutral Ports, 3 Vols. (March 1863–March 1871). Public Record Office, London, England.

———. Foreign Office. General Correspondence: America, United States. Series II, F.O. 5. Case of the "Labaun" Seized at Matamoros, Vol. 3 (1869, 1870). Public Record Office, London, England.

———. Foreign Office. General Correspondence: America, United States. Series II, F.O. 97. Case of the "Labaun" Seized at Matamoros, Vols. 1 & 2 (March 1862–August 1865). Public Record Office, London, England.

———. Foreign Office. General Correspondence: America United States. Series II, F.O. 5. Case of the "Springbok," 2 vols. (February 1863–May 1869). Public Record Office, London, England.

———. Foreign Office. General Correspondence with Mexico. F.O. 50. Public Record Office, London, England.

———. Foreign Office. Consular Reports from Mexico, 1827–1869. F.O. 207. Vols. 21, 25, 43. Public Record Office, London, England.

———. House of Commons. *State Papers.* 1863, Vol. 72, North America. No. 5. London: Harrison and Sons.

———. Parliamentary Papers. Accounts and Papers, 1861–1865. State Paper Room, British Museum, London, England.

Haas, Oscar. Manuscript. Eugene C. Barker Library of Texas History, University of Texas, Austin, Texas.

Hotze, Henry. Letter Books, 1861–1864; 1864–1865. Manuscript Division, Library of Congress, Washington, D.C.

———. Papers, 1862–1865. Manuscript Division, Library of Congress, Washington, D.C.

Hunter, John Warren. "The Fall of Brownsville on the Rio Grande, November, 1863." Unpublished Typescript, Biographical File, Eugene C. Barker Library of Texas History, University of Texas, Austin.

Kingsbury, Gilbert D. Papers. Eugene C. Barker Library of Texas History, University of Texas, Austin, Texas.

Maverick Family Papers. Eugene C. Barker Library of Texas History, University of Texas, Austin, Texas.

Murrah, Pendleton. Messages of Governor P. Murrah to the Texas Legislature. Eugene C. Barker Library of Texas History, University of Texas, Austin, Texas.

Oldham, William S. Memoirs. Eugene C. Barker Library of Texas History, University of Texas, Austin.

Plumb, Edward L. Letter Books, Misc., 1858. Manuscript Division, Library of Congress, Washington, D.C.

———. Papers. Vols. 5–6, 1858–1865. Manuscript Division, Library of Congress, Washington, D.C.

Russell Papers. Correspondence and Papers. P.R.O. 30/22, Public Record Office, London, England.

San Román, José. Letters, 1861–65. Eugene C. Barker Library of Texas History, University of Texas, Austin, Texas.

Kirby-Smith, Edmund. Papers. Southern Historical Collection, Wilson Library, University of North Carolina, Chapel Hill, North Carolina.

Stewart, William H. Diary. Southern Historical Collection, Wilson Library, University of North Carolina, Chapel Hill, North Carolina.

Stillman, Charles. Charles Stillman Papers, Houghton Library, Harvard University, Cambridge, Massachusetts.

Swisher, John M. Memoirs. Eugene C. Barker Library of Texas History, University of Texas, Austin, Texas.

United States Department of State. Consular Dispatches and Correspondence, Matamoros, Mexico, 1858–1866. Record Group 59, Vols. 7, 8, January 1, 1858–December 31, 1866.

Printed Documents

Confederate States of America. Provisional Congress, 1861–1865, *The Statutes at Large*. Richmond: R. M. Smith, 1864.

Great Britain. Foreign Office. *Correspondence Respecting the Seizure of the British Vessels "Springbok" and "Peterhoff."* London: Harrison and Sons, 1900.

Malloy, William M., ed. *Treaties, Conventions, International Acts, Protocols, and Agreements between the United States of American and Other Powers, 1776–1909,* 2 vols. Washington: Government Printing Office, 1910.

Miller, Hunter, ed. *Treaties and Other International Acts of the United States of America*. Washington: Government Printing Office, 1937.

Moore, John Bassett. *A Digest of International Law*. Washington: Government Printing Office, 1906.

Richardson, James D., ed. *A Compilation of the Messages and Papers of the Confederacy.* 2 vols. Nashville: United States Publishing Company, 1906.

———. *A Compilation of the Messages and Papers of the Presidents.* 10 vols. Washington: Government Printing Office, 1896–1899.

Robards, C. L., ed. *Synopses of the Decisions of the Supreme Court of the State of Texas.* Austin: Brown and Foster, 1865.

Savage, Carlton, ed. *Policy of the United States Toward Maritime Commerce in War.* Washington: Government Printing Office, 1934–36.

The Texas Almanac. Galveston: A. H. Belo Corporation, 1860.

United States Senate. "Journal of Congress of the Confederate States of America, 1861–1865," *Senate Executive Documents.* 58th Congress, 2nd Session, 1903–1904, Vols. 25–31, No. 234, 7 vols. Washington: Government Printing Office, 1904–1905.

———. "United States Treasury Accounts, 1862," *Senate Executive Documents.* 36th Congress, 1st Session, No. 21. Washington: Government Printing Office, 1863.

———. *Senate Executive Documents.* "Mexican Affairs, 1861–1864," 38th Congress, 2nd Session, No. 11. Washington: Government Printing Office, 1865.

———. *Senate Executive Documents.* "Mexican Affairs, 1866–1867," 39th Congress, 2nd Session, No. 26. Washington: Government Printing Office, 1866.

———. *Senate Executive Documents.* "Cotton Sold to Confederate States," 62nd Congress, 3rd Session, No. 8. Washington: Government Printing Office, 1913.

Smith, Edward D. *The Peterhoff.* (An Argument addressed to the Court by Edward Delafield Smith.) New York: John W. Amerman, 1863.

The Seizure of the "Peterhoff." London: Effingham Wilson, 1863.

The United States versus the Steamer Peterhoff and Her Cargo. New York: John W. Amerman, 1864.

United States Congress, "Condition of Mexico, 1862," *House Executive Documents.* 37th Congress, 3rd Session, No. 54. Washington: Government Printing Office, 1864.

———. *House Executive Documents.* "Mexican Affairs, 1861–1862," 38th Congress, 1st Session, Nos. 1, 3, 25, 111. Washington: Government Printing Office, 1865.

———. *House Report.* "New York Custom-house," No. 25, 38th Congress, 2nd Session. Washington: Government Printing Office, 1865.

United States Navy Department. *Official Records* of the *Union and Confederate Navies in the War of the Rebellion.* 30 vols Washington: Government Printing Office, 1894–1927.

United States War Department. *The War of the Rebellion: The Official Records of the Union and Confederate Armies.* 130 vols. Washington: Government Printing Office, 1880–1901.

Diaries and Memoirs

Alvensleben, Max Baron von. *With Maximilian in Mexico: From the Notebook of a Mexican Officer.* London: Longsman, Green and Company, 1867.

Bassler, Roy P., ed. *The Collected Works of Abraham Lincoln.* 9 vols., New Brunswick, N.J.: Rutgers University Press, 1953.

Case, Lynn M., ed. *French Opinion on the United States and Mexico, 1860–1867: Extracts from the Reports of the Procureurs Généraux.* New York: D. Appleton-Century, Co., 1936.

Fremantle, James A. L. *The Fremantle Diary.* Edited by Walter Lord. Boston: Little Brown and Company, 1954.

Gorgas, Josiah. *The Civil War Diary of General Josiah Gorgas.* Edited by Frank E. Vandiver. Tuscaloosa, Ala.: University of Alabama Press, 1947.

Grimes, Absalom. *Absalom Grimes, Confederate Mail Runner.* Edited by Milo M. Quaife. New Haven, Conn.: Yale University Press, 1926.

Johsnon, Robert U. and Clarence C. Buell, eds. *Battles and Leaders of the Civil War, Being for the Most Part Contributed by Union and Confederate Officers.* 4 vols. New York: Yoseloff, 1956.

Jones, John B. *A Rebel War Clerk's Diary.* 2 vols. New York: Old Hickory Bookshop, 1935.

Kean, Robert Garlich Hill. *Inside the Confederate Government: The Diary of Robert Garlick Hill Kean.* Edited by Edward Younger. New York: Oxford University Press, 1957.

Lubbock, Richard F. *Six Decades in Texas: or Memoirs of Francis Richard Lubbock.* Austin, Tex.: Ben C. Jones, 1900.

McIntyre, Benjamin F. *Federals on the Frontier: the Diary of Benjmain F. McIntyre, 1862–1964.* Edited by Nannie M. Tilley. Austin, Tex.: University of Texas Press, 1963.

Morgan, James M. *Recollections of a Rebel Reefer.* Boston: Houghton-Mifflin Co., 1917.

Newton, Lord. *Lord Lyons: A Record of British Diplomacy.* 2 vols. New York: Longmans, Green, and Company, 1913.

North, Thomas. *Five Years in Texas.* Cincinnati, Ohio: Elm Street Printing, 1871.

Oates, Stephen B., ed. *Rip Ford's Texas.* Austin, Tex.: University of Texas Press, 1963.

Olmstead, Frederick Law. *A Journey in the Seaboard Slave States.* New York: Dix, Edwards, 1861.

Roel, Santiago, ed. *Correspondencia particular de D. Santiago Vidaurri.* Monterrey: Universidad de Nuevo Leon, 1946.

Russell, John, First Earl. *The Later Correspondence of Lord John Russell, 1840–1848.* Edited by G. P. Gooch. 2 vols. London: 1925.

Santleben, August. *A Texas Pioneer: Early Staging and Overland Freighting Days on the Frontiers of Texas and Mexico.* Edited by E. D. Affleck. New York: Neale Publishing Company, 1910.

Semmes, Raphael. *Memoirs of Service Afloat During the War Between the States.* Baltimore: Kelly, Piet and Company, 1869.

Taylor, Thomas E. *Running the Blockade.* London: John Murray, 1869.

Watson, William. *The Adventures of a Blockade Runner.* London: T. Fisher Unwin, 1892.

Welles, Gideon. *Diary of Gideon Welles.* Edited by Howard K. Beale. 3 vols. New York: W. W. Norton and Company, 1960.

West, W. R., ed. *Contemporary French Opinion of the Civil War.* Baltimore: Johns Hopkins Press, 1924.

Williams, R. H. *With the Border Ruffians: Memoirs of the Far West, 1852–1863.* Edited by E. W. Williams. New York: E. P. Dutton and Company, 1907.

Newspapers

Austin Gazette, 1862–1865.

Boletin Oficial [Monterrey, Mexico], 1861–1865.

Cincinnati Gazette, 1865.

Cotton Supply Reporter [Manchester, England], 1861–1865.

Daily News [Galveston], 1863–1865.

Daily Picayune [New Orleans], 1885.

Daily Telegraph [Houston], 1864–1865.

Dallas Times Herald, 1864.

Fort Brown Flag [Brownsville, Texas], 1861–1865.

Journal of Commerce of Daily Shipping and Mercantile Advertiser [Liverpool], 1861–1863.

LaBandera [Brownsville, Texas], 1861–1863.

London Economist, 1861–1865.
The London Herald, 1861.
The Manchester Guardian [Manchester, England], 1861–1865.
New York Daily News, 1862–1864.
New York Herald, 1861–1865.
New York Times, 1861–1865.
Patriot [LaGrange, Texas], 1863.
Ranchero [Corpus Christi], 1862–1863.
Reporter [Tyler, Texas] 1862–1863.
Richmond Enquirer, 1861, 1863.
San Antonio Herald, 1862.
Semi-Weekly Herald [San Antonio], 1861–1865.
Semi-Weekly News [San Antonio], 1861–1865.
Texas Almanac Extra [Austin], 1861–1865.
Texas Republican [Marshall, Texas], 1863–1865.
Texas State Gazette [Austin], 1861–1865.
The Times [London], 1861–1865.
Times-Picayune [New Orleans], 1862–1864, 1937.
Tri-Weekly Herald [San Antonio], 1861–1865.
Tri-Weekly News [Galveston], 1863–1865.
Tri-Weekly Telegraph [Galveston], 1863–1864.
Tri-Weekly Telegraph [Houston], 1862–1864.
Washington Evening Post, 1865.
Weekly Ranchero [Brownsville, Texas], 1861–1865.
Weekly Texas State Gazette [Austin], 1861–1865.

Secondary Sources

Biographies

Hughes, William J. *Rebellious Ranger: Rip Ford and the Old Southwest*, Norman, Okla.: University of Oklahoma Press, 1964.

McKee, Irving. *Ben-Hur Wallace: The Life of General Lew Wallace.* Berkeley, Calif.: University of California Press, 1947.

Parks, Joseph H. *General Edmund Kirby Smith C.S.A.* Baton Rouge, La.: Louisiana State University Press, 1954.

Roeder, Ralph. *Juarez and His Mexico.* 2 vols. New York: Viking Press, 1917.

Stillman, Chauncey D. *Charles Stillman, 1810–1875.* New York: Privately published, 1956.

Tyler, Ronnie C. *Santiago Vidaurri.* Austin, Tex.: Texas State Historical Association, 1973.

Woodman, Lyman L. *Cortina: Rogue of the Rio Grande.* San Antonio, Tex.: Naylor Company, 1950.

Special Studies and Monographs

Adams, Ephraim D. *Great Britain and the American Civil War.* 2 vols. New York: Longmans, Green and Company, 1925.

Andreano, Ralph L., ed. *The Economic Impact of the American Civil War.* Cambridge, Mass.: Harvard University Press, 1962.

Arnold, R. A., Sir Arthur. *The History of the Cotton Famine.* London: Saunders, Otley and Company, 1864.

Bernard, Montague. *A Historical Account of the Neutrality of Great Britain During the American Civil War.* London: Longmans, Green, Reeder, and Dyer, 1870.

Black, Robert C. *The Railroads of the Confederacy.* Chapel Hill, N.C.: University of North Carolina Press, 1952.

Bonham, Milledge L. *The British Consuls in the Confederacy.* Columbia University Studies, Vol. 43. New York: Longmans, Green and Company, 1911.

Bradlee, Francis B. C. *Blockade Running During the Civil War.* Salem, Mass.: The Essex Institute, 1925.

Briggs, Herbert W. *The Doctrine of Continuous Voyage.* Baltimore: The John Hopkins Press, 1929.

Bulloch, James D. *The Secret Service of the Confederate States in Europe.* New York: Thomas Yoseloff, 1959.

Chevalier, Michel. *France, Mexico, and the Confederate States.* Translated by William Henry Hulbert. New York: C. B. Richardson, 1863.

Clark, Joseph L., and Elton M. Scott. *The Texas Gulf Coast.* 2 vols. New York: The Lewis Historical Company, 1955.

Cochran, Hamilton. *Blockade Runners of the Confederacy.* Indianapolis, Ind.: Bobbs-Merrill Company, 1958.

Carse, Robert. *Blockade: The Civil War at Sea.* New York: Rinehardt and Company, 1958.

Case, Lynn M., and Warren F. Spencer. *The United States and France: Civil War Diplomacy.* Philadelphia: University of Pennsylvania Press, 1970.

Chapman, Sydney J. *The Lancaster Cotton Industry: A Study in Economic Development*. Manchester, University Press, 1904.

Chatfield, W. W. *The Twin Cities—Brownsville, Texas and Matamoros, Mexico—of the Border, and the Country of the Lower Rio Grande*. New Orleans, La.: E. P. Brandao, 1898.

Evans, Clement A., ed. *Confederate Military History*. 12 vols. Atlanta, Ga.: Confederate Publishing Company, 1899.

Freeman, Douglas S. *Lee's Lieutenants: A Study in Command*. 3 vols. New York: Scribner, 1942–1944.

Goff, Richard D. *Confederate Supply*. Durham, N.C.: Duke University Press, 1969.

Goodrich, Carter. *Government Promotion of American Canals and Railroads, 1800–1890*. New York: Columbia University Press, 1960.

Hammond, M. B. *The Cotton Industry*. New York: Macmillan Company, 1897.

Henderson, Harry McCorry. *Texas in the Confederacy*. San Antonio, Tex.: Naylor, 1955.

Henderson, William O. *The Lancashire Cotton Famine, 1860–1865*. Manchester, England: University Press, 1934.

Horgan, Paul. *Great River, the Rio Grande in North American History*. 2 vols. New York: Rinehart and Company, 1954.

Huse, Caleb. *The Supplies for the Confederate Army: How They Were Obtained in Europe and How Paid For*. Boston: R. R. Marvin and Son, 1904.

Jordan, Donaldson, and Edwin J. Pratt. *Europe and the American Civil War*. New York: Octagon Books, 1969.

Kerby, Robert L. *Kirby Smith's Confederacy: The Trans-Mississippi South, 1863–1865*. New York: Columbia University Press, 1972.

Lea, Tom. *The King Ranch*. 2 vols. Boston: Little Brown and Company, 1957.

Lonn, Ella. *Foreigners in the Confederacy*. Chapel Hill, N.C.: University of North Carolina Press, 1940.

Low, Alfred M. *Blockade and Contraband*. Washington: Columbian Printing Company, 1916.

Mahan, Alfred Thayer. *The Gulf and Inland Waters*. New York: Scribner, 1863.

Martin, Michael R., and Lovette Martin and H. Gabriel, eds. *Encyclopedia of Latin American History*. New York: Bobbs-Merrill Company, 1968.

Monaghan, James. *Diplomat in Carpet Slippers: Abraham Lincoln Deals with Foreign Affairs*. New York: Bobbs-Merrill, 1945.

Nichols, James L. *The Confederate Quartermaster in the Trans-Mississippi.* Austin, Tex.: University of Texas Press, 1964.

Owsley, Frank L. *King Cotton Diplomacy.* 2nd ed. rev. Chicago: University of Chicago Press, 1959.

Pierce, Frank C. *A Brief History of the Lower Rio Grande Valley.* Menasha, Wisc.: George Banta Publishing Company, 1917.

Porter, David D. *The Naval History of the Civil War.* London: Sampson Low, 1887.

Potts, Charles S. *Railroad Transportation in Texas.* Austin, Tex.: University of Texas Press, 1909.

Pray, May M. *Dick Dowling's Battle.* San Antonio, Tex.: Naylor Company, 1936.

Reed, S. G. A. *A History of the Texas Railroads.* Houston, Tex.: St. Clair Publishing Company, 1941.

Rippy, J. Fred. *The United States and Mexico.* New York: Alfred A. Knopf, 1926.

Robinson, William M. *The Confederate Privateers.* New Haven: Yale University Press, 1928.

Sargent, Fitzwilliam. *England, the United States and the Southern Confederacy.* London: Hamilton, Adams and Company, 1864.

Schwab, J. C. *A Financial and Industry History of the South During the Civil War.* New Haven, Conn.: Yale University Press, 1913.

Soley, James R. *The Blockade and the Cruiser.* New York: Charles Scribner's Sons, 1885.

Thompson, Samuel B. *Confederate Purchasing Operations Abroad.* Chapel Hill, N.C.: University of North Carolina Press, 1935.

Vandiver, Frank E. *Confederate Blockade Running Through Bermuda.* Austin, Tex.: University of Texas Press, 1947.

Ward, W. W., and G. P. Gooch, eds. *The Cambridge History of British Foreign Policy, 1783–1919.* 3 vols. New York: Macmillan and Company, 1922–1923.

Watkins, James L. *King Cotton: A Historical and Statistical Review, 1790–1908.* New York: J. L. Watkins and Sons, 1908.

Watts, John. *The Facts of the Cotton Famine.* London: Simkin, Marshall and Company, 1866.

Webb, Walter P., ed. *The Handbook of Texas.* 3 vols. Austin, Tex.: The Texas State Historical Association, 1952.

Wooten, Dudley G., ed. *A Comprehensive History of Texas.* 2 vols. Dallas, Tex.: Scarff, 1898.

Wright, Marcus J. *Texas in the War, 1861–1865.* Edited by Harold B. Simpson. Hillsboro, Tex.: Hill Junior College Press, 1965.

Articles

Abbey, Kathryn T. "Incidents of the Confederate Blockade." *Journal of Southern History* 11 (May 1945): 214–19.

Aldis, O. F. "Louis Napoleon and the Southern Confederacy." *North American Review* 129 (October 1879): 342–60.

Barr, Alwyn. "Confederate Artillery in the Trans-Mississippi." *Military Affairs* 27 (1963): 77–83.

Baxter, James P. "The British Government and Neutral Rights, 1861–1865." *American Historical Review* 34 (October 1928): 9–29.

———. "Papers Relating to Belligerent and Neutral Rights." *American Historical Review* 34 (October 1928) 77–91.

———. "Some British Opinions as to Neutral Rights, 1861–1865." *The American Journal of International Law* 23 (July 1929): 517–37.

Belloff, Max. "Historical Revision No. CXVIII: Great Britain and the American Civil War." *History* 37 (1952): 40–48.

Bernath, Stuart W. "British Neutrality and the Civil War Prize Cases." *Civil War History* 15 (1969): 320–31.

Bonham, Milledge L. "The French Consuls in the Confederate States." *Studies in Southern History and Politics.* (Inscribed to William Archibald Dunning by His Former Students, the Authors.) New York: Columbia University Press, 1914.

Cotterill, R. S. "Southern Railroads, 1850–1860." *Mississippi Valley Historical Review* 10 (1924): 398–405.

Crook, Carland Elaine. "Benjamin Theron and the French Designs in Texas During the Civil War." *Southwestern Historical Quarterly* 68 (1965): 432–54.

Delaney, Robert W. "Matamoros, Port for Texas During the Civil War." *The Southwestern Historical Quarterly* 58 (April 1955): 473–87.

Diamond, William. "Imports of the Confederate Government from Europe and Mexico." *Journal of Southern History* 6 (November 1940): 470–503.

Elliott, Claude. "Union Sentiment in Texas, 1861–1865." *Southwestern Historical Quarterly* 50 (1947): 449–77.

Ellis, L. Tuffly. "Maritime Commerce on the Far Western Gulf, 1861–1865." *Southwestern Historical Quarterly* 77 (October 1973): 167–226.

Erikson, Edgar L., ed. "Hunting for Cotton in Dixie: From the Diary of Captain Charles E. Wilcox." *Journal of Southern History* 4 (1938): 493–513.

Ginzberg, Eli. "The Economics of British Neutrality." *Agricultural History* 10 (1936): 147ff.

Gipson, Lawrence H. "The Collapse of the Confederacy." *Mississippi Valley Historical Review* 4 (1917–1918): 437–58.

Hanna, K. A. "The Role of the South in the French Intervention in Mexico." *Journal of Southern History* 20 (1954): 3–21.

Henderson, William O. "The Cotton Famine on the Continent, 1861–1865." *Economic Historical Review* 4 (1933): 195–207.

Larios, Avila. "Brownsville-Matamoros: Confederate Lifeline." *Mid-America* 40 (April 1958): 67–89.

Miller, Edmund T. "The State Finances of Texas During the Civil War." *Quarterly of the Texas State Historical Association* 14 (1910): 1–23.

Miller, Robert R. "Matias Romero, Mexican Minister to the United States During the Juarez-Maximillian Era." *Hispanic American Historical Review* 65 (1915): 228–45.

Newton, A. P. "Anglo-American Relations During the Civil War, 1861–1865." *Cambridge History of British Foreign Policy* 2: 488–521.

Oates, Stephen B. "John S. Ford: Prudent Cavalryman, C.S.A." *Southwestern Historical Quarterly* 64 (1961): 289–314.

———. "Supply for the Confederate Cavalry in the Trans-Mississippi." *Military Affairs* 25 (1961): 94–99.

O'Flaherty, Daniel. "The Blockade That Failed." *American Heritage* 6 (August 1955): 38–41.

Owsley, Frank. "America and the Freedom of the Seas, 1861–1865." *Essays in Honor of William E. Dodd*. Edited by Avery O. Craven. Chicago: University of Chicago Press, (1935), pp. 220–43.

Potts, Charles S. "Railroad Transportation in Texas." *University of Texas Bulletin*, No. 119, Austin, 1909.

Price, Marcus W. "Ships That Tested the Blockade of the Gulf Ports, 1861–1865." *American Neptune* 11 (1951): 262–90; 12 (1952): 229–38.

Ramsdell, C. W. "Internal Improvements in Texas in the Fifties." *Proceedings of the Mississippi Valley Historical Association* 9 (1917): 104ff.

———. "The Texas State Military Board, 1862–1865." *Southwestern Historical Quarterly* 27 (April 1924): 253–75.

Roberts, A. Sellow. "The Federal Government and Confederate Cotton." *American Historical Review* 32 (January 1927): 262–75.

Sears, Louis, ed. "The London Times' American Correspondence in 1861; Unpublished Letters of W. H. Russell," *Historical Outlook* 16 (1925): 251–57.

Sibley, Marilyn McAdams. "Charles Stillman: A Case of Entrepreneurship on the Rio Grande, 1861–1865," *Southwestern Historical Quarterly* 77 (October 1973): 227–40.

Smith, Mitchell. "The 'Neutral' Matamoros Trade, 1861–1865." *Southwest Review* 37 (Autumn 1952): 319–24.

Tyler, Ronnie C. "Cotton on the Border, 1861–1865," *Southwestern Historical Quarterly* 73 (April 1970): 456–77.

Van Zant, Lee. "Early Economic Policies of the Government of Texas." *Southwestern Studies* 4, No. 2 (1966): 3–48.

Wandrus, Harry. "Firearms, Facts and Fancies." *Hobbies,* August 1905, pp. 129–31.

Windham, William T. "The Problem of Supply in the Trans-Mississippi Confederacy," *Journal of Southern History,* 22, May 1961, pp. 149–68.

Unpublished Theses and Dissertations

Cowling, Anne. "The Confederate Cotton Trade with Mexico." Master's thesis, University of Texas, 1929.

Dickenson, Sherrill L. "The Texas Cotton Trade During the Civil War." Master's thesis, North Texas State University, 1967.

Evans, Elliott A. P. "Napoleon III and the American Civil War." Ph.D. diss., Stanford University, 1940.

Felger, Robert F. "Texas in the War for Southern Independence, 1861–1865." Ph.D. diss., University of Texas, 1935.

Futrell, Robert F. "Federal Trade with the Confederate States, 1861–1865." Ph.D. diss., Vanderbilt University, 1950.

Graf, LeRoy. "The Economic History of the Lower Rio Grande Valley, 1820–1875." Ph.D. diss., Harvard University, 1942.

Heberlain, Ruby Lee. "Railroad Building in the State of Texas During the Civil War." Research paper, University of Texas, n.d.

Irby, James A. "Line of the Rio Grande: War and Trade on the Confederate Frontier, 1861–1865." Ph.D. diss., University of Georgia, 1969.

Shaver, Alethea Wanda. "The Cotton Bureau in the Trans-Mississippi Department." Research paper, University of Texas, 1938.

General Works

Bancroft, Hubert H. *History of the North Mexican States and Texas.* 2 vols. San Francisco: The History Company, 1890.

Bemis, Samuel F. *Diplomatic History of the United States.* New York: Henry Holt and Company, 1936.

Callahan, James M. *American Foreign Policy in Mexican Relations.* New York: Macmillan Company, 1932.

———. *The Diplomatic History of the Southern Confederacy*. Baltimore: The Johns Hopkins Press, 1901.

Eaton, Clement. *A History of the Southern Confederacy*. New York: The Macmillan Company, 1954.

Herring, Hubert. *A History of Latin America*. New York: Alfred A. Knopf, 1968.

INDEX